JATANI ALI
TANDHU

Jatani Ali Tandhu

JATANI ALI TANDHU

LIFE & LEGACY OF A BORANA STATESMAN

TADHI LIBAN

Published by Vivid Publishing
P.O. Box 948, Fremantle
Western Australia 6959
www.vividpublishing.com.au

National Library of Australia cataloguing-in-publication data:
Creator: Liban, Tadhi, author.
Title: Jatani Ali Tandhu : life & legacy of a Borana statesman / Tadhi Liban.
ISBN: 9781925209280 (paperback)
Subjects: Ali Tandhu, Jatani.
            Statesmen--Ethiopia--Biography.
            Assassination--Africa--History.
            Ethiopia--History--20th century.
            Kenya--History--20th century.
Dewey Number: 963.0721

Contents

Preface

What prompted me to write this biography? Armed assassins killed Major Jatani Ali Tandhu at Ngera Hotel in Nairobi on 2 July 1992; where he lived as a refugee, following a violent regime change in Ethiopia. This unfortunate date on Borana people's calendar was the catalyst for me to ponder on Jatani Ali as a person and his legacy.

Many people came to know Jatani – simply and popularly known as 'Shalaaqa' – through work and socially. Most regarded him as a towering figure in life and in his career achievements. The prominence of an individual is manifested through both tangible and intangible contributions s/he has made to society. Tangible legacies of an individual are out there for all to appreciate, in the form of monuments built for the good of the community. Intangible legacies are those that remain etched in the collective memory of those who witnessed them. Schools, student hostels, roads and clinics built in Borana towns and region are some of the monuments with which to remember Jatani Ali's tangible contributions to society. Since intangible contributions are more difficult to quantify, occasions or events are required to point them out. To this effect, I would like to recount three instances to help highlight Jatani's lasting effect on people who knew him and, by extension, on the wider society.

The first instance involves Colonel Solomon Abay, one of my interviewees and an employee of the Ethiopian Police Force. Jatani Ali and Colonel Solomon did not work in the same unit but I knew that they travelled together abroad to partake in police-related study tours and conferences, for about a month in duration. I asked the Colonel what he knew about Jatani. The first response to the inquiry was, 'Mebatsion[1] was

---

[1] Mebatsion is the name by which Jatani was known in the Police and

a great man. Please compile everything you find about him and give me a copy of the final product."

What made Jatani a great man, according to the Colonel, was intangible to many others but was not to him, given his first-hand experience in working with him.

The second instance relates to an event that highlighted the respect and lasting positive effect Jatani had on people he had worked with or on those who came to know him. When the news about his assassination was made known, it struck a raw nerve, triggering unprecedented anger and spontaneous outpourings of public grief, in both Ethiopia and Kenya. The tragic news triggered a massive protest rally in Nairobi against the agency suspected of having a hand in the assassination plot: the Ethiopian Embassy in Nairobi. It was the focus of the protest rally and it was attended by thousands of angry Ethiopian refugees and Kenyan citizens. The rallies led to widespread violence in Nairobi where Kenyan riot police were called to avoid further bloody disturbances. In Ethiopia, still stunned by a violent regime change and under martial rule, expressions of grief were more subdued and private.

The third instance is an anonymous person's web-based take on Jatani's legacy:

Jatani Ali Tandu: Borana-Oromo leader, former Provincial Governor of Borana Province in Southern Oromia, shot dead... He was an extra-ordinary public servant even through the most difficult times. He served our people with distinction. That is why he is one of the most beloved sons of Oromia and history will remember him in that light.[2]

I knew Jatani from our school days right up to the time when he fled Ethiopia, following a violent regime change, to live as a refugee in the city of Nairobi, where he fell victim of an assassin's bullet. I knew Jatani's childhood. I knew his birth place in Borana and the social, cultural and

---

Government Service.

[2] *Jatani Ali Extraordinary Public Servant,*
     http://www.geocities.ws/oromosociety/Jatani_Ali_Tandu.html

political context in which he grew up. I knew him through his school years as we both attended the same boarding school. I witnessed his life as he went through Aba Dina Police Academy and served in the Ethiopian Police force. I was present when he enrolled at Haile Selassie I University. I followed the progress of his career through the Ethiopian Ministry of the Interior as he was posted to serve in various capacities and in different provinces.

Though he had a lasting effect on people wherever he was posted, his legacy as Governor in Borana Administrative Region of southern Ethiopia was paramount. Jatani has developed a cult-like aura amongst the Borana who remember him with deep affection and respect, decades after his demise. He has been perceived as a leader, a guide, a beacon of hope and an ardent advocate of Borana rights. This community holds his name in high esteem for all the work he undertook to improve their lives. He strove to make perceptible inroads into raising Borana people's awareness regarding their standing in Ethiopia and Kenya. He worked hard to educate the community so that they are equipped and empowered to fight for their individual and collective rights. He made tangible strides in introducing agents of modernity aimed at improving the social and economic life of the people. He spearheaded the construction of schools in remote rural areas for boys and girls coming from neglected nomadic pastoralist communities. He was an enlightened leader who organised communities to build students' hostels to accommodate students arriving from these remote pastoralist communities who, otherwise, wouldn't have benefited from such schools. Under Jatani's leadership, various primary health care facilities were established in rural areas. Roads were paved to link far-flung corners of the province with major towns with schools and other facilities. He worked tirelessly to facilitate inter-community or inter-tribal dialogue to avert and peacefully solve conflicts. Both traditional and innovative conflict resolution techniques were employed in such dialogues. He campaigned hard to highlight what communities had in common and to reduce aspects that divided them. He advocated the need for mutual respect and stressed the benefits of peaceful co-existence between communities.

By enlisting the help of professionals in rural development, he organised educational campaigns aimed at improving the health and economic life of nomadic pastoralists. This effort included: campaigns to eradicate communicable diseases by teaching the basics in primary health care for rural areas; ways in diversifying existing food production techniques; better resource conservation practices; and better marketing techniques of products aimed at improving communities' ability to reduce the effects of recurrent droughts and poverty.

I am sure there are many others who also have something to say about Jatani Ali and his legacy. But the impetus for me to write this biography emanates from the encouragement I received from Borana persons who have observed the anniversary date of Jatani Ali's death every year since 2 July 1992. Many knew that Jatani and I had been close friends over the years. In particular, Liban Wako Adi, a Borana person who now resides in Australia, knew about my close relationship with Jatani both as he was growing up in Yaballo and through our correspondence. His father, the late Wako Adi, also went to Medhane Alem School with Jatani and me. On 2 July 2013, Liban sent me an email seeking information on Jatani Ali, as part of a worldwide effort to celebrate his life and to highlight his legacies. In a sense, my reply to his email started the process of writing this biography. Here is an extract from that email message:

Dear Tadhi,

...I often wonder if there is any written biography of the late Jatani Ali Tandhu whenever the anniversary of his assassination approaches. Recently, some Borana people sent me an email asking me if I had a biography of him to mark the anniversary. I told them that I didn't have one nor have I seen any before. Do you know if there is any written biography of Jatani Ali?

Considering that people of your generation (even of my generation) are ageing fast, the window of opportunity to record even a fraction of the life stories of Jatani Ali and/ or that of your generation is closing ever narrower every year. I know it is a difficult task but I thought that you are the best person with whom to even canvass the possibility of recording the story/biography of Jatani Ali, perhaps in the context of the collective history of the "ijoollee bulguu kennani" Borana persons and the recent history of the Borana people.

Do you think that such a project is beyond our scope? If we tried to approach it as a collaborative effort, we might at least get to collect and record [a] few things on Jatani Ali before it is all too late. For example, if you still have some energy left to move about to gather bits and pieces of information towards such a biographical work, I would be able to put it together. I might have to find some money to cover the cost of your transportation to gather information, somehow.

Personally, I cannot think of a better person than you to even float such an idea with amongst all the Borana persons I know. What do you think? Does it sound too optimistic or too difficult to even contemplate such a task? Please let me know. Hope to hear from you soon and thank you.

Nagaa waaqa keesa ooli bullii.

Liban Wako Adi

I do not claim to know everything about Jatani Ali nor all places he'd been to in life. However, given my longstanding contact with Jatani – from primary school to our last encounter in Nairobi few months before his assassination – I have considerable information in my head regarding his life trajectory, career achievements, political views and even some life anecdotes. Additionally, I had already compiled and written an outline of Jatani's life history, and I have kept some photos over the years.

So, in response to Liban's request in that email, I sent him a rough outline of Jatani Ali's biography. Liban expressed his appreciation for the material and added a note of encouragement for me to expand on the draft at hand so as to end up with a more tangible biographical account of Jatani Ali. I was aware that the outline I sent him was too general and barely canvassed the myriad contributions Jatani had made to communities he so devotedly served. Though I did not come across any significant written material about Jatani, I was fully aware how his contributions, achievements and legacy were not held in a book, but rather in the memories of all those who had come to know him over the years. I know several persons who are still alive who once knew or worked with Jatani, who could tell lively stories about his work and life. However, I was also aware of how it is only a matter of time before they take their memories with them to the grave. Therefore, I decided to persevere with the idea of expanding on the biographical outline I had on hand with the hope of making it into a decent biography of Jatani Ali.

Attempting to write a biography of such a notable public figure by relying on my own personal knowledge alone doesn't do justice to the history and stature of the person. If available, the use of primary and secondary data on the subject would make the final product more germane. As mentioned above, I knew Jatani nearly all his life. Our relationship was not of a social kind alone but extended to our mutual concern for and efforts to overcome some of the hardships affecting Borana society. As the result, whenever we met while he was the governor of Arero *Awraja* (Province) or that of Borana Administrative Region, he shared with me the challenges he faced, his achievements and setbacks.

I am not sure whether a documentary evidence of his efforts and the work challenges he faced are open to the public. Nor do I know how much of it has been recorded and kept in government files somewhere. Even if they did record these things, I was unable to locate any files that could have served as secondary data towards this biography. Often a wanton destruction of government files accompanies the usually violent regime change processes in Ethiopia. It is possible that many government files in offices where Jatani Ali served as a governor might have been destroyed in such circumstances.

I have managed to conduct interviews with individuals who knew Jatani first-hand over the years in the context of work and socially. Such interview notes have been used here as subjective field data towards the biography. The subjects of such interviews included Jatani's fellow students from his elementary and secondary school days, police cadet course-mates, colleagues in the police service, employees who worked with him in provincial and regional administrations, notable elders from Borana and Gujii pastoralist communities and casual friends. The names of these informants are listed at the end of this document. Elders from Gabra and Garri communities who knew him were not available for interview. I previewed a few books and some documents which provided some insights into Jatani's work as a leader and life. His personal files in the Ethiopian Police Headquarters and the Ministry of the Interior were inaccessible for assessment or to be used as references.

The Ethiopian Ministry of the Interior has gone through various upheavals and does not exist in its original form. That Ministry was in charge of public administration and was Jatani's employer, when he was a governor of both provinces and administrative regions.

Jatani was born in Borana but educated in Addis Ababa. He travelled from Borana to Addis Ababa with a group of boys whom I call "Borana Pioneers of Modern Education". Informally, the group was also known as *ijoollee bulguu kennani* and was made up of 65 boys in total. The boys left Borana country in two separate cohorts to attend boarding schools in Addis Ababa, by order of Emperor Haile Selassie. The first batch arrived in 1947 and the second in 1952. A brief discussion on the background of this group of boys and how they came to access modern education have been included in Appendix 1 of this book to provide context.

Some readers of this book might wonder at the merit of including information on the "Borana Pioneers of Modern Education" group here. Jatani's prominence has been pointed out in this preface. The prominence of an individual will have significant weight if presented in the context of his upbringing and social settings. Jatani Ali shared the earlier years of his formative years with this group of Borana students. I also believe that the story of this group of Borana boys forms an integral part of Borana's modern history. I used the occasion as an opportunity to inform on the past as well as the current status of Jatani's contemporaries.

I also opted to add the story of the "Borana Pioneers of Modern Education" to demystify the stories around their selection and their trip to the alien and distant Addis Ababa. Perhaps due to a lack of information, myths, half-truths and distortions surround the circumstances in which the group of boys to which Jatani Ali belonged was selected from all over Borana country to attend boarding schools in Addis Ababa. There are stories that allege that the first batch of boys was taken from poor families or recruited from street children to fulfil the official quota order from the then Emperor of Ethiopia. This is a baseless claim and far from the truth. The selection process of the boys was conducted by following established Borana traditional norms and government rules.

All the same, the process was instrumental in producing capable leaders such as Jatani Ali whose legacy is far-reaching, even long after death. Arguably, Jatani's concern for the welfare, justice and fair treatment of the down-trodden made him into the most revered leader in the recent history of the Borana. To many young Borana, the mere mention of Jatani Ali's name conjures up an image of a legendary figure from a distant past. Jatani Ali was not the only one from his cohort to have had the opportunity to serve as provincial and/or regional governor. Four other members of the "Borana Pioneers of Modern Education" group served as district, provincial or regional governors in Borana country and in other parts of Ethiopia. However, Jatani Ali is by far the most memorable of these leaders, one who had a long-lasting effect on the communities he served. His stature and legacy as a leader put him in an entirely different category to leaders who came before him, during his tenure or since. His character and his tangible legacies have become a benchmark with which people measure the mettle of current and future leaders in Borana country. He will be remembered as the very first indigenous Borana governor to lay the foundations for modern education, economic development and social advancement focused on the indigenous peoples in the area. He will also be remembered as a charismatic, effective, hardworking and dynamic leader who possessed immense persuasive abilities to change old attitudes.

This biography will give readers a glimpse into the life and work of an outstanding Borana, Oromo and Ethiopian leader. More importantly, it is hoped that many young Borana will be inspired to follow in the footsteps of Jatani Ali, in having the determination, attitude, courage, education, skills and wisdom to lift their people out of demeaning poverty, years of misrule and hopelessness. An everlasting monument to Jatani is not a bronze statue but a legacy that lives on in people's minds; to inspire current and future generations of Borana to follow his example in serving the public honourably.

Tadhi Liban
Addis Ababa, May 2014

Acknowledgements

In writing Jatani Ali's life history, efforts have been made to use varied primary and secondary sources of information including written documents and input from individuals. So many people have made contributions in compiling the biography; I would like however to mention the name of a few individuals whose input and encouragement were vital in enabling me to produce the final product.

Firstly, special thanks go to Liban Wako Adi for encouraging me to put pen to paper about what I knew about Jatani, as well as for helping me with the process of editing and publishing the book, including the financial costs involved in publication. Thanks too to Liban's wife Dale Gietzelt for her assistance in formatting the final document. Financial support from Liban, Dhiba Guyo and Halakhe Ganyu allowed me to travel to Borana country to gather first-hand information on Jatani Ali and his accomplishments, by interviewing individuals who knew Jatani intimately, both through work and socially.

I also thank Colonel Solomon Abay for making available photos featuring Jatani Ali as a member of the Ethiopian Traffic Police Officers delegation which toured Japan and Western Europe in 1970. My heartfelt thanks go to Dr Boku Tache who offered his time to read an earlier draft of this biography and provided valuable advice. Though not mentioned by name, there were many individuals who gave me verbal encouragement and moral support to persevere with the task of getting this book published. I would like to extend my gratitude and a sincere thank you to them all.

Introduction

The name "Borana" features a great deal in this book as Jatani Ali was born into a Borana community and that was where he left his most significant mark. "Borana" refers to both a country and a community of people. Borana country is in southern Ethiopia and straddles the Ethiopia-Kenya border. The name and provincial boundaries of this region have been altered according to the whims of successive despotic regimes which have alternated in ruling Ethiopia. As a community, Borana is a segment of a much larger cultural group or tribe called Oromo. The Borana community is found in both Ethiopia and Kenya. During the reign of Emperor Haile Selassie, the Borana community in Ethiopia was governed from adjacently located provinces (*Awrajas*) named Arero and Borana. Arero Province had the town of Yaballo as its capital with a jurisdiction that included the districts (*woredas*) of Yaballo, Teltele, Arero, Hagere Mariam and Burji. Borana Province had the town of Nagelle-Borana as its capital and comprised districts named Liban (now in Gujii Zone or regional administration), Dirre, Moyale and Dolo (now part of Somali Regional State or *Kilil*).

The regime of the Emperor was removed from power via a military coup leading to the installation of a junta named *Derg* that ruled the country from 1974 to 1991. Colonel Mengistu Haile Mariam was the leader of the *Derg* for most of this time and it too was removed from power violently. The *Derg* regime retained pre-existing provincial jurisdictions, except when it put the districts of Dirre and Moyale under Arero Province during the Ethio-Somalia war in the late 1970s. The regime that replaced the *Derg* in 1991 changed the Amharic name for a province, *Awraja*, or Administrative Region to Zone. Today, the bulk of the Borana community falls under the jurisdiction of Borana Zone except the Borana community of Liban district who are now part of Gujii Zone. In Kenya the Borana community mainly lives in Moyale, Marasbit (Saku) and Isiolo counties or divisions.

This book is made up of three broad parts spread over 18 chapters. The first part documents the life and career of Jatani Ali from childhood to the day of his assassination. The second part comprises what has been written about him after the assassination. This includes the attorney's reports, what newspapers in Nairobi reported on the assassination plot, tributes by fellow Borana and others who knew him, and commemorative notes from diaspora Borana who have been remembering him every year on the anniversary of his assassination. The third part ponders on virtues that defined Jatani as a person and a leader, through the views expressed by people who had worked with him, met him or heard about him. Assessment of his character and measures of his quality as a leader complete the third part. Documents directly taken from different sources and reproduced here are put in italics and smaller fonts.

In the first part, the chapters of the book follow the life trajectory of Jatani Ali chronologically from childhood to his death. The book begins with his name and early childhood. This is followed by his travel to Addis Ababa for education. His career trajectory is described starting from his training at Aba Dina Police Academy through to his service in the Ethiopian police force. His stint at what is today Addis Ababa University in pursuit of higher education and his participation in the Literacy and Development Campaign (LDC) are covered. His services as provincial and regional governor, as part of the Ethiopian Ministry of the Interior, follow, where his career achievements are described. This section culminates with a chapter dedicated to his exile and assassination. This last chapter includes reports on his assassination, various attributes highlighting his character as a human being and a leader. This is followed by appendices that remember Borana boys who gained access to modern education along with Jatani Ali, accompanied by their photos, and a poem dedicated to Jatani by a student from "Jatani Ali Students' Hostel". The book finishes with a page indicating my sources of information and a brief note about me as the author.

1: Early Childhood

Jatani was born in 1941[3] in a locality called Melbana, in Dirre District of Borana Province. His exact date of birth is not known as the family did not keep such records.

His name

Jatani Ali Tandhu is the complete name of Jatani that most Borana people are familiar with. Jatani was the name his parents gave him at birth according to Borana culture. His first name was changed from Jatani to Mebatsion as part of his baptism and assimilation into the dominant culture of Ethiopia. However he has been known to many as both Jatani Ali and Mebatsion Ali, depending on the context in which the name is used. In bureaucracy or in formal official papers he was addressed as Mebatsion Ali. Mebatsion was the Christian name his godfather, the late General Gashaw Kebede, forced him to take after he graduated from Aba Dina Police Academy with a rank of second lieutenant.

From his childhood in Borana country and as he moved through schools and the police cadet course in Addis Ababa, all those who knew him called him Jatani Ali. Acquaintances in his birthplace of Borana, schoolmates and police cadet course mates thus called him Jatani Ali. After graduation from the Police Academy, his name was officially changed to Mebatsion. Thus his personal files in the police force and government administrative jobs in the Ministry of the Interior carry the name Mebatsion Ali. Affectionately, many Borana refer to him simply as 'Jaato' or 'Shaalaqa' ("the major" in Amharic). Throughout this book the

---

[3] The European or Gregorian calendar is used with all dates in this book.

---

name Jatani Ali is used except where his name is quoted from official files as Mebatsion Ali.

Family

Jatani had six brothers and one sister; he was among the youngest. His father Ali Tandhu was a prominent Borana elder in the locality.[4] His mother was Karu Ali, a housewife.[5]

Jatani never married. He thought of it when he was in the police service, but it did not happen. After he got involved in public service outside Addis Ababa, he did not seriously consider about settling down and having a family. He gave priority to serving the public with unreserved dedication wherever he was assigned to work. Towards the end of his life, however, close friends urged him to get married. He accepted the idea and started courting a girl whom he hoped would be his future wife. Before the marriage materialised, however, the *Derg* regime[6] was toppled, and his career and eventually his life terminated. However, his fiancée had conceived and gave birth to a girl while he was in the bush. He never saw his daughter. The girl was brought up by her mother and was admitted to a local university in September 2012, to undertake an undergraduate degree course in sociology.

Growing up as a Borana child

Borana is a community of semi-nomadic herders that primarily depends on livestock resources for its livelihood, by rearing cattle, goats,

---

[4] 'Ali' here is not a Moslem name but a name commonly in use long before the introduction of Islam in the region. In this case, 'Ali' is derived from Afaan Borana verb "ala" (outside) and given to a child born outside a family home.

[5] Unlike in other parts of Ethiopia, in Borana culture, a married woman drops her biological father's name and takes up that of her husband's.

[6] A military junta that ruled Ethiopia between 1974 and 1991.

sheep and, to a lesser extent, camels. In Dirre district some families, including that of Jatani, raise horses.

From a tender age to adolescence, a Borana child grows up looking after the family's livestock. At around the age of six years, the child looks after small animals such as baby goats and calves within and around a homestead. By the time he is nine years old, he can look after cattle not far from home.[7] As he advances in age, he drives the animals, first goat and sheep and later cattle, to grazing sites far away from home. Jatani Ali grew up in his family home and village as a typical Borana boy until he was 11 years old. The people who knew him then described him as a bright, active and responsible child for his age.

Borana boy holding on to a goat
(Photo: Argaw Ashine, OXFAM – © OXFAM)

---

[7]   Reference is made to a boy here to illustrate the process of growing up as a child but most of it applies to girls as well, at least until they marry.

2: The Schooling and Training Era

In 1947, by order of Emperor Haile Selassie, 34 boys travelled from Borana to Addis Ababa for the purposes of gaining an education. They were part of a scheme that sought to create an educational pathway for marginalised nomadic herders in the farthest corners of Ethiopia. These Borana boys were lodged in boarding schools in Addis Ababa, together with other boys from other nomadic herding communities such as the Somalis. In September 1952, after the Emperor had exhorted these 34 boys to recruit their younger brothers as a second cohort, 31 Borana boys were recruited and arrived in Addis Ababa. Jatani Ali was one of these boys in the second and last batch of Borana students to attend boarding schools in the capital.

Among the boys in the first cohort, Jarso Halakhe was a member of Jatani's clan or subset of a tribe. As Jarso was the last son in his family, he did not have a young brother who would go with him to Addis Ababa to fulfil the Emperor's pledge. The clan members met to discuss who would go with Jarso. Reportedly, Jatani's father highlighted young Jatani's potential to become a good student given his alert demeanour and resourcefulness in completing all undertakings from a tender age. On that basis, Ali Tandhu, Jatani's father, gave his permission and requested members of his clan to allow Jatani to travel to Addis Ababa with Jarso.

Jatani attended two boarding schools in Addis Ababa: Medhane Alem from Grades 1-9 and General Wingate Secondary School, in Grades 10-12. Thereafter he undertook a three-year Police Cadet Officers' Training Course at Aba Dina Police Academy.

At Medhane Alem School

In September 1952, Jatani was admitted to Medhane Alem School, together with his compatriots. In this school there were already 34 boys from Borana who had come to Addis Ababa five years earlier in pursuit of education. At Medhane Alem, Jatani attended Grades 1 to 9. During this period, his school-mates recall that he was one of the most popular with fellow students, as well as with teachers and the school administration. He was articulate as a child and fond of telling stories he had heard and events he had witnessed while in Borana. Because of this attribute, close friends called him "Livy", a nickname after an ancient Roman historian who lived from 59 BC to 17 AD

Jatani at Medhane Alem School

After he completed Grade 9, the Ministry of Education closed secondary-level education at Medhane Alem. As a result all the boys requiring a secondary education from this school were dispersed to other boarding secondary schools in Addis Ababa. Jatani and some other boys were transferred to General Wingate Secondary School.

At General Wingate Secondary School

At General Wingate Secondary School Jatani was admitted to Grade 10 as he had already completed Grade 9 at Medhane Alem. In the new school, it did not take him long to gain popularity with fellow students as well as the school administration. His popularity was never of an opportunistic nature, but that of a person who has a love for people and positive attributes to influence people around him.

Jatani at General Wingate Secondary School]

The school had four residential halls, designated as Red, Yellow, Blue and Green houses. Each house had a capacity to accommodate around 50 boys. The school had a tradition of appointing a captain to each house. A teacher who was assigned as a supervisor of a hall also nominated a captain for it with the consent of the majority of the boys concerned. The appointment of a nominee was subject to the approval of the school director. The teacher who was in charge of the Red House where Jatani was hosted nominated him as a house captain. The director who, it can be assumed, knew Jatani's character and behaviour, endorsed the teacher's nomination.

Jatani attended Grades 10 to 12 in General Wingate Secondary School. Completing Grade 12, he sat for the Ethiopian School Leaving Certificate

Examination (ESLCE), but he did not get the required marks for automatic admission to Haile Selassie I University (now Addis Ababa University).

Jatani decided to study on his own to make up for the additional marks he needed for university admission. At the same time Dr Asmarom Legesse, an anthropologist who later became a prominent authority in Oromo culture, was a lecturer at Haile Selassie I University. He was preparing to carry out fieldwork on the Oromo *Gada* system, specifically in Borana country. He was looking around for a research assistant with some knowledge of Borana society and who could act as translator in dealing with Borana subjects. Incidentally, I was a student at this same University at the time. Dr Asmarom asked his students to look around for a Borana student who might help him find a translator. One of my fellow students introduced me to him. The anthropologist briefed me on the nature of his research and the type of person he was looking for as a translator. I promised to find one for him but was aware of the challenges where only a handful of ethnic Borana had gone to school at this stage. At that time, I knew about Jatani's effort in getting additional marks that would allow him direct admission to that University. I met up with Jatani and explained how an academic was looking for a translator in the research he was doing on Oromo culture, focussing on Borana society. At first Jatani showed reluctance to take up the job. I tried different approaches to persuade him, by highlighting its merits and future opportunities that such a job could lead to. I pleaded with him to not turn down the offer. I knew of Jatani's keen awareness of the conditions of life in Borana country and his passion to improve them. With this in mind, I tried to convince him how assisting the anthropologist in his research in Borana country would be a good opportunity towards his own personal development as well as his aim to improve the lot the Borana people. I further pointed out to him how Borana society would not be immune from all the changes in the world and stressed their need to embrace changes to secure the continuity of their culture and way of life. In an attempt to influence him; I added how the Oromo or Borana has a beautiful culture worth preserving for the benefit of current and future generations. I pointed how Borana was the only segment of the Oromo people where such a culture has remained unadulterated or mostly intact. I reasoned how the anthropologist's attempt to record such a culture for posterity was a noble undertaking. Our sessions of considering the pros and cons of working with the anthropologist helped Jatani in deciding to take up the job offer as a research assistant cum translator.

I introduced Jatani to Dr Asmarom and assured him how he wouldn't find a better person for the job than Jatani at that time. As expected Jatani shone during his initial contact with the anthropologist, which was partly an interview. The academic was impressed by the eloquence and behaviour of the young man and decided to employ him for a monthly wage of 200 Birr – a respectable sum in those days. He also promised to assist him in his preparation for exams for university admission. The anthropologist briefed Jatani on the scope of his research and how studying Borana culture was the focus of his study. Assessing the economic effects of change on Borana society from an anthropological perspective also featured as part of his study.

It was all a short-lived promise as Jatani's work contract with Dr Asmarom was terminated due to unexpected budgetary problems at the University. Dr Asmarom was very disappointed about these developments and with deep regret terminated Jatani's employment contract. Professor Asmarom (an academic title he later attained) travelled down to Borana and found Tari Jarso, a student at the time, to assist him with the translation. He carried out the preliminary research for eight years and produced a book entitled *GADA: Three Approaches to the Study of African Society* (published by the Free Press in New York in 1973). This book is regarded as a classic document in the study of the Oromo *Gada* instittion. He continued with the study of the Oromo culture and published another book entitled *Oromo Democracy: An Indigenous African Political System* (published by the Red Sea Press in Asmara in 2000). In this book the Professor discussed the fundamentals of Oromo democracy, how this system operated in the past and the effects of alien forces that had eroded it at the time of study.

Though only for a brief time, Jatani enjoyed his job working for Dr Asmarom, not least because it provided him with an opportunity to travel to Borana country. The same would allow him to study his own culture with a perspective of an ethnic Borana who went to school and experienced other cultures.

Following the end of his employment with Dr Asmarom, Jatani looked around for other jobs and training opportunities.

At Aba Dina Police Academy

At the time the Aba Dina Police Academy was recruiting young men who completed a Grade 12 level of education for a three-year police officers' training course.[8]

Emperor Haile Selassie had been forced to live in exile in Britain for five years following Mussolini's invasion of Ethiopia in 1935. Upon his return, his administration embarked on a mission of modernising the country through education and by building modern institutions. Aba Dina Police Academy was an example of this effort and was inaugurated on 15 October 1948.

To attract the best recruits, Aba Dina promised its cadets would get all the facilities and benefits those enrolled in the more prestigious Harar Military Academy were getting. Jatani was attracted by the promise and joined a three-year police cadet course at Aba Dina Police Academy in September 1962. His course was the eighth in the series and the first to enrol only those who completed Grade 12-level education with high marks. The training focussed on producing competent police officers for

---

[8] At first the academy recruited police cadets who completed at least a Grade 8 level of education but over the years this requirement changed to the completion of a Grade 12 level of education.

the modern age. Trainees acquired skills in basic policing, military and academic courses. He successfully completed the cadet training course in 1965, as a second lieutenant in rank in the Ethiopian Police Force.

While attending the course he showed much interest in sport and other police and social activities. It did not take him long to gain popularity among fellow cadets, instructors and the administration. There used to be a tradition in the cadet course where a graduating class would elect the most popular cadet through a secret ballot. The late Colonel Workineh Belihu and Major Eshetu Damote, both Jatani's course-mates, reported that, out of 42 graduating cadets, 92 per cent voted for Jatani. According to these two, this was the highest number of votes ever recorded in the history of Aba Dina Cadet School up to that point. The prestige of the school was such that Emperor Haile Selassie himself used to be the guest of honour at the graduation ceremony of the cadets. The same was an occasion when the cadet chosen as the most popular was awarded a gold watch by the Emperor. Jatani was a winner of such a coveted trophy and was awarded by the Emperor himself.

Emperor Haile Selassie with graduating cadets from Aba Dina Police Academy (6th Cadet course, 1959)

3: In the Service of the Ethiopian Police Force

Following his graduation from the Police Officers' Training Academy, he served in the Ethiopian Police Force for seven years at several places in different capacities.

Gamu Goffa

2nd Lt Jatani Ali in Gamu Goffa

Jatani's first assignment was in Gamu Goffa Administrative Region where he served for about two years. Ethiopia was divided into fourteen administrative regions or provinces at the time. It was one of the least developed and accessible provinces at the time, even by Ethiopia's poor standards. Jatani and one of his close cadet friends, Paulos Bogale, were reportedly assigned to Gamu Goffa for disciplinary reasons or transgressions. Jatani's role as student leader and campaigner against the unfulfilled promises to the students by the police cadet school was a reason for this punitive posting. As I mentioned earlier, in a bid to attract the best candidates, Jatani's police cadet school carried out a publicity campaign that promised candidates the provision of excellent training facilities and benefits similar to those accepted into a more prestigious Harar Military Academy. But the promise was not fulfilled. The new recruits persistently kept up their complaints with the Academy administration about unfulfilled promises. Jatani Ali and Paulos Bogale were amongst the most outspoken, and they spearheaded demands for the realisation of the promises. The cadet academy's administration did not like the persistent demands by Jatani and Paulos on behalf of other cadets. This militant behaviour presumably put the two cadets on the disciplinary black list.

After his stint in Gamo Goffa, Jatani lived and worked in Addis Ababa for several years, sharing a rented house with colleagues named Colonel Workneh Belihu and Major Eshetu Damote. Colonel Workneh recalls Jatani's behaviour that was likely to have put him on the black list at the Police Cadet School. The Academy had instructors in different disciplines or courses. Among them was a fellow named Colonel Legesse Wolde Mariam who provided training in law and was also in charge of disciplinary measures at the Academy. According to Colonel Workneh, Jatani found the law course too boring and did not like the style of its delivery. He was absent from some of the sessions and this was noted by the instructor. According to Colonel Workneh, it was Colonel Legesse who was suspected of having put Jatani on the disciplinary register of the Academy. Jatani and Paulos Bogale's first posting in the province of Gamu Goffa was thus a kind of mild punishment for their disciplinary transgressions.

Let me briefly highlight certain characteristics of Gamu Goffa where Jatani was assigned. At the time, the infrastructure in that province was so poor that it was one of the most inaccessible parts of the country by road. During the main rainy season that lasted about four months, the province was effectively cut off from the rest of the country. There were virtually lawless districts in the southern parts of the province straddling the Ethio-Kenya and Ethio-Sudan border regions. Some police stations in settlements such as Bume were only accessible during the dry season or by a light plane when high-ranking officials visited.

By far, the southern districts of Gamu Goffa were the least pacified region in Ethiopia at that time and even today. It was also a region made up of a polyglot of cultures and languages. Skirmishes and bloody wars were common between the various tribes. Some cattle-rustling parties raided deep into Kenya and Sudan creating diplomatic crises between these neighbouring countries and Ethiopia. The Hamar were the most war-like of these tribes and fought against all their neighbours. The Hamar's raids were not limited to their immediate neighbours but extended to other regions such as Borana to their east, a branch of an Oromo ethnic group, then ruled as part of the Sidamo Administrative Region (Sidamo *Teklay Gizat*). Residents in Borana and Gamu Goffa shared a fair bit in terms of their isolation, marginalisation and neglect by the central governments of Ethiopia, Kenya or Sudan. Communities in these remote areas lagged behind all others in Ethiopia in terms of their economic or social development parameters. There were virtually no roads, schools or health clinics in these two sub-regions. In most districts of Gamo Goffa or Borana, police stations – mud-wall structures held together by sticks – were the only institutions representing distant bureaucracies. Their main function was to reduce inter-tribal and/or cross-border raids and wars. Raids, counter-raids and livestock rustling were so common that some districts remained ungovernable for an extended period of time. Jatani's first post as a rooky police officer was in the country of the Hamar tribe, by far the most difficult of districts to govern even by Gamo Goffa's standards of remoteness and lawlessness.

Jatani did not bemoan his assignment in Gamu Goffa. He rather did his best to diligently execute his responsibilities. Although posted at Hamer district, he moved around to different stations in the area as there was a drastic shortage of trained police officers willing to go to this remote and lawless corner of Ethiopia. As part of his duties, Jatani attempted to instil the idea of peaceful co-existence between the warring tribes by encouraging dialogue between tribal leaders. His effort to stop warring and cross-border raids between the Hamar and Borana tribes was an example of this. But his tenure in Gamu Goffa lasted only two years and was hardly long enough to make a lasting impact on centuries-old feuds and wars between various communities. During his two years of posting in Gamu Goffa, it was reported that he discharged his duty with diligence and earned high respect from his superiors, colleagues and the communities he served.

Incidentally his compatriot, Paulos Bogale, stayed behind in the region for several years. He became so popular among the communities that they elected him to represent them in the Ethiopian parliament for one term lasting four years. Paulos not only represented the communities he came to serve as a police officer few years back, he became an ardent advocate against severe human rights abuses, complete lack of development and neglect endured by communities he came to represent at the parliament in Addis Ababa. He became one of the most outspoken members of the parliament against the Emperor's unjust and deeply oppressive rule. He ran for the second term and was re-elected to the parliament. However his outspoken stance was too much of an irritant to the conservative and feudalistic rulers of Ethiopia. The Electoral Board, apparently with a pressure from the emperor's court, created an excuse and barred him from serving out his second term in the parliament.

In Addis Ababa

Addis Ababa had become Jatani's home town as he had grown up and gone to school there. Most of his friends and mentors lived in and around the city. After his rather challenging post in remote districts of Gamu Goffa, he sought a posting in or near Addis Ababa. Given his knack for making friends and leaving a positive impression on people he met, Jatani managed to quickly find a posting in Addis Ababa police force.

He was transferred to the city's Traffic Police Unit where he served for about five years as an assistant officer in the accident investigation unit and as an organiser in the motorcycle traffic service. He provided regular police services at the city's 3rd and 4th police stations for some yime.

In the Addis Ababa Traffic Police Unit

Captain Jatani Ali in the Addis Ababa Police Service

At Addis Ababa Traffic Police Office, Jatani was first assigned to the motorbike service unit where his immediate supervising officer was Captain Yadate Gurmu, now a retired officer with the rank of Brigadier-General. His unit's routine operations involved the use of motor-bikes to monitor and manage the flow of the city's growing motor vehicle and pedestrian traffic. Around this time, the city was showing spurts of modernisation resulting in an increase in traffic and traffic accidents. This development owed in part to Addis Ababa's status as the 'diplomatic capital of Africa' and the seat of various international agencies such as the Organisation for African Unity (OAU) and the Economic Commission for Africa (ECA). Jatani's job as part of the city's traffic police department included organising the schedule and deployment of motorbike units as part of the city's traffic management. In addition, his unit provided official motorbike escorting services to the Emperor's entourage. This could be when the Emperor moves about in the city, travels to or from the city's airport, attends public rallies in celebration of national holidays or leaves the city to visit the provinces or foreign countries. Frequent visits by foreign dignitaries to the city kept the unit busy in escorting official entourages to and from the airport or around the city.

As a traffic police officer investigating accidents, Jatani became a very popular and trusted officer in Addis Ababa. He was always fair in carrying out accident investigation and solving any conflicts that arose from such incidents. The involved's social or class status mattered little to him in passing judgement. This was one of the virtues many motor vehicle owners he dealt with remember him for since. On one occasion, Emperor Haile Selassie travelled to the resort town of Bishofitu (Debre Zeit) with other members of the royal family for a weekend. On the return trip to Addis Ababa, the royal entourage included the grandson of the Emperor. The young prince was driving his own car but was delayed along the way. To catch up with the royal entourage, the prince drove his car recklessly and collided with a taxi. The taxi driver was detained for the accident and Jatani was appointed by his superiors as an investigating officer of the incident. He went to the site with an assistant officer named Teferedegn Yigezu (my informant on Jatani's character and performance while serving in Addis Ababa traffic police unit). After assessing the incident, Jatani told the prince that he, not the taxi driver, was the offender, according to the county's traffic rules and regulations. The prince accepted the verdict and requested Jatani and Teferedegn inform the Emperor's office about the matter. Jatani determined that it was neither his nor his superiors' business to go to the Emperor for such a common traffic accident. He simply recorded the incident by following normal procedures and advised his superiors of the innocence of the taxi driver. That was that. However, given the reverence and god-like aura with which the Emperor and his family were held in Ethiopia, this unusual approach in dealing with the royals left an indelible impression on all who worked at Jatani's traffic police unit.

Jatani Ali in a ceremonial police officer's uniform

As a delegate to international events

Jatani soon found himself travelling to other countries to take part in police-related symposia and conferences. One such was the 70th World Expo of Osaka, organised and sponsored by Japan in 1970. The organisers invited traffic police officers from all over the world to attend an international conference as part of the Expo. The Ethiopian traffic police received a formal invitation to the event and this was accepted by the country's Police Headquarters. As the matter directly concerned the traffic police unit, it was determined that four officers would be chosen to represent Ethiopia at the Osaka Expo. Three officers were chosen from

Addis Ababa Traffic Unit and the fourth was a co-ordinating officer of traffic affairs in the provinces at the National Police Headquarters. This four-man delegation was made up of Colonel Negussie Wolde Michael (head of Addis Ababa Traffic Police Unit); Major Abera Ayana (deputy to Col. Negussie); Lieutenant Jatani (Mebatsion) Ali (the officer in charge of the accident investigation unit of Addis Ababa Traffic Police); and Major Solomon Abay (co-ordinator of provincial traffic affairs from National Police Headquarters). Colonel Negussie was the team leader and all four were graduates from Aba Dina Police Academy, in the following serial course order: Colonel Negussie: 2nd; Major Solomon Abay: 3rd; Major Abera: 4th; and Lieutenant Jatani Ali: 8th. Jatani was by far the most junior member of the team in terms of both rank and age. His selection reflected his stature as a capable and respected officer in the Ethiopian police force.

I had the privilege of having been invited by Jatani to the pre-trip party organised by his cadet course-mates in his honour. Addis Ababa's Police Officers' Club was the venue for the party and it was an evening of tributes and enjoyment. It was an occasion for me to witness the exceptionally high and warm regard with which Jatani was held by his colleagues and friends alike. Clearly he was a natural at parties and was admired by many. His love for life was palpable.

The Delegation in the Conference Hall

The major theme of the conference at Osaka was an exchange of traffic and accident management matters by delegates from different parts of the world. The Ethiopian delegation presented their report. The findings and resolutions reached were published as a chapter in a book about policing, written in Amharic and published in Ethiopia in 1972. The author of the book was Brigadier General Moges Beyene and the book was entitled **Policina Gize** (*Police and Time*) (1941-1971). The chapter on the Osaka conference runs from pages 386 to 410. According to the report, 54 countries participated in the conference. The delegations from all over the world exchanged their experiences regarding the management of motor vehicle accidents via agenda items that included:

- How to protect children from traffic accidents;
- Actions to be taken to reduce accidents caused by drivers who are under the influence of alcohol;
- Actions to be taken to reduce accidents on pedestrians while walking on or crossing roads;
- Actions to be taken to reduce rear-end car crashes; and,
- General trends of traffic accidents in participating countries, whether it is increasing or decreasing,

Jatani at the conference dinner reception in Osaka, Japan

After extensive deliberations on the agenda topics, the following nine points appeared as part of the resolution:

1. In the 20th century, human beings have made impressive progress in motor transport services leading to improvements in people's livelihood all over the world.

2. Motor vehicle accidents have increased tremendously with the world-wide increase in motor vehicle ownership. Mistakes made by pedestrians, coupled with defects in motor vehicles, have resulted in millions of victims from motor vehicle-related accidents.

3. The human race has invented the motor vehicle for its many benefits. At the same time, humans are forced to make tremendous efforts to reduce direct or indirect damage caused by motor vehicles to human life, mutilation of bodies and destruction of property.

4. We, the traffic officers, see the effects of traffic accidents on people on a daily basis. Directly or indirectly, we are affected by these accidents. We often see how horrific traffic accidents are the result of bad driving behaviour, lack of respect for traffic rules, pedestrians' lack of knowledge on traffic rules, the lack of safe road-crossing points for children, etc.

5. The success of this traffic safety conference depends on our ability to educate the wider community on the perils of reckless driving and their failure to maintain motor vehicles in good condition. We request continued worldwide sharing of ideas and experiences to better manage traffic in our respective countries.

6. A reduction in motor vehicle accidents depends on improvements in driving skills, good behaviour of drivers, improved roads and on having adults and children who know the fundamentals of traffic rules.

7. On behalf of the participants this world traffic safety conference, we appeal to the higher authorities of concerned countries to pay more attention to the issue of traffic accidents and assist with the

efforts to reduce them.

8. With due respect, we ask the United Nations to look at the resolutions of this conference and to support world-wide efforts to reduce traffic accidents.

9. Finally, we appeal to worldwide drivers to educate themselves in safe driving techniques as the cars they drive are potentially as lethal as loaded guns.

The Ethiopian delegation to Osaka successfully completed its tour. Before travelling to Japan, the Ethiopian team was scheduled to visit the traffic police departments of Britain, France and West Germany to learn from these countries' well-established traffic and accident management techniques. The team visited police departments in the cities of London, Paris and Bonn. The following photos were taken during the team's tour of the three countries.

Three members of the Ethiopian Delegation

The British Police Unit was the host which gave them the following photograph with the attached note.

BRITISH OFFICIAL PHOTOGRAPH: CROWN COPYRIGHT RESERVED
ISSUED FOR INFORMATION SERVICES BY THE CENTRAL OFFICE OF INFORMATION, LONDON

A PARTY OF SENIOR POLICE OFFICERS FROM ETHIOPIA

Recently visited Britain for eleven days and followed a programme of arrangements made for them by the Central Office of Information, on behalf of the Foreign and Commonwealth Office,

The party comprises:

Lt. Col. Negusie Wolde Michael   *Chief of Traffic Police, Addis Ababa*

Major Aberra Ayana   *Deputy Chief of Traffic Police, Addis Ababa*

Major Solomon Abay   *Traffic Officer for the Provinces*

Lt. Meba-Tsion Ali   *Chief of accident investigation, Addis Ababa*

Mr. L. Coulstock Chief Maintenance and Installation Officer at GEC/Elliott Traffic Automation Ltd., explains an outside traffic light system to the visitors during their tour of the Company's factory, East Lane, Wembley, Middlesex.

The Delegation in Britain
From left to right: Maj. Solomon Abay, Maj. Abera Ayana, Col. Negussie Wolde Michael and Lt. Jatani Ali (respective ranks during the trip)

The Delegation in Germany

Jatani (on far left) with Traffic Officers in Germany

The Delegation in Paris, France

These tours highlighted personal qualities, human touch and competence that came to define Jatani as a leader. As indicated earlier, Jatani was the youngest and most junior member of the delegation. The fact that he was chosen to be part of this senior team of officers was indicative of the high esteem with which he was held by senior and junior police officers alike. He had a warm and magically engaging personality that made people gravitate towards him. His talent to tell a story with a humorous streak put even total strangers at ease. His likeable personality, mastery of languages and knack of discussing a wide range of topics made him an asset that the Ethiopian police delegation came to appreciate during their travels to Japan and Europe. He had an ability to make friends wherever he went regardless of language barriers. Here are some incidents of his travels that he told me on his return to Addis Ababa.

While in Japan he reported an incident that reflected his ability to easily relate to and influence people. In Osaka they met with many young and old Japanese who asked the guests for their autographs. Among these was a young Japanese lady who asked Jatani for an autograph and showed unique interest in him. She could not communicate her true feelings toward him because of the language barrier. Still she was able to convey her interest in him non-verbally or through the use gestures. She gave him her picture and a traditional wooden shoe for walking on snow as a memento. In exchange, she took his heart! With regret they departed forever. His house-mates Colonel Workneh Belihu and Major Eshete Damote reported that Jatani and his Japanese admirer kept up exchanging letters for quite a while afterwards.

Another incident showed Jatani's already well-honed people skills in solving conflicts. Relations between the members of the Ethiopian delegation were not always cordial. At times, the senior officers in the delegation did not get along well; often there were clashes of ego between the team leader and his deputy. As indicated above, Jatani was a very junior office of the team in terms of age and rank. Regardless, he soon emerged as a neutral arbiter of the team whenever conflicts arose. Jatani told me how many of the misunderstandings were on minor issues that should have been overlooked by persons of their age, experience and rank. Regardless of his own age and rank, Jatani's arbitration was upheld by the feuding individuals at least momentarily. One day, Jatani and I were walking along a street in Addis Ababa. We came upon Major Solomon Abay (now a Colonel) who had been member of Jatani's team during their travels. He was sitting at a bar with his colleagues and friends. The Major jumped up from his seat and greeted Jatani warmly. He told his friends at the bar how Jatani and he had been members of a delegation that travelled to Japan and Europe representing the Ethiopian police force. He added fondly, 'As you can see, he is younger than all of us gathered here today as he was the youngest member of that delegation then. Had he not been part of our delegation then we wouldn't have returned home in one piece. We would've finished each other off in foreign lands!'

There was another incident that might demonstrate the rather tense relationship between the senior officers in the delegation that travelled with Jatani. During a visit to a remote site far from a major city, it so happened that there was a shortage of single bedrooms for every member of the team at the hotel where they stayed. They were told that they would have to share rooms. Colonel Negussie, head of the delegation and senior member of the team, chose Jatani to be his roommate, even though protocol and expected norms would have required him to share a room with one of the senior officers. Jatani told him, 'Sir, after work and in the evening, I would like to go out to the town to unwind or just to look around. I might come back late at night and disturb your sleep.' The Colonel replied with a smile, 'You can go out and return at any time you wish, that won't disturb me at all.' One evening when Jatani returned to the room rather late, his roommate was not asleep but simply lying in bed. Jokingly and with a senior police officer's tone, he asked, 'Anything to report back from your inspection of the town?'

Campaigning for Borana representation in parliament

Jatani possessed a natural aptitude for persuasion way beyond his age. The small community of Borana persons residing around Addis Ababa often chose him as a delegate or a spokesperson in matters concerning the Borana people as a whole. For example, while Jatani was a chief investigating officer at Addis Ababa Traffic Police Unit, he was chosen by the community to assist with an electoral campaign of a fellow Borana for a seat in the Ethiopian Parliament. As part of the modernisation effort of the country and also to fend off political unrest, Emperor Haile Selassie's regime allowed a nationwide election of candidates to the national parliament in 1957. The parliamentary term lasted four years but several candidates competed against each other to represent their constituencies at the national parliament in Addis Ababa. Borana country, then ruled as part of Arero and Borana provinces, was allocated two parliamentary seats. As a rule, all candidates vying to represent the mainly Borana constituency were not ethnic Borana but wealthy members of the settler communities who resided in major towns such as Nagelle or Yaballo. The small community of Borana persons living in Addis Ababa realised this anomaly and resolved to encourage one of their own to stand for a parliamentary seat in Arero or Borana provinces. They started canvassing for suitable, young and educated ethnic Borana candidates in Addis Ababa and from Borana country as well. Unfortunately, only a handful of Borana had been to school at that time and even fewer of those would be ideal candidates given their place of residence outside Borana constituencies. The Borana community was not ready to nominate one of their own as a candidate for the first parliamentary election in 1957. However, the community found a promising young ethnic Borana candidate for the 1961 term of parliamentary elections. He was Dhera Jatani, a teacher who lived in Yaballo town with his wife and young children. Dhera Jatani, like

Jatani Ali and this author, was one of the Borana boys sent to a boarding school in Addis Ababa.[9]

Dhera Jatani stood for parliamentary elections of 1961 but failed to win a seat. It appears that this was in part due to his limited exposure to and brief campaign among the mainly rural Borana electorates who were unfamiliar with electoral politics. For the 1965 election, the Borana people in Addis Ababa pledged once again to support Dhera's candidacy. This time round, though, they went further to do something tangible to back Dhera's electoral campaign. The small Borana community in Addis Ababa gathered and sought ways of enhancing Dhera's chances of winning a parliamentary seat. One of these was to send Jatani Ali to Borana country to campaign on behalf of Dhera Jatani. He was also given a brief to lobby key Borana tribal leaders to support Dhera's candidacy, as well as educating community leaders on the fundamentals of electoral politics. Jatani was the right person to educate Borana people on the realities of Ethiopian political life and to highlight their unfavourable position within it. Jatani took 15 days' leave from his Traffic Police Office and travelled to Arero and Yaballo districts to assist Dhera's campaign. He met up with local chiefs and community leaders in both districts. Back in Addis Ababa, he briefed the community on the challenges of election-eering in the region and his efforts at supporting Dhera's candidacy. He told those of us who sponsored his trip to Borana how he managed to persuade community leaders to support Dhera and their pledge to back him. Unfortunately Dhera was unsuccessful again.

---

[9] See the Appendices for the list and pictures of Borana boys sent to boarding schools in Addis Ababa.

Dhera Jatani, candidate for parliament

4: At Haile Selassie I University

In its early history, Addis Ababa University used to be called Haile Selassie I University. Jatani did not go to the university as early as he wished as other engagements occupied his time. However, he did not abandon the dream of getting a university degree one day. Having fulfilled the requirements for admission to the university, he requested the Ethiopian Police Force for leave to pursue a university education. The Police Force granted him a leave of absence and he was admitted to the University in 1972, enrolling in the School of Social Work.

Jatani at Haile Selassie I University

Jatani stayed at the University for two academic years, 1972 and 1973. After he completed the first year and during the summer vacation, he led a group of high school boys from Addis Ababa to Harar in a kind of youth social development program. Getahun Metaferia, the head of Hararge Regional Education at the time, reported the story thus.

In the early 1970s, while Jatani was at the University, a person called Yigezu Oda initiated a youth leadership development program. Yigezu used to get funding for the program from businessmen, including from his own well-to-do family, and other philanthropists. During the summer vacation of 1973, 35 high school boys were chosen to take part in the program. Jatani was chosen from the University's School of Social Work to lead this team. The boys were hosted at Harar Teacher Training Institute. Jatani organised different activities in and around Harar that would demonstrate the concepts and styles of leadership to the students within the cultural contexts of the communities they visited. The activities included meeting with community leaders and notable residents. These leaders shared their approach at leading a private or a community-based meeting with the boys. Jatani planned to widen the scope of leadership concepts to practical application in government offices. In order to relate theoretical concepts of leadership to their practical application, he invited several high-level government officials in the city to share their leadership style and experience with the boys. Among such officials was Getahun Metaferia, the head of Hararge Regional Education Office and my informant about Jatani's role in the Harar youth development program. Getahun gave a lecture on the concept of leadership and used practical cases from his own line of work to illustrate the ideals of effective leadership. After a brief lecture he opened the floor to questions. Getahun recalled a question one of the boys asked him. It was: 'How can a person attain authoritative power?' His reply was, 'There are four possible ways of attaining authoritative power'; he added how these ways were: 'inheritance, legal election, education and use of force.' According to Getahun, the boys enjoyed the lecture and asked for its repetition on another day. Apparently, the boys showed such an intense interest in the lecture to enhance their own understanding about the nature of the oppressive bureaucratic regime in the country against which they were waging a campaign of civil disobedience.

One of the major activities in the social services program was cleaning the old quarters of Harar town known as Jegol. Harar is one of the oldest historical towns in Ethiopia and Jegol formed a core of an Islamic walled city around which the rest of the town grew. The old section of the town lacked facilities for sanitation and local streets were strewn with rubbish. Reportedly, the boys did a commendable work in cleaning Jegol and the activities of that year's program were lauded as a huge success. On the last day of the program, the organisers awarded Jatani Ali an expensive wristwatch as a token of appreciation for his superb leadership qualities in implementing that summer's youth development program.

5: The Literacy & Development Campaign

Shortly after the Harar program, Ethiopia experienced unprecedented political turmoil as the result of a military *coup de état* in September 1974 that toppled Emperor Haile Selassie I and the Solomonic dynasty that he led. The military committee or junta that removed the Emperor was locally known as the *Derg*. The Literacy and Development Campaign (LDC) was one of the major and controversial undertakings by the *Derg* regime immediately after toppling the ancient feudal monarchy that ruled Ethiopia for centuries. The same was meant to serve as a conduit through which the regime explained its ideology and actions to the vast majority of Ethiopians who lived in rural areas.

Background

Emperor Haile Selassie was a monarch who held absolute power over every aspect of life in the country. However, many regarded him as a benevolent ruler. The 1974 military coup that deposed the Emperor was preceded by a failed coup in December 1960, spearheaded by officers from his own Imperial Bodyguards. The 1960 *coup d'état* lasted briefly and was violently put down by loyalists from other branches of the imperial army and police forces. However, it was enough to galvanise sections of the society that have been pressing for political reform or even regime change for years. For example, many university and high school students supported the ideals of the coup then, as they did during the later coup, which successfully ridded Ethiopia of the monarchy in 1974. The failure of the 1960's coup did not put out the flame of opposition against the despotic regime of the Emperor but only pushed it underground. First university students and later high school students kept alive the movement against the monarchy for years after the first coup was put down.

Such broad-based popular opposition against the feudal regime served as a catalyst for the military coup to remove the Emperor from power some 14 years later.

Leading up to the coup, the first moves in undermining the authority and rule of the Emperor took place in February 1974 when the Emperor's incumbent Government, led by Prime Minister Aklilu Habte Wolde, resigned *en masse*. The Emperor appointed Endalkachew Makonnen as the Prime Minister and instructed him to form a new, ostensibly more progressive, government. But nothing short of total regime overhaul would satisfy those who were pressing for political change in the country. Protests against the new Prime Minister continued unabated and spread to different parts of the country. Endalkachew appeared not to be effective in quelling mass unrest and he was replaced after only a brief stint at the post. The Emperor appointed Michael Emiru as a new Prime Minister hoping that he would be more acceptable to the public, to no avail. Students who sought a radical regime change pressed on with their protests as the country's social and economic crisis worsened with the skyrocketing in the price of gasoline. At the same time, a large swathe of the country was gripped by a severe famine and the news of this was kept under wraps from the rest of the public.

Under such turmoil and confusion, certain self-appointed individuals from a military barracks in Addis Ababa took the initiative to organise other progressive elements from the army and police forces into a committee to tackle the country's worsening political turmoil. To this end, the individuals called a meeting of delegates representing various units of the army and police forces at a military barracks in Addis Ababa. In a bid to alienate high-ranking officers perceived to be loyal to the Emperor, they stipulated that only officers with ranks of a major or below should be sent as delegates to the convention. In response to the invitation, 109 delegates assembled at the 4th Army Division Headquarters in Addis Ababa. They called themselves the *Derg*, an Amharic word that roughly translates as "a committee". Their influence grew over the following months and they staged a peaceful coup that removed the Emperor from his throne on 12 September 1974, imprisoning him in the same army barracks.

Early days of the *Derg*

One of the *Derg*'s immediate undertakings was to declare that theirs was a socialist revolution. For that, they enlisted all university and senior high-school students in Grades 11 and 12 to educate the populace on the virtues of this revolution. To this end, universities, colleges and senior high schools suspended their normal teaching programs for two consecutive years.

Thus, Jatani's aspiration for a university degree came to an end. He did not return to his job in the Police Force but was drafted to join the *Derg*'s campaign locally known as *idget be hibret zemecha* (development through collective effort). The campaign's aim was to free Ethiopia from centuries of misrule, illiteracy and poverty through a campaign that focussed on mass literacy and rural development programs. The English version of *idget be hibret zemecha* was the LDC and Jatani joined it, not as a student but as a leader of a contingent dispatched to Arero *Awraja*, then part of Sidamo Administrative Region (Sidamo *Kifle Hager*).

From the onset, the campaign was received with equal measures of enthusiasm and scepticism. Some sections of the population saw it as a deliberate act on the part of the *Derg* to strengthen its grip on power by sending its opponents to rural areas under the guise of the LDC. The soldiers who took the reins of power knew very well the vital role students played in the downfall of the Emperor. At the very least, the presence of students in major cities was viewed as an irritant to the military junta that was trying to consolidate its grip on power.

Many believed the years of the students' movement was the force that precipitated the demise of the Emperor's regime. Students saw the soldiers as usurpers of a cause for which many students had been killed by the feudal and conservative regime presided over by the Emperor. At the time, I was a school director at Shimelis Habte High School in Addis Ababa. I overheard students openly lamenting how the group who made the least contribution to the downfall of the regime, ended up, by default, becoming the supreme authority in the country. They reasoned that this happened simply because there was no better organised or agreeable entity in the country to take power from the Emperor. They would say "the house was empty" to indicate how there was a power vacuum and how this was filled by the least desirable of all forces (the same military that used to shoot at student protesters). Students held raw memories of fellow students killed by the army and police while protesting against the oppressive regime. Leaders of the military junta, who moved by chance into the palace, were fully aware of students' hatred for them and their ability to agitate the public to rise against a dictatorial regime.

Many students believed that the LDC was a decoy by the military junta to get rid of the very force that was likely to oppose their grip on power: namely, the students. The LDC was meant to last for just one year but the military regime extended it to two years. This action reinforced even further the view held by some that the main goal of the campaign was not a concern for the impoverished masses in rural areas, literacy or rural development but to undercut popular opposition to the *Derg*.

The Campaign

In Ethiopia the academic year used to start on the third week of September. However, this routine was altered following the coup. That year, educational institutions were not opened as usual and university and high school students hung around for two months without knowing what to do. Actually, the new regime was completing plans to send students to rural areas of the country as part of its LDC. No official data are available to establish the exact number of students and teachers who participated in the scheme. However, it is understood that tens of thousands took part. Thousands of university and senior high school students were dispatched to all administrative regions of the country (except to Eritrea due to the ongoing war between rebel forces and the Ethiopian state). The *Derg* neither took ample time to organise nor had the experience to mobilise such a large number of students to rural areas for an extended period of time. It lacked a formula to keep these young people motivated for such a long time away from their families. The whole thing was put together hurriedly in about two months. The regime put a Major named Kiros Alemayehu in charge of the mobilisation for the LDC and Major Dawit Wolede Giorgis was appointed his deputy. I have not managed to access any detailed reports or studies done on the achievements or failures of this campaign. One way or the other, the military regime managed to keep students they perceived as troublemakers away from the centres of power for about two years.

Given the haphazard manner in which the students were unleashed on unsuspecting and culturally alien rural communities, it was not clear how much control the regime had on what hordes of students were meant to do. There was little to suggest that enough consideration was given to clearly delineate the mandate of the students and ways of regulating their behaviour in their interaction with rural communities. There were all kinds of wild rumours floating about where students on this campaign had become a law unto themselves in dealing with villagers. There were reports of students interfering with or taken over the governance of the entire Administrative Region of Arsi, then headed by a governor named Tesfa Bushen. The students marched into the office of Tesfa Bushen and ordered him to do something outside his mandate as governor. Arsi was one of the 14 Administrative Regions into which the country was divided at the time. He told the students to leave his office as he only received orders from the central government or the military junta that ruled the country. The students forcefully removed him from office and sent him to Addis Ababa. In fact, rumours about students acting outside the guidelines of the campaign or simply running amok in rural areas were rife at the time. There were worrisome reports whereby students allegedly interfered with centuries-old marriage institutions or disrupted domestic family affairs. According to a rumour from Arsi, a region where many people followed Islam and polygamy was the norm, students told a Muslim husband with several wives to change his attitude and keep only one wife.

Major Dawit and officials of the *Derg* "head-hunted" individuals with local knowledge, experience in public or community service and leadership qualities to serve as coordinators in its LDC. Jatani was exactly the kind of person they were looking for. Fellow Social Work student Mesele Dhaba and he were from Borana country and they later became the governor and deputy governor of Arero Province respectively.[10] Mesele indicated how both showed reluctance to be sent to their home province, given all the political angst associated with the campaign, the curse of familiarity, entrenched attitudes and personal security. Major Dawit however managed to persuade them by highlighting the pros of working for the good of a community they both knew a great deal about.

Jatani was assigned to lead the campaign in Arero Province which was then part of Sidamo Administrative Region.[11] He established the provincial main station of LDC at Yaballo town and organised sub-stations at Yaballo, Hagere Mariaim, Teltele, Mega, Hidi, Tuqa and Moyale districts. He assigned senior university lecturers as station coordinators and mentors of students allocated to these sub-stations. Thus, he started his duty as a coordinator of LDC in Arero Province according to the guidelines from the *Derg*. Jatani appointed Mesele Dhaba first as a program coordinator at Yaballo sub-station and later transferred him to Teltele sub-station.

This was a time defined by chaos and political uncertainty following the military coup that removed the old imperial order. Getting rid of the

---

[10] According to Mesele, it was specifically because they were both native to Borana country that they were assigned to Arero Province as part of the LDC.

[11] Political configurations and administrative structures in Ethiopia have undergone changes since then.

Emperor was the easy part. Undoing established norms, attitudes and power relations soon become a far more complex and bloodier undertaking than anticipated. The country was in a revolution instigated from the capital and was wading through uncharted waters of political, ideological, class and ethnic turmoil. The huge human and material cost of all these dramatic and sudden social upheavals had yet to be felt. Things were fluid and no one knew with relative certainty as to where the country was headed at this stage. Defections of government officials and ordinary citizens to neighbouring countries started and soon grew in intensity. Many students and college instructors assigned to Arero province as part of the LDC easily crossed the border into nearby Kenya. Such defections affected the conduct of the campaign during the first year. Relative stability was attained during the second year, albeit with a great deal of micro-management of campaign programs by Jatani.

Captain Jatani Ali:
Chief Coordinator of 'idget be hibret zemecha' (LDC)
in Arero Province]

Jatani told me about the challenges he faced while acting as a campaign manager in a remote province that bordered Kenya. In particular I remember the story he told me when he went to campaign headquarters in Addis Ababa to brief Major Dawit. The major told him how they were up to their necks in sorting out all manners of hiccups and complaints coming from all corners of the country. He added that he and all staff at the campaign head office felt harassed both from above (regime leaders) and from those sent to provinces to help the people. Realising how things were moving along relatively smoothly in stations where Jatani was a coordinator, he asked, 'What techniques do you employ at your station to contain or solve problems that other stations keep on complaining about, seeking our intervention?' Jatani told Dawit that he was not using any miraculous techniques in handling problems that do crop up except the use of participatory approach in finding solution. He went on to say,

First I made sure that all participants are made aware of the magnitude of the tasks at hand. Second, I highlighted the social, cultural, political and resources constraints to be overcome in order to complete set tasks. Third, I indicated the extent of resources at hand and what I thought was an efficient way of using them. Fourth, I assured all sub-stations would get their fair share of resources and I would do all possible to secure vital resources for the campaign.

Jatani concluded his answer by discussing how he handled problems that might locally crop up, saying,

At all sub-stations, I organised committees consisting of teachers and students who would deal with any matter that was out of line and I was often invited to such committee meetings to have my input.

He added, 'By luck or design, no issue went out of our hands to seek intervention from the headquarters.' Reportedly, the campaign headquarters in Addis Ababa rated Jatani's unit as one of the most successful in terms of the smooth management and achievement despite the remoteness and close proximity of the site to both Kenya and Somalia.

This was not to suggest that serious matters didn't arise at Jatani's main station or sub-stations from time to time. One such involved embezzlement of campaign funds and defection of key members to Kenya. University and senior high-school teachers assigned to his stations would be given tasks in which they led a group of students to various localities. One day, a teacher who acted as a treasurer withdrew several thousands of Birr for himself and defected to Kenya. By that time, political conditions in Ethiopia were becoming so volatile that defections to neighbouring countries were becoming the norm. It was often difficult to tell which among the defections owed to a legitimate fear of persecution at home and which an opportunistic search for a better life in a foreign country.

A high-profile defection

There was another high-profile defection that involved a native Borana named Major Salesa Jallo. The fellow was a contemporary of Jatani Ali from boarding schools in Addis Ababa and was in charge of an LDC contingent dispatched to the neighbouring Borana province, with its capital of Nagelle Borana. Halfway through the campaign, he decided to quit and defected to Kenya with three other Borana men named Boru Dinne, Mamma Waqo and Saar Jarso. On their way to Kenya, the defectors met up with Jatani in Mega town. They explained their intention, asked him to reject the regime and to join them in seeking exile in neighbouring countries. He declined the offer. This was what Jatani told me in terms of his reasoning for choosing to stay back in Ethiopia. He said, 'I didn't see how I could possibly help the Borana people from the outside. For me, the best way to help them would have to be by living among them in the same country.' The defectors crossed into Kenya and obtained asylum. They stayed in Nairobi for about five months and moved to Somalia to join ethnic liberation fronts operating from there. Siad Barre was the president of Somalia at the time and his regime backed various ethnic liberation fronts operating within Ethiopia. These included the Eritrean Liberation Front (ELF), the Tigray Peoples' Liberation Front (TPLF), the Oromo Liberation Front (OLF) and Liberation Fronts for Ethiopia's Somali region (that is, in the Ogaden). His support was conditional and linked to his own agenda of carving out a huge chunk of territory from Eastern Ethiopia as part of his 'Grand Somalia' scheme. In Mogadishu, the Somali capital, Salesa Jallo and his friends met up with Galassa Dilbo who was then the OLF Commander. The OLF was said to have some rebel fighters operating in some outlying areas of Hararge, in eastern Ethiopia. Salesa and his friends didn't quite find what they had hoped for. Galassa told them that the movement he led had difficulty in establishing an effective line of communication with their supporters at home. He reportedly told them that, had he known about their intentions to come to Somalia ahead of time, he would have advised them to refrain from doing so. According to Galassa, Somalia did not provide the OLF with genuine and encouraging support. That was so because Somalia's and OLF's agenda clashed badly. Somalia supported liberation fronts that would actively assist Somalia's overarching agenda of territorial expansion. Fronts whose mission was the liberation of a different people such as the Oromo, without it also helping to advance Somalia's expansionist agenda, didn't interest Siad Barre.

Major Salesa was a highly-trained army officer in the Ethiopian army and was an instructor of Ethiopia's army officers before he was enlisted in the LDC. Given Salesa's knowledge of the army and his opposition to the military junta ruling Ethiopia, he was a valuable asset to Somalia. As expected, Somalis welcomed Salesa and appointed him a deputy to a Somali colonel tasked with the invasion of southern Ethiopia. His name was Colonel Abdullah Yusuf and he was the Commander of the Somali Southern Military Command with the specific mission of invading southern Ethiopia, including Borana and Arero provinces. This way, Salesa and his friends were dispatched to Borana country. On their way to fulfil their mission, Mamma got ill with a malarial infection. They left him behind at the Somalia-Ethiopia border and moved into the interior of Borana province. After slight recuperation, Mamma ran away from the recovery site and surrendered to Ethiopian forces in the area.

The other three marched into Borana province with the Somali command force they joined. After several months in the front, Colonel Abdullah Yusuf was ordered to arrest Salesa and his friends and to send them to Mogadishu. It was reported that there were various soldiers who served in the same command alongside Salesa but belonged to various ethnic groups in the area that were not particularly friendly to ethnic

Borana. It was alleged that such anti-Borana persons had instigated the arrest of Salesa and his colleagues. They were: Ali Badia (nickname), who was in the service of the Somalia National Security; Mohammed Hassan, a Garri chief (Garri are claimed by some to be a Somali clan); Tahir Shake Hussein, a Dgodia chief (a Somali clan); Takale Utura, claimed to be a Gujii chief (an Oromo clan) and Nura Arero, an ethnic Borana who represented nobody but himself. These plotters and others fabricated allegations that claimed that Salesa and his friends were not genuinely working for Somalia but had a separate hidden agenda that upheld Oromo interests. Without explanation, Colonel Abdullah was ordered to immediately arrest Major Salesa Jallo and his colleagues and hand them over to concerned authorities in Mogadishu.

Eventually, Somalia was defeated in its war against Ethiopia and its forces and collaborators were driven out of the country. A few years later, some senior officers planned a *coup d'état* against Siad Barre but the plot was discovered before it was implemented. Siad Barre killed some of the plotters while others were arrested. Colonel Abdullah Yusuf – the commanding officer of the Somali invasion to southern Ethiopia – was one of the plotters but fled to Ethiopia to save his life. He was given fair treatment in Ethiopia and was associated with an Ethiopian high-ranking official to whom he narrated the circumstances of arrest and the charges against Major Salesa and his colleagues.

Major Salesa and colleagues were thrown into a Mogadishu prison in which another well-known and celebrated Ethiopian Air Force pilot was also imprisoned. His name was Major Legesse Tefera and he was captured by Somali forces as the air force jet plane he was flying exploded mid-air before reaching its target, according to his account. Major Legesse and Major Salesa knew each other from earlier while both were in Asmara, the capital of the war-torn province of Eritrea in northern Ethiopia. Their units jointly fought Eritrean rebel forces from the air and on the ground. Major Legesse remained in Somali detention for 11 years. After his release and return to Ethiopia, the *Derg* promoted him to the rank of Brigadier General. I had an opportunity to meet General Legesse who told me a little about his prison life in Mogadishu, how he was in the same prison with Major Salesa Jallo and Salesa's two other colleagues for three years and how afterwards they moved them out of that prison. Legesse hadn't heard about them since then.

The defection of Salesa to Somalia put Jatani Ali under a cloud of suspicion with some members of the *Derg* who did not know him well. The ramifications of this suspicion against Jatani and how it was eventually resolved will be discussed later.

Jatani's success in the LDC

Let me mention some of the key achievements of Jatani as part of the LDC. The *Derg* regime tried to re-organise the social fabric of Ethiopians, living both in rural and urban areas, in the hope of improving their living standards. The *Derg*'s new land reform decree enacted during this period introduced radical changes to the prevailing economic, social, and political relations in the country. Grass-roots organisations cropped up to assist the regime in tackling some of the social, economic, security and political problems facing the country. People in urban areas were organised through a grass-roots organisation called *kebele* while those in rural areas were organised under the umbrella of the Peasant Association (PA). Those partaking in the LDC tried to teach peasants how to sustainably manage plots of lands allocated to them by a decree from the military regime (also referred to as revolutionary regime). For example, they showed farmers how to terrace their farms to reduce the effects of soil erosion.

Under the rule of feudal monarchies, presided over by emperors from the Christian northern half of the country, Ethiopia had two distinctive landholding systems. One was called *rist* and applied to the northern half of the country. Under the *rist* system, land was owned by a head of the family and passed to his/her descendants down the generations. Both the sub-dividing of the original plots down through the generations and population growth led to the creation of ever-smaller plots of farms that were hardly enough to sustain those who owned and cultivated them. The loss of topsoil, as the result of the hilly nature of the terrain and centuries of ploughing these same farms, gradually reduced the yield from such plots. Unless new territories were added to the overall landholding of these northern regions through conquest, the prospect of widespread poverty and famines was real. An acute shortage of arable land and famines in northern Ethiopia were the economic impetus that led to the emergence of warlords-cum-kings hell-bent on expanding the Ethiopian empire through conquest. Newly-conquered lands were then allocated to soldiers and collaborators who assisted with the conquest, pacification and colonisation of these conquered territories. These newly-landed colonists and former soldiers were known as *neftegna* and/or *gultegna*, they become the landowning class in territories they helped to conquer.[12]

Hence, southern provinces of Ethiopia were added to the empire through a series of bloody acts of conquest. As expected, the former *gultegna-neftegna* class and their descendants emerged as the main foci of resistance against the *Derg*'s land reform policy and all it set out to do, to improve the lot of former serfs (*gebar*), landless tenant farmers (*chisegna*) and nomadic pastoralists who basically roamed on crown-owned lands in the central-southern regions. Thus, it was no mere coincidence that the *Derg* regime faced its stiffest resistance either from the northern half of Ethiopia or from colonist settlers in southern Ethiopia (with their roots in northern Ethiopia).

Resistance to the *Derg* regime and policies were comparatively mild in southern Ethiopia as the locals in these regions stood to benefit from the reforms. In the end and not surprisingly, the *Derg* regime was defeated by armed rebels from the north of Ethiopia. The land reform decree by the

---

[12] The term *gultegna* literally means he who 'owns' a *gult* land or farm in exchange for his services to the king or emperor. The term *neftegna* literally

Derg was lauded as the most important legislation ever undertaken by any regime in Ethiopia. Farmers in these central-southern provinces of Ethiopia however didn't end up becoming the outright owners of land that was forcefully taken from their ancestors following conquest. The reform merely transferred land ownership from the mostly northern landlords to the Ethiopian state. Suddenly, farmers in central-southern Ethiopia found themselves working land that now belonged to the state, as distinct from working for "parasitic" settler landlords from northern Ethiopia (*neftegna*). Even today, land remains the property of the state and therefore the most effective economic means of political control over most Ethiopians who happen to be farmers.

One of the most important undertakings by those involved in the LDC was to assist with the implementation of the *Derg*'s land reform policy. This included the act of formally reclaiming tracts of land from the landlords and distributing it to former serfs (*gebar*), tenant farmers (*chisegna*) and landless squatters. Trying to implement the *Derg*'s radical land reform policy was by far the most dangerous undertaking by those involved in the LDC. It often led to violent clashes between disgruntled but armed landlords and a band of students and teachers from the LDC trying to redistribute land. The process invariably pitted the new forces of change (LDC and the peasants they tried to empower) against those determined to defend the *status quo* (furious, still-armed former landlords and the communities they represented).[13]

The *Derg* embarked on a multi-pronged agenda to improve the lot of the severely impoverished peasants of Ethiopia. In order to achieve this goal, the regime needed the support and resources of these peasants. One way of achieving this was by organising them into peasant associations,

---

means 'he who carries a *neft* [rifle]' and implies the person's role as a soldier of the conquering king or emperor.

[13] Ethiopia's exploitative feudal land tenure system will be discussed further in a later chapter.

farmers' self-defence militias, farmers' cooperatives and the like. The task of organising communities into such organisations or cooperatives was another responsibility of those taking part in the LDC. Starting a basic illiteracy program for all those who didn't have an opportunity to go to schools was another undertaking of the LDC. In those days, access to formal education was the preserve of a tiny town-based minority. Most school children in central-southern regions of Ethiopia emanated from the settler communities that lived in towns that grew around the *gultegna-neftegna* feudal system. Very few students – if any – from indigenous and rural communities in these southern regions went to school. Ethiopia had one of the lowest rates of literacy in the world despite being the only country in black Africa to have its own writing system in use since before the birth of Jesus Christ.

Under the conditions highlighted above, it would be easy to imagine all sorts of crises and conflicts thwarting Jatani's ability to fulfil his duty as a coordinator of the LDC in Arero province. In reality, Jatani's station held together relatively very well compared to most other LDC stations in the country. Many observers attributed this positive atmosphere in Jatani's sector to his nature as a "people person", his rare ability as a leader, his ability to easily negotiate competing cultural imperatives due to his multicultural upbringing or knowledge and his strong sense of duty.

6: In the Ministry of the Interior

Biographical accounts of Jatani Ali touch the reigns of three successive regimes in the recent and dangerously fluid history of Ethiopia. Those individuals who managed to make a difference to the lives of people in the regions or provinces of Ethiopia would have to have the skills, patience and courage to negotiate Ethiopia's distinctly byzantine bureaucracy and Machiavellian intrigues. Jatani was one such governor.

Structure of the Ethiopian Government

Each regime that has ruled Ethiopia changed the naming of and the overall structure of the country's administrative system to reflect its ideological outlook, the parochialism of the ruling tribe or simply the whims of the dictator of the time. For example, all three regimes changed the Amharic word for a province as though they wanted to remove the scent mark of the regimes they violently replaced and brush the country with their own scent marks. Such changes by decree of Amharic terms to represent the country's administrative units was nothing more than a wasteful act of window dressing that added nothing useful except more confusion for the population. Despite all the name changes, the essence of Ethiopia's system of government remained top-down, dictatorial, militaristic and despotic. To varying degrees of cruelty, all regimes ruled the country through the use of state-instigated violence. Notwithstanding all name changes, the country more or less retained its four-tiered levels of government: central, regional, provincial and district. During the rule of the Emperor, the country was divided into 14 Administrative Regions referred to as *Teklay Gizat* in Amharic. Administrative Regions comprised Provinces known as *Awrajas* and the Provinces broke down into districts called *Woredas*.

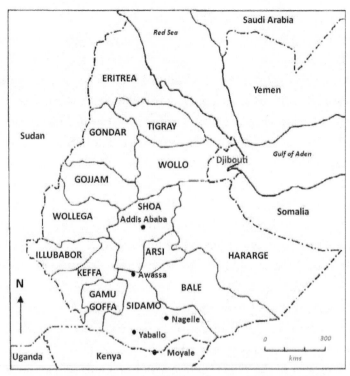

Administrative Regions of Ethiopia between 1952 and 1987
(Adapted from "The Ethiopian Revolution, 1974-91" by Teferra Haile Selassie)

The *Derg* that deposed the Emperor and later called the country the Socialist Democratic Republic of Ethiopia, more or less retained the administrative structure it inherited from the previous regime. However, the *Derg* did make some alterations to this administrative structure in a bid to give rebellious provinces such as Eritrea and Afar a semblance of autonomous rule and renamed *Teklay Gizat* as *Kifle Hager*. It also made attempts to reduce administrative red tape and hasten the delivery of services to the population through the creation of grassroots organisations named Peasant Associations (PAs). People living in towns were organised along *Kebele* Associations (KAs). The *Derg* regime was defeated by the combined rebel armies of two ethnically-related groups from northern Ethiopia. They were the Eritrean People's Liberation Front

(EPLF) and the Tigray People's Liberation Front (TPLF).[14] Ethnic Tigre people made up the bulk of the population both in Tigray Administrative Region and in the neighbouring Eritrean Administrative Region. As well as ethnic commonality, people in both regions have long questioned the very legitimacy of those ruling Ethiopia (ethnic Amhara) from Addis Ababa. This was so because these northern regions had historically been the political epicentre of the Ethiopian empire. The elite of the Tigre tribe saw themselves as the legitimate inheritors of the Ethiopian throne. However, for over a century or so, the epicentre of Ethiopia's state power shifted from the Tigre region to ethnic Amhara regions just south of them. Though both Tigre and Amhara tribes share a great deal in terms of culture and religion – both are staunch followers of the Orthodox branch of Christianity – they fought over Ethiopia's imperial throne. In the eyes of ethnic Tigre elites, ethnic Amhara (the ruling tribe of Ethiopia from Addis Ababa) usurped their region's status as the legitimate and God-given king-makers of Ethiopia. Additionally, people in Eritrea and Tigray felt neglected and oppressed by successive Amhara rulers, namely the Emperors and the *Derg*. These northern regions also suffered from frequent famines due to recurrent droughts and brutality from Ethiopian army units stationed there to suppress dissent. Despite the fact that most neglected and most oppressed communities were concentrated in the southern half of Ethiopia, the *Derg* regime was defeated by rebel armies from the north, dominated by ethnic Tigre from Eritrea and Tigray Administrative Regions. One of the first undertakings by the rebels-turned-rulers of Ethiopia who ousted the *Derg* regime was to facilitate the secession of Eritrea from Ethiopia. They too proceeded to re-arrange the administrative structure of the country and came up with their own terms to rename the country's administrative tiers of government.

---

[14]   *Shabia* (EPLF) and *Woyane* (TPLF) are the less formal names most Ethiopians use for these rebel movements.

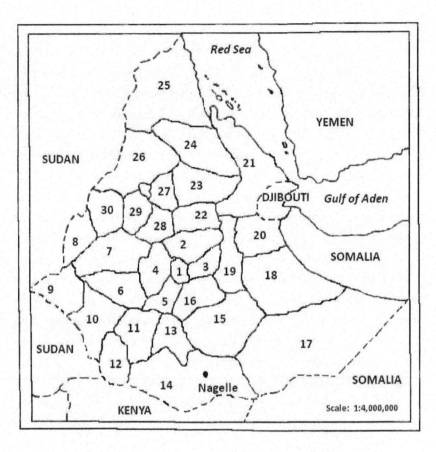

1. Addis Ababa	11. Northern Omo	21. Aseb
2. Northern Shoa	12. Southerm Omo	22. Northern Wollo
3. Eastern Shoa	13. Sidamo	23. Southern Wollo
4. Southerm Shoa	14. Borana	24. Tigray
5. Western Shoa	15. Bale	25. Eritrea
6. Illubabor	16. Arsi	26. Northern Gondar
7. Wollega	17. Ogaden	27. Southern Gondar
8. Assosa	18. Eastern Hararge	28. Eastern Gojjam
9. Gambella	19. Western Hararge	29. Western Gojjam
10. Keffa	20. Dire Dawa	30. Metekele

Ethiopia's Administrative Regions from 1987 to 1991
(Adapted from "The Ethiopian Revolution, 1974-91" by Teferra Haile Selassie)

The country became the most populous landlocked country in the world following Eritrea's separation from Ethiopia. The rest of the country was divided into nine ethnically defined regions the new rulers called *Kilil* and two city-based special administrative regions or *Kilil*. Each *Kilil* was divided into Zones (provinces) and each Zone into districts (*Woredas*). It is not clear why an English word "Zone" was chosen to designate a province when the names for the rest of administrative tiers were all derived from Amharic-sounding words, Ethiopia's *lingua franca*. The *Derg*-era grassroots PAs and KAs were retained but other and more intricate layers were added to them to enhance the regime's ability to control what went on in the country, at neighbourhood and individual levels. These last tiers were called "teams "or "1 to 5" and were akin to "neighbourhood watch" organisations such as found in totalitarian countries like North Korea, China and Cuba. The "1 to 5" was an organisational cell made up of 5 persons and led by a regime-approved convener from among them. The convener of such a cell was himself/herself a member of another cell higher up the chain of organisational hierarchy. Such a cell had the task of gathering information on the comings and goings in a neighbourhood or locality, to be passed onto the next level of organisation, until it reached the central government's security officials.

A brief glance at the political panorama of the country at the time is useful to describe Jatani's role as a governor. As mentioned above, the fall of the Emperor from the throne created a power vacuum for which many groups vied. The country was rattled by a series of protests by students and workers seeking a radical overhaul of the ancient feudal regime. Young Ethiopians who went to Europe and North America for education formed political parties in exile and kept the flame of protest against the despotic feudal regime alive. Many of these students returned home to join the popular resistance and became leaders of these movements. Some of them went on to create political parties of their own. However, the ideological divide that characterised these movements would also create a rift and even bloody feud between such groups or the political parties they founded. At least five significant political groups fought to emerge as a dominant political force to rule the country. Three of them played prominent roles in this contest. They were: the *Derg*, the Ethiopian People's Revolutionary Party (EPRP) and the All Ethiopian Socialist Movement (AESM). All three aimed for a revolutionary regime change in Ethiopia and espoused varying degree of leftist ideologies fashionable at the time. Debate raged as to whether a Stalinist, Maoist and even Albanian version of socialism suited Ethiopia best. It was an unequal contest from the onset and the *Derg* consolidated its grip on power and proceeded with its self-assumed mission of transforming the country from a feudal monarchy to a socialist republic. The two civilian parties questioned the very legitimacy and style (brutal military dictatorship) of *Derg*'s rule of the country. They debated whether the *Derg* had legitimacy, the necessary experience or the right temper to rule over disparate tribes and keep the country united. Both these parties stated their determination to wrestle political power from the inexperienced junta but opted for different strategies. AESM forged a strategic alliance with the *Derg* with the ultimate and covert aim of dislodging them at an opportune time. The *Derg* became aware of their malicious intention and knocked them out of their political perch. For its part, the EPRP came up with a manifesto known as a "revolutionary gospel" and a rallying motto of "democracy now!" It hoped to galvanise its young supporters and grasp political power immediately. It organised its members into a secretive cells and communicated its intentions and strategies via a highly covert underground message delivery system. Their motto appealed to educated young people in all parts of the country, including some in the military. They also went one step further and sought to eliminate members suspected of spying for their opponents and high-profile persons who sided with the *Derg*. These newly-minted parties and other civilians who used violent tactics to undermine the *Derg*'s rule failed as it was an unequal contest from the start. The *Derg* unleashed the might of state power at its disposal and violently crushed all opponents.

Jatani's roles in the Ministry of the Interior

Jatani joined the Ethiopian public service and ended up serving as a governor of Arero Province, in the context of such a volatile political climate that characterised the post-imperial period. His appointment as a governor came on the heels of his role as the coordinator of the LDC in Arero Province, a responsibility he discharged with diligence and merit. After the campaign, he neither returned to the university to resume his studies nor to the police service.

He joined the public service through a full-time post in the Ministry of the Interior. This ministry was responsible for public administration in Ethiopia. A rigid hierarchy of power prevailed and a top-down line of command linked all tiers of government. Power flowed from the head of state down to the minister, and from him to regional, provincial and district governors. Reports were passed on up the chain of command. He served in the Ministry in different capacities and regions of the country. These included a posting as a governor/administrator of a province (*Awraja*), as deputy governor of a region (*Kifle Hager*) and as a chief governor of a region. There were other less well-known duties he fulfilled as part of the general public service duties in the Ministry of the Interior. In this last duty he acted as a special appointee of the Ministry, providing training and consultancy services to prepare new recruits to posts in public administration. In this role, he trained and mentored persons recruited to serve as district or provincial governors. His input in training and mentoring would-be governors in the neglected and marginalised parts of southern Ethiopia received special accolades by all those who came to know him in this context. Those who knew him at the Ministry reported how he excelled in just about every task he was given and outshone even his superiors. They stressed how he was loved and respected by all those who worked with him and envied by some. Being highly knowledgeable, likeable, able to influence those around him, having superb skills at organising and completing tasks, and having a positive outlook on life, despite all the gloom that often surrounded him, were some of the personal attributes that cropped up whenever I interviewed people who had worked with Jatani. Economic and social development of marginalised communities in the country was by far his main preoccupation, towards which he channelled most of his energy. His determination to serve as an advocate for and a defender of the underdog defined his character both as a person and a governor. In the following chapters are more detailed accounts of Jatani's life as a public servant.

7: As Governor of Arero Province

When Jatani joined the Ministry of the Interior, Ethiopia was divided into 14 administrative regions. Sidamo was one of these and it shared its southern boundary with the troublesome Republic of Somalia and Kenya. The Sidamo Administrative Region itself was divided into six provinces (*Awrajas*). Three of these *Awrajas* – namely Arero, Borana and Jemjem – had majority ethnic Oromo communities such as Borana, Gujii, Gabra and other smaller *Afaan Oromo*-speaking communities, including Garri, Burji and Konso. People from other parts of Ethiopia also resided in major towns in these provinces as employees of the state, as merchants or owners of small businesses. As discussed above, Jatani carried out his duties as a coordinator of the LDC in Arero Province from campaign headquarters based in Yaballo, then in the capital of Arero Province. Reportedly, Jatani established a favourable rapport with the then-governor of Sidamo Administrative Region, General Desta Gamada. When the provincial governor of Arero Province named Major Takele Wolde was removed from his position, a vacancy was created. General Desta nominated Jatani to replace Major Takele and advised the Ministry of the Interior to appoint him as the Governor of Arero Province in March 1976, just before the completion of his LDC tasks. Jatani served in that post until 1984.[15]

The *Derg* expected him to govern according to the official revolution-ary ideology of the state and to implement its policies. However, the bureaucratic system and the personnel that Jatani inherited in the prov-ince still operated according to the norms of the old imperial regime before it was replaced by the military junta. He knew that it was not

---

[15]   "Administrator" and "governor" are used interchangeably in this document.

possible to change the entrenched administrative culture of the bureaucracy overnight. He needed to make the system more dynamic, modern and less resistant to change by injecting fresh blood (personnel) into the system. He began the process by recruiting dynamic and educated young men to key posts in the provincial and district administrative posts. Alemayehu Legesse, Huqa Garse, Mesele Dhaba, Teshome Dahesa and Wario Galgalo were some of these. All of them were native to the province and had a very good understanding of local culture, language, history and challenges. Their appointment represented a radical move from old practices where nearly all government officials to the province were sent from other parts of Ethiopia. They therefore were unable to operate efficiently because of language or cultural barriers. However, the fact that his new recruits were young and inexperienced in public administration was not lost on Jatani. Nevertheless, he believed that they are more attuned to the new times and to the communities in the province than the old guard. The young recruits were given different posts that included acting as district governors, facilitators of political affairs and managing pubic security offices. Regardless of their youth and inexperience, they did not betray him and quickly grew into their posts. Jatani's expertise in training and mentoring people for a career in public service on behalf of the Ministry of the Interior also came in handy in bringing these rooky officials up to speed. I must indicate here that some of these officials were among my key informants of the years when Jatani was a governor of Arero Province, both during periods of wars and peace.

Like Jatani, many of his young officials such as Alemayehu, Mesele and Wario were undertaking university studies when they were drafted into the LDC. They too discontinued their university education to find employment in provincial public administration. By far they were the most educated crop of officials to be appointed to posts in the province up to that point. The fact that they originated from the province was a bonus. Their proven leadership qualities while serving in the LDC was also a factor in their recruitment. After their stint at posts in public administration, many of them managed to return to their old "alma mater" (universities) to complete their studies. Regardless of the intervening years outside academia and the distracting influences that came with life as a salaried employee of the state, all managed to complete their studies with flying colours. It too is an indication of the calibre of people with whom Jatani surrounded himself. Wario and Alemayehu returned to university to resume their studies after serving for about two years. Mesele returned to it more than a decade later. Mesele Dhaba was first appointed as a district governor of Teltele for a year and started a job as a deputy governor of Arero Province in 1978 following Jatani's endorsement. He held the post for three years up to 1981. Jatani often spoke highly of Mesele's trustworthiness, strong work ethic and commitment to the cause of improving the life of people in the province.

Governor Jatani Ali

When Jatani was appointed as a governor of the province in 1976, he faced the following four major challenges:

(a) The political and security problems in the province following a change of regime in Ethiopia;

(b) Challenges in implementing the radical land reform policy enacted by the new revolutionary regime. This included managing conflicts and, at times, armed violence between landlords (whose estates had been confiscated by government decree) and landless peasants (who stood to benefit from the policy);

(c) Dealing with the devastating effects of the Ethiopia-Somalia war of the late 1970s. The war unleashed hordes of heavily armed ethnic Somali and pro-Somali bandits in the province that uprooted many communities from their villages. Pacification of large areas of the province and restoration of law and order were major undertakings by provincial administration; and,

(d) Tackling the effects of years of neglect and marginalisation endured by the people in this remote province of Ethiopia. Heroic efforts were made to reduce the compound effects of economic, social and political factors affecting the province's overall development.

Jatani tackled these challenges as they arose and overcome many of the hurdles to put the province back on the road to recovery from the combined effects of wars and lack of development. Let us look now at how he went about tackling these challenges.

Conditions in Arero Province

The fall of the Emperor and the *Derg*'s mission of embarking on a radical socialist revolution instigated instability all over the country. Groups that opposed the *Derg* regime agitated for popular uprising. Some hoped to replace the military junta with a democratic civilian regime. Others fought for the restoration of the old feudal regime headed by kings and emperors. Still others fought to free their communities or regions from the oppressive clutches of the Ethiopian state, often dominated by a tribe with a monopolistic control over guns and resources ostensibly owned by the state. The party known as the EPRP had managed to appeal to a significant section of young people in Ethiopia and its message of covert and overt mass revolt against the regime was gaining momentum. Those who served and benefited from the old feudal regime were up in arms and tried to undermine every measure the new regime took to unshackle peasant populations from centuries-old, slave-like servitude.

The bulk of the population in Arero Province were semi-nomadic pastoralists and farmers. Lowland regions of the province were home to the semi-nomadic Borana community and smaller communities that spoke the Borana dialect of the Oromo language. Better watered highland regions of the province were home to Gujii-Oromo community who farmed the land to grow crops and raise some cattle. Borana and Gujii communities shared a great deal in terms of language and culture for being segments of the large Oromo people of Ethiopia and Kenya. As indicated elsewhere, Jatani was born into the Borana community and the province was not used to having a native-born as governor. Nearly all provincial and districts governors before Jatani were non-locals sent there from other parts of Ethiopia by the decree, whim or favouritism of regional or central government officials based in Awassa (Hawassa) and/or Addis Ababa. Kegnazmach Galagalo Doyo was an exception to this rule when he was appointed a governor of Arero province during the last years of Emperor Haile Selassie's reign. Galagalo Doyo was a major in the Ethiopian Army and a native Borana who attended boarding schools in Addis Ababa just like Jatani Ali. As expected, Jatani's appointment as a governor of the province displeased chauvinistic elements who belonged to the ruling tribe or town-living communities associated with the old feudal regime. Some didn't even think that members of local indigenous communities had what it takes to become governors. In their eyes, such communities were good only to serve the ruling group in Ethiopia as serfs, landless tenant farmers working for alien landlords or naïve nomadic herders who roamed the land that in fact belonged to the Ethiopian crown. The pro-*status quo* elements or sympathisers of the old regime found it hard to grasp the novel idea that these communities should be treated as citizens of Ethiopia, not as its subjects. Reportedly, there were chauvinists who openly questioned the very competence of a person such as Jatani, native of a nomadic pastoralist community, to become a governor of a province. To disrupt Jatani's appointment, the chauvinistic elements in towns such as Yaballo agitated the town's people to a public rally where abusive ethnic slurs were chanted against Jatani's appointment as a governor. The protesters called out the names of Jatani and the young men he recruited and demanded their immediate dismissal. They carried slogans and cried out, "Down with Jatani", "Down with Ifa", "Down with Mesele" and so on. Furthermore, Jatani was a staunch supporter of the revolution; like many progressive young men of the era, he believed the revolution would help bring justice to Ethiopia's down-trodden masses and solve the country's major social and economic problems. He wasn't a naiveté who imagined that the revolution would be a smooth process and necessarily led by only genuine or competent individuals. After all, he had gone to school in the heart of the empire, went to the top police academy in the country and worked as a police officer in Addis Ababa to have a good understanding of the culture, social upbringing, attitude and limitations of those who embarked on a revolutionary course. He also grew uneasy and disappointed as the Emperor's autocratic regime was replaced by another equally autocratic military junta headed by Colonel Mengistu Haile Mariam. Jatani believed that the new regime had a chance of improving the lot of the subjugated peasant populations and that one has to be part of the process in order to channel its forces to benefit neglected communities in remote provinces of Ethiopia.

Opposition to Jatani's appointment as a governor was set to grow as the military regime enacted proclamations that nationalised all plots of land in rural areas as well as some plots of land and extra (rented) houses in urban areas of Ethiopia. These and other decrees affected the mostly town-residing landlords, their families and their communities. Many were infuriated by the loss of their possessions and declared an outright war on the regime. Some even went to the bush to fight the revolutionary regime for usurping what they thought was their legitimate and God-given land and other possessions. Most of the rural population who stood to benefit from the reforms by the ruling military junta welcomed the appointment of Jatani as a governor and even rejoiced to see one of their own as governor. Those who opposed the new regime also exploited the old inter-tribal feuds and the chaos that accompanied these changes to undermine the *Derg*'s revolution. Taking advantage of the chaos to fulfil its expansionist agenda, Somalia was preparing to invade eastern and southern Ethiopia, including Arero and Borana provinces. This was the general context into which Jatani was appointed a governor of Arero Province: to uphold law and peace, provide vital services, build schools or roads, pay the wages of government employees on time, deliver emergency food aid to reduce the effects of famines caused by droughts and wars.

Before the *Derg* regime felt settled on the "throne" and some degree of stability was restored to Arero Province or to the country, the Gujii community was racked by a series of conflicts with disgruntled former landlords and with neighbouring communities such as the Burji. Major Takele Wolde was the governor of Arero Province at the time. According to Utukan Malo, a Gujii elder, Major Takele asked the authorities higher up the chain of command for armed support to suppress the militant behaviour of Gujii farmers. A military contingent was sent to Gujii country from an Ethiopian army garrison based in Nagelle Borana town. A meeting of Gujii leaders and people was called at a place called Sorora in Hagere Mariam district. The sent army contingent first disarmed the people who came to that meeting carrying their guns. Of course, carrying a spear or a gun by men was a normal practice in the province as it was in many parts of Ethiopia. According to Kassa Chirqisa, a Gujii elder, the army rounded up and killed 353 Gujii men on the spot. Further, the military reportedly burnt the bodies of those murdered, as a punitive measure. The Gujii community complained to the higher officials of the *Derg* about the actions of the army in massacring Gujii men. The *Derg* sent Major Atnafu Abate, the deputy chairperson of the *Derg* at the time, to the area to cool down the matter. Major Atnafu carried out an investigation of the incident and determined that the actions of Major Takele were wrong and illegal. To appease the community, he ordered the public hanging of Major Takele at a locality called Finchawa. Local supporters of the EPRP, a movement with a support base mainly amongst the disgruntled and town-based elements opposed to the *Derg*, were incensed by the hanging of Major Takele. The already volatile situation in the province was inflamed even further as the fear that the ruling could lead to civil war was voiced. The hanging of Major Takele also created rifts in the police units and other institutions in the province. Jatani was appointed as the governor of Arero Province, replacing Major Takele. The disgruntled elements even made an attempt to detain Jatani as a protest against the hanging. This was an example of the sort challenges he faced during the initial stages of his stint as the governor of Arero Province.

As mentioned above, to put the administrative machinery of the province in motion, Jatani recruited educated young men who were native to the area. Let us have a glance at how he recruited some of these and what they had to say as to what was happening in the province at the time.

Wario Galgalo in Dida Hara

Like Jatani, Wario Galgalo served in the LDC in Dirre district. Wario told me how, after his services in the LDC, he returned to Addis Ababa University and registered in the Faculty of Science. Jatani came and told him how he would like him to consider returning to Arero province to serve the people. Jatani then arranged Wario's withdrawal process from the university with Dr Abiy Kifle who was in charge of that university's students' registrar office. After Jatani left, Dr Abiy contacted Wario to complete the withdrawal formalities.

On arriving back in the province, Jatani first assigned Wario to a post created to carry out educational campaigns to raise community awareness of the virtues of the *Derg*'s revolution. One of the functions of Wario's unit was to strengthen the capacities of producers' and consumers' cooperatives organised in towns (*Kebele* Associations or KA) and rural areas (Peasant Associations or PA). One of the missions of groups opposed to the *Derg*, such as the agents of EPRP, was to dismantle any organisation that the new government had established. In Yaballo, they went further than disrupting the operations of established organisations; in a bid to make the province ungovernable, they run a campaign of disinformation by concocting false accusations against Jatani and his new recruits. They agitated local people to rise against Jatani on trumped-up charges. One of the agents vowed to assassinate Jatani. It was clear to Jatani that, if such an act was committed, it would have led to vicious cycles of attacks and counter-attacks that were devastating to the whole community. To thwart the destructive intentions of such agents, Jatani and his young recruits had no choice but to leave the area and seek temporary refuge in Awassa, the capital of Sidamo Administrative Region. As well as being for safety concerns, their trip to Awassa was to brief the authorities on the unfolding crisis in Arero Province that could lead to bloodshed. According to Wario, Jatani and his "refugees" spent two weeks in Awassa without getting a hearing from persons in authority. Given the lack of response from the authorities, they decided to do something on their own. Jatani and his team held a meeting at the nearby town of Shashamane to explore feasible options. They came up with two: firstly, to keep up the complaint process through legal channels; and secondly, to mobilise the manpower and material resources of communities living in the countryside of the province – their main support base – against the arrogance of *agents provocateurs* in towns. For the first option, Jatani was chosen to go to Addis Ababa. For the second, Wario Galgalo and Ifa Diriba were assigned to go to Dida Hara, a rural locality near Yaballo, to facilitate the mobilisation of their rural supporters. Galgalo Arero, who was in charge of the elementary school construction program in the province, secretly assisted with the transportation of the two to Jirmo Dida's village in Dida Hara.

Wario and Ifa's mission was to stay amongst rural villagers to explain what *agents provocateurs* living in major towns such as Yaballo were doing to undermine Jatani's authority and the policies of the new regime. With the help of their rural supporters, they set out to design strategies to counter the disinformation campaign of those hell-bent on undermining Jatani's appointment as a provincial governor. Jirmo Dida's village in Dida Hara was an ideal place for the mission. Jirmo was a Borana elder and a respected community leader. Wario described the actions they took as follows. Wario, Ifa and Jirmo met to discuss the unfolding events in Yaballo and what could happen to the interests of rural communities if the town-based agitators succeeded in undermining Jatani's authority. The three figured most residents in Yaballo town owned farms and other properties in nearby rural areas. They reasoned that one way of counter-ing the anti-Jatani plotters in Yaballo must involve tactics that would impact on urban residents' access to their farms in adjoining rural areas. They agreed that such farms or access routes to them constituted a weak link for their opponents. They entrusted a capable local agitator and supporter of their cause named Yota Doyo to mobilise the rural people to carry out their tactical move. The main message to urban residents who owned farms in rural areas was this: "Unless you do something against those town-based plotters and would-be assassins, your properties (crops and animals) in rural areas would constitute a legitimate target by rural communities who support Jatani." Yota and his band raided some of the farms to register their intention. Some farm fence-posts were removed and a herd of cattle was made to graze on some of the growing crops. The town residents could not figure out what brought about such a sudden behavioural change in the otherwise peaceful rural villagers around Yaballo.

To further widen the scope of the operation, the instigators arranged with Jirmo to call a meeting of Borana residents in the area at *Qaallu* (*Qallu*) *Karrayu*'s village.[16] While the meeting was in progress, a Yaballo businessman named Ele Yaya arrived in his car, bearing gifts for the *Qaallu*. Apparently the town-based farm owners had noted the protest by

---

[16] *Qaallu* or *Qallu* is a Borana spiritual leader.

rural communities and sent Ele Yaya to plead with the *Qaallu* to calm down the angry Borana pastoralist villagers. Those at the meeting with the *Qaallu* excused him to meet up with his guest and they proceeded with their deliberations without him. Wario did not know what Ele and the *Qaallu* discussed. Ele came out of the session with the *Qaallu* and marched to the venue where the meeting was taking place. He drove away shortly after having been denied attention at the meeting. The gathered felt that the agenda of the meeting didn't concern him.

At the meeting, it was decided that the rural community would totally boycott Yaballo township. It was agreed that villagers should refrain from sponsoring town-based businesses and selling their products to the residents of that town unless those residents flushed out the troublemakers amid them or handed them over to the authorities. This boycott by pastoralists seriously scared business owners and consumers in the town. Another planned option was to storm the town as a show of force. For this, armed men on horseback were made ready to pounce on the town if conditions didn't change. The town's people called a meeting at the civic hall. Jatani had in the meantime arrived back in town with an escort of army trucks with the list of the plotters. The names of the suspected culprits were called out from the hall and they were thrown on the trucks and taken to jail. Peace was restored and the meeting was adjourned. The rural contingent of armed men on horseback proceeded with their march to the town as planned. It was a successful show of force and was enough to register their determination to resist any challenges against the new administration led by Jatani. Thereafter, peace was restored in the province and normal life resumed.

Sometime later, Jatani summoned the residents of Yaballo town to a general meeting at a church hall in the town. He informed the audience that the *Derg* had ordered him to disarm those who owned firearms. He instructed them that they should bring their firearms to the government offices and hand them over, to comply with the new gun ownership laws passed by the *Derg*. Many residents obeyed the order. However, provisions were made in case there were some gun owners who might defy the orders. To make sure all firearms had been handed over, a house-to-house search was conducted. Several hidden guns and even machine guns were discovered in many homes. Jatani told me how, while searching for guns, a huge stockpile of contraband teabags was found and seized. He sold the tea for Birr 17,000 and used the money to build a small store where essential consumer goods were sold at discounted prices to residents. The store would counter shortages and price hikes of essential goods that were negatively impacting on the lives of the townspeople and villagers alike. The store was a successful venture and it was replaced by a much larger store built by the Ethiopian Domestic Distribution Corporation (EDDC). However, the tea venture didn't succeed without a hitch. The existing government policy demanded that any contraband goods seized should be handed over to the customs office. Such goods would then be auctioned and the money sent to the coffers of the central government. The local customs office head accused Jatani for violating the official policy. Jatani managed to persuade the *Derg* authorities to drop the case on the grounds that the money obtained from the sale of seized contraband goods was spent on a vital infrastructure that would benefit the public.

In the meantime, the agents of the EPRP stepped up their sabotaging the actions of the new regime to reform the country. They also started to murder supporters of the *Derg* all over Ethiopia. By using the jargon of leftist revolutions in other parts of the world, the *Derg* defined the murderous actions of the EPRP agents as a "white terror" and its own counter-measure as a "red terror". The red terror campaign of the regime was swift and brutal. The government used the full resources of the state to kill hundreds of young people suspected of being agents of the EPRP, mainly in Addis Ababa but also in other parts of the country. The measure was so harsh that hundreds of targeted young people fled the country. However, in Arero Province no one was killed in the red terror campaign. Even those who publicly plotted to assassinate Jatani were generally left alone to freely move about and work in the community.

The EPRP agents in towns were not the only destabilising elements the provincial administration had to deal with. Somalia was preparing to embark on its war for territorial expansion against Ethiopia. It was sending scouts of armed men to outlying regions in the province as a vanguard force for its impending invasion. Wario recalled one such incident where they faced and repelled Somali agents from establishing a base in Haro Kafara (Kafara pond), a locality in Dida Hara. At the time, Wario lived in Yaballo and worked as a facilitator of cooperative affairs as part of the local government. Alemayehu Legesse was the district administrator or governor of Yaballo at the time. Wario and his colleagues in government offices learned how Somali agents raped young girls and women at Haro Kafara pond under the pretence of buying milk. They led a task force to deal with the Somali agents to the area and secretly observed their movements to determine their number and fire power. One morning they rounded them up, opened fire, killed 8 of them and captured one machine gun. Those who survived the surprise assault fled in disarray.

Alemayehu Legesse in Yaballo

After the winding up of the LDC, Jatani got hold of Alemayehu Legesse just as he had with Wario Galgalo. He was indigenous to Dirre District. Like Wario, he suspended his university studies and went to work in Jatani's new administration. He was appointed as the governor of Yaballo District. Alemayehu described the chaotic situation in the province just as Wario and others did. Soon after his appointment, Gujii tribesmen rustled over 1,000 head of cattle from Borana. Traditionally, Borana used to avenge such actions by carrying out a similar counter-action of their own, against members of the offending tribe. To restrain the Borana from taking retaliatory action, Gujii elders and local government officials intervened with a promise of recovering all the looted animals. Alemayehu reported that 700 of the animals were recovered. Before they were able to recover the remaining 300 head of cattle, the propaganda barrage of the Somali government attracted many Gujii young men, urging them to go to Mogadishu to collect automatic guns with which to fight the Ethiopian regime or their 'tribal enemies'. This disrupted the recovery of the remaining animals. To make things even more complicated, the Somali government resorted to exploiting the brutal mistreatment of the Gujii community by Major Takele Wolde as a propaganda coup, to attract as many young Gujii men as possible to its cause of undermining Ethiopia's regime and to invade the country. [17]

As indicated elsewhere, Borana and Gujii are closely-related sub-groups of the much larger Oromo people. The province was home to smaller groups that also spoke the same language as the Borana and Gujii. However, the relations between these groups weren't always of a peaceful nature. They often fought each other over grazing land and water resources. A delicate act of balancing inter-group power relations was critical to keeping the peace in the province. The Somali practice of arming some of these groups as an extension of their expansionist agenda was set to disrupt this delicate balance of power. Elements of ethnic Gujii were not the only ones who aligned themselves with the Somali and received arms from them. The Gabra and Garri groups, Oromo-speaking smaller ethnic groups in the province with some cultural and religious affinity with the Somali, had also been getting arms from Somalis. With their new supply of guns, the Gujii felt emboldened and less willing to live in peace with their neighbours such as the Borana. This condition, coupled with the disruptive actions by the agents of the EPRP, made the process of governance very challenging, according to Alemayehu. Due to

---

[17]   As mentioned earlier, Major Takele was the Governor of Arero Province who carried out the cold-blooded massacre of 353 Gujii men at Sorora. He was found guilty and hanged in public.

the frequent attacks by Somali bandits and their supporters, towns such as Surupha and Arero (Mata Gafarsa) had to be temporarily abandoned.

Alemayehu pointed out that Jatani would not have been able to buy time or quickly restore law and order in the province without the support of the young men he employed in his administration. Alemayehu served in the province for two years and returned to Addis Ababa to resume his university studies.

Huqa Garse in Yaballo and Mega

Huqa Garse was another young fellow recruited by Jatani to assist in the tasks of stabilising and governing the province. Huqa too was native to the province and one of the handful who managed to go to school at the time. He started his secondary-level education at Bishoftu (Debre Zeit) Evangelical College and completed it at a school in Yirgalem. He too was forced to discontinue his studies as the result of the chaos following the military coup that deposed the Emperor. He returned to Yaballo and got caught up in the process of fighting the enemies of the people and of the revolution. He was given brief training in the skills of using a firearm and went to fight against Somali agents at Dida Hara with individuals such as Sara Jirmo. After partaking in a few clashes here and there, he was assigned to Dirre as a facilitator of political affairs in that district. His post was charged with the tasks of educating the public in the virtues of the revolution and conducting public awareness campaigns to help implement the revolutionary policies of the new regime. Wario Galgalo was the district governor of Dirre at the time. Wario left the position to resume his studies at a university while a teacher named Kinfu Tesfaye was appointed to replace him in 1980.

The town of Mega was chosen as a strategic command post to organise operations to weed out both Somali agents and invading forces in Arero and Borana Provinces. For this purpose, an Ethiopian army contingent under the command of a general moved eastward towards the border with Somalia in an attempt to flush out the invading forces. Borbor was one of the localities freed from the control of Somali invaders. However, some residents of this locality lodged a complaint against certain individuals who mistreated them while collaborating with Somali bandits. Some of the accused were members of Borbor PA or held some position within the PA. According to Huqa, around 25 alleged culprits were rounded up by members of the Ethiopian army in the area to answer for their alleged role in mistreating the locals by collaborating with the enemy. Some members of the community feared that a bloody act of retribution would be taken against the accused the following night. The local people who disapproved of the intended plan informed Huqa about the developments and their grave fear of what might happen to the accused. He went to the general and asked him why he intended to take such a serious measure against the accused people without proper and fair investigation. The general told Huga that Dirre district governor Kinfu Tesfaye gave him the names of the accused and signed the orders for him to take the necessary action. Huqa demanded to know whether Kinfu produced any substantial evidence for the charges against the alleged collaborators. However, Kinfu was not able to do so; he pretended that he was ill and left the area. The detained individuals were released and set free, thanks to the insistence of Huqa.

Consequently, Kinfu resigned from the position of district governor of Dirre and Jatani appointed Huqa in his place. Huqa served in that position from December 1980 to 1982. Under Huqa's leadership, the district recorded some notable achievements in terms of good governance and community development. It also experienced administrative challenges as the result of Ethiopia's top-down dictatorial system of governance and its byzantine bureaucracy. For instance, Dillo PA was a neglected and remote locality in Dirre district. The district itself was part of one of the least developed, remote and neglected provinces in Ethiopia.[18] While

---

[18]   Dirre and Moyale districts were part of Borana Province, ruled from Nagelle, before being made part of Arero Province.

Huqa was a district governor, Dillo was struck by a severe and life-threatening drought. Huqa took the initiative to tackle the problem before the conditions worsened. Waiting for the authorities higher up the chain of command in the Ethiopian bureaucracy to act would have led to worsening of drought conditions and even deaths. Huqa told me that he proceeded to borrow Birr 64,000 from merchants in the area to purchase sacks of grains from Shashamane to help the drought-stricken people in Dillo PA. The sacks of grain were transported to the district but the pastoralists did not have the cash to pay for the grain. An arrangement was made whereby pastoralists would barter a certain quantity of grain with an estimated sale value of live animals they brought. The animals the locals brought for barter were in bad condition or too skinny due to the drought. Huqa's aim was to make arrangements whereby bartered animals where kept alive through the drought period and re-sold when their condition improved after the rains. The plan was a success and the fattened animals were later sold at a profit. Huqa reported that he got enough profit to repay the original loan and ended up with a profit of Birr 12,000. He used this money to construct a students' hostel in a more convenient location for children coming from remote parts of Dillo PA to attend school. Many locals laud this entrepreneurial flair of Huqa's to this day.

Huqa is remembered for the smooth and efficient running of the routine administration of Dirre district. He also demonstrated a determination to stand his ground against officials who tried to bully him. For example, the then Governor-General of Sidamo region, Tefera Endalew, ordered him to raise Birr 10,000 from the district for the construction of a community hall at Awassa, the distant capital of Sidamo Administrative Region. Huqa refused to cooperate on the grounds that the people in the district were only just recuperating from the double effects of severe drought and invasion by Somali forces. Besides, he didn't see how a community hall for the people of Awassa would benefit the people of Dirre, living hundreds of kilometres away. Tefera threatened to imprison him for insubordination. To get Huqa out of trouble, Jatani moved him from Dirre district to a post in Yaballo, to work as head of the provincial state security office.

During this time, Jatani travelled to East Germany to participate in a three-month-long leadership training program. His deputy, Mesele Dhaba, was delegated as acting governor of the province. Huqa told me how he was not on good terms with the person in charge of political party organisation in the province. Huqa reported that people alerted him to be watchful of the fellow as he had a secret plan to kill him. Huqa took some precautions against the alleged threat and fortunately nothing serious happened to him. Soon after, he got a scholarship opportunity to study in Czechoslovakia and went abroad. Jatani spoke highly of Huqa as a committed and very resourceful person, able to discharge his responsibilities with great efficiency.

A crack in inter-communal relations

During times defined by volatile and unpredictable political developments, a minor event can act as a trigger to exacerbate pre-existing rifts between sections of the community. Events associated with the killing of a notable local businessman in Yaballo were an example of this. Etenesh Gebere Giorgios was a relatively wealthy businessman from Yaballo who belonged to the Oromo ethnic group. One day, while driving in the town, he was involved in a fatal motor vehicle accident that killed the son of another wealthy merchant from the same town named Ele Yaya. The latter belonged to the Burji tribe. A bloody inter-family feud resulted from the accident with nasty ramifications for inter-communal relations in that town (i.e. Burji v. Borana/Oromo). Ele Yaya's son was riding a bicycle, ran into the car driven by Etenesh and was killed. The police investigation attested that the incident was nothing but a traffic accident. Etenesh apologised to the deceased's family. To cool down the matter, Etenesh asked Borana traditional leaders and elders to plead with the grieving family for forgiveness. However, the Ele family refused the gesture and indicated that nothing short of Etenesh's death would satisfy them. The traditional leaders were disappointed with this behaviour and told the grieving family how Ele family's attitude was totally opposed to Borana's cultural norms of solving disputes. The deceased's family opted to take the law into their own hands to avenge their dead, conforming to their tribal (Burji) code of conduct (a "blood for blood", "eye for an eye" sort of thing). Accordingly, an older brother of the deceased boy, who was undertaking a university education in Addis Ababa at the time, returned to Yaballo and murdered Etenesh. In response, a sympathiser of Etenesh killed an uncle of the deceased boy as a vendetta. The local police could not trace this vendetta killer. At the time, Jatani was not in Yaballo but was on duty in Addis Ababa and unable to cool down the spiralling blood feud. In the meantime, some members of the Burji community inflamed the matter and turned it into an inter-communal strife between the Oromo and the Burji. The Borana, being a branch of the Oromo people, were tagged as the enemy of the aggrieved family and the Burji community in general. Their tribal vendetta attacks also targeted innocent Borana people who lived in faraway places such as Mega. They went so far as to poison water sources used by ethnic Borana villagers for human and livestock consumption. For instance, at Madhacho, near Mega, some animals died from drinking such poisoned water. The people became furious against this malicious act and couldn't grasp the extreme to which some people or tribe would go to, to avenge their dead. Persons suspected of putting poison in water sources were arrested by police and punished. The matter seemed to cool down. What started as a family feud had evolved into a full-blown feud between the Burji and Borana communities.

The Burji's home district formed part of Arero Province. However, the Burji community had been leaving their home district in large numbers in search of better opportunities elsewhere in the area. Many early migrant Burji families settled as farmers around major towns in Borana-Oromo and Gujii-Oromo countries. They lived according to the norms of the host community and many were even "adopted" into the clan system of the host communities. The descendants of these settlers started small businesses such as shops and were partially assimilated into Oromo culture. Over time, many Burji families grew wealthy and came to own many herds of cattle. As they were essentially town-based or lived around towns as farmers, many entered into contractual arrangement with the pastoralist Borana to look after their cattle. Ele and other members of his Burji community around Yaballo had a lot of cattle they entrusted to Borana families for their upkeep. This longstanding collaboration and mutual help between the two communities didn't stop Ele and his Burji community from treating Borana people with an inflated air of arrogance, disdain and disrespect. Such behaviour infuriated Borana community leaders. They reminded him how he or his ancestors came to Borana country penniless and yet they grew arrogant and looked down upon the very people that helped them out of the life of degradation and shameful misery. Borana community leaders tried to emphasise how Ele's unto-ward behaviour towards the Borana was totally unacceptable and could lead to hefty penalties according to traditional Borana norms. They urged him and his Burji community to reconcile with the Borana community. They warned him that he could lose some of the cattle he entrusted to Borana villagers if he continued with his arrogant and disrespectful demeanour.

The Burji community took their grievances against the Borana and Jatani's rule to the chief Governor of the Sidamo Administrative Region. In response, the Sidamo Governor came to Yaballo and called a meeting that had representatives of the two feuding communities as well as relevant administrative personnel in Arero Province. In the meeting, some outspoken individuals from the Burji community accused Jatani of not caring for their community and not even visiting their homeland of Burji district. They went on to say that he and others in his administrative team should be killed. The regional security officer refuted their wild statements by pondering, 'How could they expect the person whom they thought of killing in public would visit them?' He added, 'Should he go to the district to be slain?' He stressed how the behaviour and actions of some members of the Burji community were totally "out of order" and illegal. He quoted the case where members of the Burji community took the law into their own hands and murdered another person who had accidentally killed a Burji boy. He said that this was against the law of the country. He noted how traffic vehicle accidents are common all over the world and Ethiopia had laws to deal with them through law-enforcing agencies. He concluded his deliberations by emphasising how traffic accidents must be handled through legal channels, not by ethnic vigilantes. The Burji community lost the case but their bitterness continued.

Jatani's battle against the landlords

Background

Detailed discussion of the land tenure system in Ethiopia during Jatani's lifetime is outside the scope of this biographical work. However, a brief outline of land tenure and the *Derg*'s attempt at reforming it is necessary, as a context to Jatani's role in land reform processes. Jatani and his administration battled with landlords who were reluctant to part with their land possessions.[19] This went hand-in-hand with efforts to organise peasant farming communities – the beneficiaries of the land reform policy – to defend their newly-given rights. This section starts with a brief outline of the landholding system that was installed in the southern part of the country by Emperor Menelik II, following the conquest of this region by armies from northern half of Ethiopia. Except for a brief period when Ethiopia was occupied by the Italian forces just before the Second World War, the *gult* and related land tenure system imposed on

---

[19] The term "landlord" is broadly used here to designate a person who owned a substantial piece of land on which another person (or family) worked for him as a tenant farmer.

the southern provinces of Ethiopia – as outlined previously – remained intact right up to the *Derg*'s 1974 Revolution.

The north has historically been the king-making region of Ethiopia, and is home to two culturally and religiously related ethnic groups, the Amhara and the Tigre. The majority of ethnic Amhara and Tigre belonged to the Ethiopian Orthodox Church, the state religion of Ethiopia for centuries.[20]

As mentioned earlier, before the *Derg*'s land ownership decree of 1975 that made all land the property of the Ethiopian state, there existed two radically different land-owning systems in Ethiopia. In the northern half, land was generally owned privately by the head of a family unit or extended family. Such landholdings, known as *rist*, were redistributed to both male and female descendants of the original owner(s) through inheritance.

The southern half of Ethiopia was historically seen as frontier land of "savage" tribes, with fertile lands and resources, all for the taking by conquest by warlords-cum-emperors. So, a distinctive land and labour tenure system known as *gult* (pronounced, "goolt") was imposed on southern Ethiopia following conquest. A person who was given a title to a *gult* land or farm was a salaried employee in the service of the Ethiopian crown, known either as *gultegna* or *neftegna*

Those who served the conquering emperors of Ethiopia as soldiers or officials were paid through this system. It was a slave-like system akin to European medieval feudalism where those who worked the land were serfs. (Also, the *gultegna-neftegna* system has remarkable similarities with the *encomienda* system through which Spanish conquistadores combined land

---

[20]   The relationship between these kindred groups has rarely been a cordial one. The two competed and fought over Ethiopia's political power and the spoils that flowed from being the tribe that emerged as the king-maker in the empire.

and the slave labour of indigenous peoples in the Americas to finance their conquest and colonisation there.[21])

In order to finance and facilitate a smooth administration of conquered lands, the officials of the crown or emperor divided the areas they occupied into regions, provinces, districts and sub-districts. They appointed the *neftegna* of different ranks to administer these segments of the conquered territories.

Thus *neftegna* (a person with a gun) is an Amharic word commonly used in Ethiopia's southern regions to denote a settler-landlord. The term refers to persons who arrived in the southern provinces as armed colonist-settlers from northern Ethiopia. It expresses at once the class- and ethnic-based hierarchy between the ruling people (from northern Ethiopia) and the subject peoples (of southern Ethiopia).

Clear ethnic, linguistic, religious and cultural boundaries delineated the two groups. A master-and-servant-type relationship evolved between the *gultegna-neftegna* class of people and indigenous families assigned to work land that sustained this class, as *gebar*.[22] *Gebar* were a kind of slave labour similar to that of *serfs*, forced to work on *gult* farms. Hence, *gult* farms were created by combining crown-owned land taken from vanquished tribes and *gebar* families who used to own such lands. Resources extracted from *gult* farms paid the "salaries" of soldiers and other officials helping with the conquest and colonisation of the colonies.

In this administrative arrangement, the life of a *gebar* was almost identical to that of a slave in terms of serving a master. The main difference was that, while a slave was like a commodity to be sold in open markets, a *gebar* and/or his family were not sold. A *gebar* and his family were the

---

21 The *Encyclopædia Britannica* defines *encomienda* as a "legal system [in colonial Spanish America] by which the Spanish crown attempted to define the status of the Indian population in its American colonies... in practice it became a form of enslavement" (http://www.britannica.com/EBchecked/topic/186567/encomienda).

22 Also known as *gabar* or *gabbar*.

property of the Ethiopian Emperor just like tracts of land conquered by his *neftegna* soldiers in what became the southern provinces of Ethiopia.

Table 1: Number of *gebar* families allocated to a corresponding size of an estate or farm known as "gult"[23]		
Rank of neftegna	*No. of* gebar *families for each* neftegna	*Size of land allocated to a* neftegna *in* gasha[24]
Regional administrator	Above 1,000	1,000 (= 40,000 hectares)
Provincial administrator	300	300 (= 12,000 hectares)
District administrator	100	150 (= 6,000 hectares)
Sub-district	50	50 (= 2,000 hectares)
Ordinary soldier	15-20	2 -20 (= 80-800 hectares)

Source: Yewugana Dirsetoch and Yetarik Ewinetawoch ('Biased Essays and Historical Facts') by Tabor Wami, pp 507-510.

As I mentioned, Ethiopia – then called Abyssinia – was invaded and briefly colonised by the fascist forces of Mussolini-ruled Italy from 1936 to 1941. The Italians did a great deal to abolish the slave trade and the widespread institution of domestic slavery during this period. At the same time, they put in motion the process of dismantling the oppressive *gultegna-neftegna* system in many parts of southern Ethiopia, where many *gebar* families had a chance to escape the clutches of their *gultegna-neftegna* overlords.

The Italians were expelled from Ethiopia in 1941 by a combined effort of Ethiopian patriots and British forces. After Emperor Haile Selassie returned from exile in Britain, he found he couldn't entirely reverse the reform in the *gultegna-neftegna* and the slave-holding systems started by the Italians. His regime half-heartedly tried to implement a land reform decree that would render the former *gultegna* class into private landlords or *ristegna*. A select group of individuals who remained loyal to the Emperor

---

[23] Such a farm generated a "salary" that sustained a "*neftegna*" official and his family for serving the Ethiopian Emperor. A person who was given a right to a "*gult*" farm was known as a "*gultegna*".

[24] *Gasha* is a type of land measurement.

during his exile and patriots who staged guerrilla warfare against the Italians, benefited from large land grants (*rist*) in southern Ethiopia as a reward for their loyalty and services. Thus, over time, *gult* land was gradually converted into privately-owned land (*rist*) and came to be owned by the former *gultegna-neftegna* class. This way, the *gultegna-neftegna* class morphed from being a class of salaried employees of the Emperor to private owners of *rist* land known as *ristegna*. The *ristegna* were the rich landlords against whom Jatani and his administration fought in an effort to implement the *Derg*'s land nationalisation policy.

Parallel to that, indigenous populations also underwent their own metamorphosis in terms of their status. They started as citizens of sovereign nations or tribes before conquest and ended up as *gebar* of the Ethiopian crown. Decades later, former *gebar* become landless tenant farmers (*chisegna*) who toiled on land that was turned into *rist* land owned by landlords known as *ristegna*.

Two decades later in the 1960s, the government of Haile Selassie passed a decree that stipulated that every Ethiopian was entitled to get at least half a *gasha* of land (20 hectares) in southern Ethiopia. The underlying logic of this was that fertile land was in abundant supply in the south and every Ethiopian had the right to such land without needing to consult the indigenous owners from whom such land was taken by force. According to the decree, land was available to anyone who applied for it and not limited to people who might be prepared to work as farmers. People had to get title deeds to legally own a piece of land from state authorities charged with land administration matters. Once title deeds were issued in the name of applicants, such plots of land were officially recognised as private property on which owners would pay a land tax. Any Ethiopian engaged in any business or profession was entitled to apply for a parcel of land in southern Ethiopia and hold it as private property. In a country where nearly all the rural population were illiterate, only persons who lived in major towns and were closer to the ruling class stood to benefit from the Emperor's land privatisation policy. In theory, indigenous peoples in the south could also apply for a plot of land. Most however had no clue about the policy, much less the means to negotiate the convoluted bureaucratic red tape to acquire a piece of land that previously belonged to their ancestors. In reality, the status of the former *gebar* families, allocated to *gult* farms, changed little over the years. By the time the *Derg* enacted its own radical land reform in 1975, the bulk of *gebar* families didn't have title deeds to the plots of land they continued to farm or lived on.

As the result of the *Derg*'s land reform decree, landlords in southern Ethiopia lost their entitlements to their *rist* lands. Indigenous peoples, who up to then existed on such lands as *gebar*, *chisegna* or mere squatters, gained the right to hold and work a plot of land for the benefit of their families. However, the *Derg*'s land reform policy didn't make indigenous people outright owners of land. The *Derg*'s decree proclaimed that all land in Ethiopia was to become state-owned property and citizens gained the right to work a piece of land if they wished to live as farmers. The status of tenant farmers changed hardly at all as the indigenous people merely shifted from being tenants who farmed plots of land that once belonged to private landlords, to tenant farmers on land that now belonged to the Ethiopian state. However the state appeared a more benign landlord to farmers in comparison to the often absentee private landlords.

The *Derg* also tried to improve the living conditions of farmers in many other areas in its sweeping land reform policy. Ethiopians willing to work as farmers were entitled to a piece of land and were meant to reap the benefits of their labour; at least, that was the initial hope. Financing years of protracted wars and the need to feed growing numbers of people in urban areas forced the regime to extract more and more resources from farmers, thereby cancelling out the positives of its land reform policy. Still, the *Derg*'s radical land reform decree abolished once and for all what was left of the old *gultegna-neftegna* and the post-Italian-era *ristegna* systems. The *Derg* improved the life of most tenant farmers who had been at the mercy of exploitative landlords, some of whom were a law unto themselves. Most of the affected landlords in the south of Ethiopia were settlers who either themselves arrived from central-northern Ethiopia, or were the descendants of such settlers. The *Derg*'s decree only had a marginal impact on farmers in the northern half of Ethiopia where the *rist* land-ownership system predominated.

The terrible treatment of tenant farmers in southern Ethiopia at the hands of brutal landlords featured prominently in the Ethiopian students' anti-feudal regime protest movement. In their protest rallies leading up to the military coup that removed the monarchy, students chanted "Land to the Tiller" alongside slogans that demanded the establishment of a democratic and just society. It is believed the *Derg* regime enacted its land reform policy to satisfy the demands of the students and other enlightened Ethiopians who called for a less exploitative land-owning system for peasants. Tenant farmers who were once at the mercy of harsh landlords ended up with a more benevolent landlord (the revolutionary state) that restored some of their dignity. At the same time, former landlords and the community of people they supported felt that the *Derg* took away properties they owned legitimately without even paying compensation for what was taken. To reclaim land 'illegitimately' taken from them, many landlords began to resist the regime from their town bases. Others went to the bush to mount guerrilla-style warfare against the *Derg*. Jatani Ali and his administration waged at times bloody battles against such disgruntled landlords.

The life of a tenant farmer in Gujii country

The treatment of *gebar* and *chisegna* (tenant farmer) by landlords in Sidama, Gedeo (Darasa) and Arero Provinces, then part of Sidamo Administrative Region, was almost identical. To illustrate some of these conditions, two episodes from Gujii country are presented below. The first provides an insight into the living conditions of a Gujii *chisegna* and the second illustrates the attitude and behaviour of a landlord as witnessed by me (the author).

Utukan Malo and Mesele Basie are two Gujii elders who were tenant farmers during the reign of Emperor Haile Selassie. They described to me the life of a *chisegna* in Hager Miriam district of Arero Province during this era. According to them, rural land in the district was divided into three parts in terms of fertility and owned by landlords. These categories were: productive, semi-productive and arid lands. The tenancy practice that was exercised in the country heavily fell on those residing in areas designated as productive and semi-productive lands, with more weight on the former. The labour force of a *chisegna* family was organised to serve the landlord. Roughly, one third of the labour time of a *chisegna* family was reserved for the exclusive use of the landlord. The father and head of a *chisegna* family was at the disposal of the landlord in cultivating his land or doing whatever was required of him. His wife was required to assist the landlord's wife in domestic chores. She – and her daughters – would fetch water and firewood, grind grains and do any other household chores that the landlady directed. Older children of the tenant farmer looked after the livestock of the master. They also completed other duties around the farm and landlord's household as required. The landlord could demand not just labour but also what little material resources owned by the *chisegna* family. The landlord would demand a payment in the form of an animal from the *chisegna* whenever one of his children married, to be used in the wedding festivities. Mesele defined his father's and family's experience at the hands of their landlord as awful and bitter. In one incident, the landlord of the family punished Mesele's father for sending him to school without his knowledge. At the time, Mesele was going to Yirgalem High School and remembered his rebellious behaviour against the system. He said that once, during school vacation, he went back to his district to stay with his family. One day, he was instructed to relieve his father in fetching water from a pond used by the landlord family. Mesele found that the water container (a bowl) given to him for this task was too big for him to carry. He was then given a smaller-sized bowl. He decided on his own what he would do to make a point against the mistreatment of his family by the landlord. He went to the pond, broke the bowl, threw the pieces into the water and went to Hagere Mariam, the major town in the district. When he failed to return home as expected, the family was concerned about his welfare and went to the pond to check in case he had drowned. They found the broken pieces of the bowl in the pool. They assumed that he accidentally fell into the pond and broke the container. They reasoned that he was afraid of possible punishment and fled to the nearby town to escape it.

Ayele Gebre Giorgis: A typical landlord in Gujii country

In my travels between Addis Ababa and Borana-Gujii countries, I had many opportunities to witness the behaveiour of landlords and the mistreatment of 'their' tenant farmers. In one occasion, I witnessed the attitude and behaviour of a prominent landlord in Gujii territory.

Due to poor road conditions, travel from Dilla to Yaballo by truck was often difficult and dangerous, especially during the wet season. People who travelled along this section of road relied on the use of different means of transport to get to their destination. These ranged from a ride on a mule's back to a lift in a passing four-wheel-drive vehicle or a heavy truck. In the summer of 1964, Dhera Jatani and I travelled from Dilla to Yaballo on a heavy truck along the old Dilla-Hagere Mariam road up to a Gujii locality known as Torre. Dhera was a teacher at Yaballo elementary school at the time and he was returning to Yaballo after attending a summer course in teachers' education. Torre was the hometown of one of the area's prominent landlords named Ayele Gebre Giorgis. He claimed to be one of the patriots who resisted the Italian occupation in the south of the country. As mentioned elsewhere, the Emperor had been in exile in England and on his return, provided free land grants in the south as a reward to Ethiopians who provided patriotic services in resisting the Italian occupation. Ayele was one of the beneficiaries of such a land grant in Gujii country. Such land grants invariably reduced the indigenous peoples to the status of *chisegna* in the service of culturally and ethnically alien landlords. In linear measure, Ayele's estate stretched for more than 30 kilometres. His property started a kilometre away from Hagere Mariam town and ran all the way to Torre village, and beyond. The total area of his domain could be estimated in thousands of square kilometres. As well as the coffee, tobacco and *ensete* cashcrops produced in the locality, merchants moving Borana cattle to Gedeo-Sidama markets and other produces back to Borana also used this same road. As the road passed through Ayele's vast estate, he charged a toll of Birr 0.25 per head of animal that travelled along this route. The justification was that they consumed the grass on the side of the road the bordered on his land. Many people were puzzled by the vast magnitude of Ayele's estate and the wide-ranging powers he had in the area that included his right to collect his own toll as though he were a king. One might ask: why was one individual given that much land in the first place? Did this land grant reflect his role in resisting the Italian occupation? Who allowed him to collect the toll – the Emperor? There were no clear answers to these and similar questions that bugged many people in the area at that time. Regardless, all Gujii people who resided in the territory he claimed as his own were his tenants. Ayele behaved as though he were a king and was noted for brutalising his *chisegna*. His main goal was to extract as many resources as possible from his tenants and he had his own ways of dispensing the law. If anything went wrong among his tenants, he would not allow them to settle the matter in accordance to their traditional ways of solving conflict. Instead, he intervened in such matters and collected payment in cash or in kind for legal services he supposedly provided. At the time, many people wondered what role, if any, district or provincial governors had in dispensing law and order in vast areas that had been declared the property of this or that landlord.

Dhera and I moved around Torre town to find a means of transportation to reach our destination of Yaballo. People told us that Ayele had a Landrover that would at least take us to Hagere Mariam town. We went to his residence; introduced ourselves, and pleaded with him to give us a lift. He agreed to give us a lift to Hagere Mariam. He also told us that he might even travel as far south as Surupha, a locality some 70 kilometres away from Hagere Mariam toward Yaballo, to investigate some Gujii people accused of stealing his cattle. The people who knew a great deal about his behaviour and *modus operandi* told us that he had no cattle there. They suggested that it was more likely that the local Gujii might have stolen animals from each other. They added that whenever he heard about such an incident, he was fast to intervene to grab something for himself from the people involved.

Ayele Gebre Giorgis (Photo by Tadhi Liban)

While travelling to Hagere Mariam in his Landrover, he boastfully narrated to us his patriotic achievements. Among his deeds he cited an ambush he carried out on Italian soldiers. One day, he said, an Italian military convoy was travelling from Hagere Salam in Sidama Province to Aleta Wondo, about 30 kilometres away, along a steep escarpment. He said that he shot the driver in the head and the vehicle rolled down the steep slope, killing most, if not all, of the passengers. He added how that brave act gave him immense esteem and respect in the community, leading to a reward of the sizable land grant from the Emperor. He was one of the landlords who made futile attempts against the revolution. He refused to surrender and was killed in a fight against those supporting the *Derg*'s land reform decree.

Ayele Gebre was not the only landlord in the area who committed serious crimes against the Gujii tenant-farmers and people in general. There were several other landlords known for their gross violations of the rights of tenant-farmers in Gujii districts. Another notorious landlord was named Worku Desta and his brutality and inhumane treatment of the tenants were widely known, even outside the Gujii territory. Following the revolution that deposed the Emperor from power, victims of his brutality called loudly for his arrest. The *Derg* authorities arrested him and he was hanged in Hagere Mariam town.

Gujii country is a very fertile land and known for its cash crops such as coffee and food crops such as maize. The region is also rich in mineral resources such as gold. So much so, the capital town of Jemjem province – Gujii country – was given an Amharic name 'Kibre Mengist' that reflected its status as a rich source of gold for the Ethiopian crown or the state.[25] Before the revolution, there were hardly any Gujii who owned or participated in any meaningful business operation. It seemed as though they were destined to serve the landlords either as *gebar* and/or *chisegna*. However, the *Derg*'s revolution paved the way for some members of the local Gujii to own businesses and become patrons over their ancestral land. Kassa Chiriqisa was such an elderly man who became a prosperous merchant in coffee. He was one of my informants about the reality of life in Gujii country during the pre-Derg, during and post-*Derg* times. He informed me how he started his business on the heels of the *Derg*'s revolution that drove out the parasitic landlords and allowed locals (former tenants) to own land. In the pre-revolution era, it seemed, as though they were barred from owning a business in the same way they were not allowed to own a piece of their ancestral land. Today, some businesses in Bule Hora (Hagere Mariam) are owned by the locals. The construction of various business establishments in the town by members

---

[25] The name "Kebre Mengist" roughly means the "Golden Pride of the Crown/State".

of the Gujii community is indicative of the changing circumstances of the indigenous people.

Gujii protest against feudalism and their status as tenant farmers

Immediately, after the breaking out of the revolution in the country in 1974, the Gujii in Hagere Mariam district rose against the landlords in the area. They chased them out of the rural areas into Hagere Mariam town, home to many of the landlords, their businesses and extended families. The town became a bastion of support for the landlords. The Gujii elders got together and imposed a sanction on the town. The arrangement was that the mainly rural-living Gujii community would sever commercial transactions with the town's people. It was declared that the Gujii would neither buy from urban-based *neftegna* merchants who opposed every measure taken by the *Derg* nor sell any of their products to them. It was said that Gujii in rural areas liked to drink a honey-based wine called *tej* made by merchants living in Hagere Mariam town. Many who owned businesses in town such as those selling *tej* either sympathised with or had links to the landlords. To strengthen the sanction even further, a rumour was spread claiming that *tej* sellers were planning to put poison in *tej* drinks served to rural Gujii customers. The rumour worked in keeping most Gujii people out of town. The landlords and others who could afford to left the town and moved to other places. The sanction severely hit the low-income residents who were unable to leave the town. The government officials tried to discuss the issue with the Gujii community leaders but these refused to talk with anyone unless they knew in advance the name of the person who would come to address them. They were told that Captain Jatani Ali, who was chief coordinator of the LDC in Arero Province, would come to address them. They accepted his mediation. In this mission, Jatani was joined by another Borana fellow named Major Salesa Jallo, who was also coordinator of the LDC in the neighbouring Borana Province. Jatani informed the Gujii on the scope of the revolutionary change that had taken place in the country and its irreversible nature. He told them how the old land-tenure system that rendered the Gujii tenant farmers at the mercy of alien landlords had been abolished by law. He assured them the exploitative relationship of the past that linked landlords with tenants would never return, and advised them to go back home and live in peace.

Utukan Malo recalled how Jatani stunned the Gujii audience by addressing them in their own language. According to the accepted practices, officials addressed the local people in Amharic first and then a translator would repeat the message in a local language. Often a distorted version of the original message reached the audience. This was standard practice even if both the speaker and the audience were able to communicate via a local language such as *Afaan Oromo* (the language of the Oromo people, the largest ethnic group in Ethiopia).[26] In a sense, Jatani broke this archaic language protocol from the time when he was appointed as LDC coordinator in Arero Province. Whenever he assembled the town residents to explain to them the mission of the revolution, he would address them in *Afaan Oromo*. Most residents in towns such as Yaballo or Hagere Mariam were fluent in *Afaan Oromo* but many considered the use of local language in official settings as nothing short of a rule against nature. Jatani spoke out against individuals who suffered from ethnic or language chauvinism and highlighted the democratic nature of using indigenous languages used by the vast majority of people in the provinces. He also spoke against those who degradeed themselves and their people by denying their native languages in favour of Amharic in a bid to be accepted by the ruling people.

---

[26] Both the Gujii and Borana communities speak a closely-related dialect of *Afaan Oromo*. This dialect of *Afaan Oromo* is also spoken in parts of Kenya and Somalia.

Assaults on the rebels

As mentioned previously, the *Derg* regime's decrees of nationalising rural lands and extra houses (i.e. rental premises) in cities and towns didn't go well with the former landlords and the propertied classes, who started futile protests against the reform policies. Gujii farmers took assertive initiatives to chase out of their home districts those who resisted the new land and property ownership decree. According to Utukan, the final battle between the Gujii and the landlords took place at a Dhadacha Bulto, in the nearby Yaballo district. The landlords tried to exploit the longstanding Gujii-Borana inter-clan feud as a tactic in their attempt to fight the Gujii's determination to get rid of them. The landlords tried to enlist some Borana people to fight the Gujii with them by citing the possibility of a lucrative reward in the form of Gujii cattle. They told the Borana how easy it was to drive away plenty of Gujii cattle once they collaborated with the militias fighting the Gujii on behalf of the landlords. Few Borana believed the propaganda and even fewer temporarily sided with the landlords. However, these Borana discovered that the offer was a trick so moved away from backing the landlords. The Gujii militias killed several of those fighting for the landlords and wounded one of their leaders, Dambala Gutema. The wounded and those who survived the skirmishes fled to Teltele, a remote district west of Yaballo, to join up with other forces resisting the *Derg*'s land reform decree.

Teltele was a remote district that straddled the administrative regions of Sidamo, Gamu Gofa and Kenya. Its strategic location and remoteness made Teltele an ideal location for disgruntled landlords to gather force and mount armed resistance against the *Derg*. As outlined, fighting against the landlords started in Yaballo district, with the Gujii community playing an active role. The Gujii occupied a fertile highland region north of Borana country where the Ethiopian crown carried out vast land grants to benefit *neftegna* settlers that became landlords. The militias fighting on behalf of angry landlords continued to move to Teltele area from various points in Sidamo and Gamu Gofa Administrative Regions. Dambala

Gutama, wounded at the Dhadacha Bulto's battle, joined the landlords' militants somewhere in Teltele district. The rebel militias in the bush started to disrupt the routines of government processes in the district. For instance, they killed elected members of peasant associations to weaken the *Derg*'s ability to implement its land reform policy. More than that, they also joined hands with infiltrators (*sergo-geb*) from Somalia and helped them to reach the extreme southwest corners of Arero Province. They also attacked Teltele town but the police unit and civilians in the town fended them off.

Jatani appealed to the higher authorities in Sidamo Administrative Region in Awassa and those in Addis Ababa to provide him with military support to thwart the bold ambition of the rebels. His appeals fell on deaf ears at both centres. The situation in the country remained volatile and fluid. Jatani suspected that there could be people in the positions of authority, both in Addis Ababa and Awassa, who were against the revolutionary actions of the *Derg* and were tacitly supporting the rebels. Under such a condition, Jatani had no other option than to consider what he could do on his own. Having assessed the capacity of the rebels, he determined to take action against them with the resources at his disposal. For this purpose, he recruited a militia force under his command from peasant communities in the adjacent provinces of Arero, Borana and Gedeo.

Mesele Dhaba was District Administrator (Governor) of Teltele before he was appointed as Deputy Governor of Arero Province. He was the right-hand man of Jatani in the campaign against the rebels. He narrated the assault against them as follows. In the district the rebel forces settled at two sites named Gara Barchuma and Makanisa. The rebels appeared well organised and had amassed thousands of head of cattle to sustain their members and supporters. They were waiting for an opportune time to launch a coordinated attack on the *Derg* administration. On his part, Jatani recruited around 500 militia soldiers with guns from Gujii and Gedeo areas. He gathered about the same number of peasant militias from Borana districts. Teltele police unit under the command of Lieutenant Tekle Amde-Brihan, and a few volunteers from Harbore and Wat Wondo communities in Gamu Gofa region also joined the campaign on Jatani's side. The rebels who seemed informed about the planned action against them changed their site of operation and moved to a locality known as Garba Soya, near the border with Kenya. Jatani divided his force into two and tried to track them in the area they reportedly moved to. He led one of the groups himself and put the other under the command of Mesele. In the pursuit, one afternoon, rural people who lived around the area informed Mesele of the rebels' whereabouts. They further advised him to hold on the assault till the following morning. As per the advice of the people, Mesele waited and launched the attack on the rebels early the following morning, around 6 a.m. The shooting continued until 11 a.m. The rebels were overwhelmed and fled the area towards Kenya. The pursuit continued into Kenyan territory as far as Dukanna. By the time Jatani's group arrived as reinforcement, the battle was over and Mesele's militia force was on the chase. On the battlefield, Jatani made an assessment of war causalities and looked around for Mesele's body in case he had fallen. Mesele was unharmed but could not tell the exact size of the casualties on either side. He estimated that there were around 30 casualties on the rebels' side and 4 on his. The thousands of head of cattle they amassed from the pastoralists for provision were retrieved and returned to the legitimate owners who came to reclaim them.

With local militia force under his command, it did not take Jatani more than two weeks to totally dismantle the rebel forces of the landlords from the bush and chase them out of Teltele district once and for all. This was his second major challenge as a governor of Arero Province which he managed to overcome successfully.

An ambush on Jatani

Jatani was one of the zealous supporters of the revolution at the beginning. According to him, the revolution came to liberate the downtrodden

Ethiopian masses from the feudal yoke of emperors. He openly expressed this conviction to the masses wherever he went and urged the communities to be vigilant in defending the fruits of the revolution. He was an articulate and eloquent speaker with uncanny persuasive abilities. On one occasion, he went to Mata Gafarsa to educate people in the area about the virtues of the revolution and possible challenges it faced. The gathered came from all communities in the district, including the Borana, Gujii, Gabra, Garri and the town's people. He addressed the people and on his return trip to Yaballo, he was ambushed at a place called Hommacho, a few kilometres away from Mata Gafarsa. The Garri community, supporters of Somalia's agenda for territorial expansion, was suspected of this pre-planned attack. In a car, Jatani was sitting beside his driver when he saw someone suddenly getting up from the bush and aiming at them from a distance of about 50 metres. He ordered the driver to stop the car, got out of the car and ducked out in a nearby ditch with his gun. Three attackers fired on Jatani's convoy with their automatic rifles. They killed the driver and his two police escorts on the spot and; burned the vehicle. He found a dry riverbed which he followed to get away from the assault. He returned to the town but by the time the police arrived for help, the attackers had escaped.

Battling Somali armed infiltrators

Background

The Republic of Somalia was created by merging the former colonies of Italian Somalia and British Somaliland in the early 1960s. Soon after, the rulers of the new country spear-headed an expansionist vision of "Greater Somalia". The realisation of this vision required the bringing together of all Somali clans residing in five regions in the Horn of Africa, to be ruled under one Somali flag. These regions comprised Somalis in the former Italian, British and French colonies and; those living in eastern Ethiopia, Northern Kenya and Djibuti. This vision was symbolically reflected via a deliberately chosen emblem that appeared on the flag of the Republic of Somalia. A single white star with five arms was the emblem and the arms represented the five sub-regions that would make up Greater Somalia. Successive rulers of Somalia aspired to annex a large territory in eastern Ethiopia inhabited by different Somali clans and even territories home to various Oromo communities such as Borana. Somali rulers prepared and launched various wars against Ethiopia and Kenya to grab vast territories. In this, they resorted both to indirect (through armed proxies) and direct (through outright military assault using its regular army) forms of aggression. They made several futile attempts at sending their army to invade Ethiopia during Haile Selassie's era and thereafter. In 1963, just a few years after Somalia gained independence from Italy and Britain, its army launched an attack on eastern Ethiopia at a place in Ogaden called Togo-Wichale. This war soon spread to other areas of Hararge, Bale and Borana regions. The Somali regime also armed ethnic Somali and other groups that had grievances against the repressive feudal rulers of Ethiopia to advance their Greater Somalia project. The Somali invading army was quickly repelled and a relative peace was restored in areas affected by that invasion. However, Somalia never abandoned its mission but continued to rebuild its army to stage other outright invasions some years later while it sent bands of armed infiltrators to destabilise border regions of Ethiopia. Following a military coup in October 1969, Siad Barre became the President of Somalia and resumed the Somali aspiration to annex ethnically Somali areas in Ethiopia with a renewed vigour. Through the decades of the 1970s and 1980s, he put Somali on a war footing and made preparations to build a strong army that would allow him to capture lands from Ethiopia and Kenya. To this aim, he declared that Somalia was a Socialist Republic and forged a strategic and military alliance with the Socialist-bloc countries dominated by the Soviet Union. The Soviet Union, China, Arab and Islamic countries sent large quantities of modern weaponry to arm the Somali army. Siad Bare grew emboldened as his army grew in size and sophistication due to the military aid from its allies. This gave him full confidence to invade Ethiopia and extend his aspiration for land well beyond the lands inhabited by Somali clans. This extended land claim included lands occupied by Oromo communities in eastern Hararge, Bale and Borana. His territorial ambition was reported to stretch from the Somalia-Ethiopia border up to 700 kilometres deep into the Ethiopian interior. Borana and Arero Provinces were among the territories on which the covetous eyes of Siad Barre focused. Re-branding Oromo communities who shared an aspect of culture with their Somali neighbours was one of the tactics his regime used to claim Oromo territories in eastern and southern Ethiopia as Somali.

Siad's first move in achieving his expansionist goal was to arm members of Somali clans in Ethiopia and send them back deep into Ethiopian territory in preparation for an invasion by his regular army soon after. At the same time, his scouts tried to influence certain Oromo groups in eastern parts of the country with a promise of helping them in their fight against Ethiopia's oppressive regimes. A propaganda front was also unleashed via radio stations based in the Somali Republic to support the Somali mission for expansion. Soon, pro-Somalia militants brandishing automatic weapons were unleased on unsuspecting communities deep inside Ethiopia, including the Borana. At the time, even the standard issue rifle carried by an Ethiopian army soldier was not automatic. Most Borana and other civilians in areas invaded by the heavily-armed Somalis didn't have firearms at all. Their weapons consisted of sticks and rusty spears. Those few ethnic Oromo who claimed to have guns carried antiquated rifles used during World Wars I and II. Such ancient rifles were hardly better than spears and often failed to fire. The balance of military power decidedly favoured the Somalis and groups aligned to them. The following accounts were not on Siad Barre's wide-scale invasion of eastern part of Ethiopia per se but on what had happened in Borana and Arero provinces as part of his invasion. Siad Barre's propaganda claimed to be fighting for the liberation of the oppressed Somali, Oromo and other people in the eastern part of Ethiopia from the unjust domination of the Amhara (Ethiopian) ruling group. For this aim, he fabricated liberation fronts for ethnic or political groups purportedly fighting against Ethiopian colonial domination. Such fronts were given names that reflected the wider Somali agenda of territorial expansion. For the Oromo community, he created and fomented a Somali Abo Liberation Front. The term *Abo* is an Oromo language expression to roughly mean "you" and it was to imply the front represented a pro-Somali Oromo community. His regime spread a propaganda narrative that claimed that both Oromo and Somali people branched out from the same ancestral tree. Many Somali sleeper cells or infiltrators that waged war in Arero and Borana provinces did so under the name of the 'Oromo Abo Liberation Front'. It was a convenient arm of Somalia's invasion for territorial expansion at the expense of Ethiopia.

People in the target area

The ethnic and cultural characteristics of groups targeted by the Somali propaganda machine in Borana, Arero and Gujii provinces need to be mentioned here. The use of closely-related Oromo language dialects is by far the most important factor that defined the cultural landscape of these three provinces. Oromo communities who live in territories bordering on Somali clans shared some cultural and religious commonalities with their Somali neighbours. The reverse was also the case to a lesser extent. The ethnic distribution or layout in the three provinces was as follows: Borana province was made up of the Borana, Gujii, Garri, Arsi, Degodia, Merihan and other smaller groups. Arero province was made up of Borana, Gujii, Gabra; and other smaller groups. Gujii province was made up of Gujii, some Gabra and other smaller groups. In terms of ethnicity, Borana, Gujii, Arsi and Gabra belong to the Oromo group.[27] Degodia

---

[27]   However, some Gabra individuals do not seem to be comfortable with the idea of being associated with the Oromo group these days.

and Merihan are pure Somali clans. Garri define themselves as Somalis though many of them speak *Afaan Borana*, a dialect of the Oromo language. Some people find it difficult to recognise the Garri as Somalis.

To win over communities in his target territory, Siad Barre used different strategies. He re-defined Oromo groups with stronger cultural affinity with the Somalis, whom he deemed helpful in his scheme of territorial expansion, by giving them a generic name "Somali Abo". This was meant to stress and exploit the ethnic commonalities between Oromo and Somali groups. He applied the following distinguishing titles to different groups in Borana country:

- Garri and Gabra were called Somali *dase* (residents in mat-thatched houses);
- Borana and Gujii were called Somali *buyo* (residents in grass huts); and,
- Gabra in Golbo were called Somali *malmalo* (decorative ribbon of Gabra women of the Golbo area).

Somalia agents selected influential elders and leaders from these communities and called them *Gudi Godoma* (leaders). They were instructed to promote three fundamental missions for Somalia:

- Support the objectives of Greater Somalia;
- Recruit young people for Somalia's war efforts, purportedly to liberate oppressed Somali and Somali-like communities under Ethiopian domination; and.
- Raise funds in cash and in kind to sustain the 'freedom' fighters.

The chosen people were given further training to enhance their sympathetic loyalty towards the cause of Greater Somalia and their military skills. To entice them even more and boost their ego, they were given modern firearms and related other military gear sent from Mogadishu. To implement the mission, young men from these communities would go to Somalia to undergo military and ideological training. Once ready, they were given arms and sent back to fight to 'liberate' their communities oppressed by Ethiopia.

Gabra are Oromo and many Garri spoke the Borana dialect of *Afaan Oromo* but pretended to be ethnic Somalis. The Garri occupied the eastern part of Borana, while the Gabra lived interspersed amongst the Borana and roamed all over Borana country in search of water and pasture for their livestock. The Gabra in particular knew almost every spot in Borana and Arero provinces as well as having intimate knowledge of the larger Borana and Gujii communities. But both ethnic groups fully supported the Somali infiltrators and joined hands with them to promote Somali territorial ambitions. In addition, Somalis managed to win over some young men from Borana and Gujii communities living in areas under the influence of or occupied by the Somali invaders. Somalis also recruited Gujii and Borana young men living on the peripheries of their provinces, trained and armed them to fight for the 'Somali Abo' cause in their respective tribal areas.

As noted earlier, disgruntled former landlords attacked government forces at Teltele town. The Gabra were said to have played a key role in facilitating the infiltration of armed Somali fighters to join up with the rebel forces of the landlords. All along, many people suspected that the Gabra helped armed Somali infiltrators to move easily from eastern borderlands of Borana to its heartland, and even as far west as Teltele. Both Garri and Gabra communities played a vital role in facilitating Siad Barre's invasion of southern Ethiopia.

The Somali incursions and damages inflicted

Somalia's incursion into Ethiopia started gradually and took advantage of the chaos that accompanied the military coup that removed Ethiopia's Emperor from power. The transition from the old regime to the *Derg*'s new socialist regime was far from smooth. The country's system of government was shaken and paralysed both by open and underground power struggles. It was understood that Siad Barre was waiting for an opportune moment to invade Ethiopia while amassing armaments and building a strong army in the meantime. The political upheaval that followed Ethiopia's revolution was such a moment.

The infiltration of Arero province by Somali armed agents started before Jatani was appointed as the governor of the province. After his appointment, Jatani explained the nature of Somali encroachment on the province and presented two options of halting them to the *Derg* authorities. These were for the regime to either send military force to the area or give firearms to pro-Ethiopian pastoralists, such as the Borana and Gujii, to defend the southern borders of Ethiopia. The *Derg* regime took too long to respond to any of the options. By the time the regime tried to do something about the invasion, Somali invaders supported and directed by sympathetic groups from within Ethiopia (such as the Garri and Gabra) had inflicted serious damage on the lives and properties of local communities in the area.

Initially Somali invaders used a "softly-softly" tactic to win over the hearts and minds of the local population they set out to 'liberate' from Ethiopia's undisputed misrule and oppression. They were instructed to behave as friendly as possible toward peasant and pastoralist communities. They were advised not to take anything from them by force. They purchased whatever supplies they needed from the villagers. They would use force only if they were attacked or stopped from moving further inland. Given years of misrule and brutality with which Ethiopia's rulers treated indigenous populations in these border regions, the *modus operandi* of Somali forces seemed far more progressive to many in the area. With this approach, they managed to occupy most parts of Dirre district in Borana province and a major part of Arero and Hagere Mariam districts in Arero province. They were met with some resistance only as they approached Yaballo district and town, the capital of Arero Province. The Somali invaders stunned and overwhelmed local defences with their use of sophisticated weaponry that included automatic machine guns, grenade launchers and landmines. Automatic AK47 rifles were standard-issue weapons carried by Somalis and militias aligned to them. Rusted spears carried by Borana or Gujii men were no match to the efficient Soviet machine guns carried by the Somalis and their allies. As a result, Somalis initially seemed unstoppable in their march towards the highland areas of Ethiopia. They killed all those who stood in their way and looted resources of communities suspected of being on the side of Ethiopia. The *Derg* seemed to suffer from Nero's syndrome of fiddling while Borana burnt. The *Derg* regime was too busy trying to strengthen its grip on power at the centre rather than protect citizens or arm them to protect themselves against an open aggression from a foreign country.

Somali invaders and their allies inflicted heavy damages on the Borana. They got away with thousands of head of cattle which were the major source of livelihood to these pastoralists. For example, Jirmo Dida was a prominent community leader in Dida Hara area and one of the richest persons according to the Borana measure of wealth. Members of his family and extended family had thousands of head of cattle. According to Guro Dida, his younger brother, Somali raiders plundered 4,600 head of cattle, about 200 goats and sheep and 45 camels from Jirmo's family alone. Only a small portion of the family's assets escaped the plunder due to their location at the time. According to Guro, Doyo Dida lost 2,500, Wario Kulla 400, Guyo Boru Lalo 200 head of cattle respectively during this time. Hardly any families in the area escaped the plunder as hundreds of individuals were robbed of from ten to a few hundred head of cattle. He estimated the number of people killed in separate raids in Dida Hara area alone at 250. The following were notable members of the community killed by Somali invaders recalled by Guro: Jilo Arero, Arero Qanchora, Guyo Dima, Dida Guyo and two sons, Guyo Saphansa, Duba Saphansa, Galgalo Raso, Kana Guyo Gnaru, three sons of Arero Dabaso, and Guracha Arero.

As pointed out above, agents from Somalia recruited and armed young men from Borana, Gujii, Gabra and Garri communities to advance the Somali agenda. Many of these took part in raids on communities suspected of harbouring people who sympathised with or spied for the enemy of Somalia (i.e. Ethiopia). For instance, separate battles raged in Yaballo and Arero districts where prominent Borana elders were killed. A Borana named Dima Jilo was a commander of the Somali forces in many of these battles. According to Guro Dida, notable Borana persons such as Guyo Aba Sara, Jilo Arero, Chachu Wadare, Arero Qanchoro and Guyo Boru Lalo (the retired Hawatu *Abba Gada*) were among those killed by forces commanded by Dima Jilo. After the Somali forces were finally defeated, Dima surrendered to Ethiopian authorities and lived peacefully among the community he harassed and ravaged so much. Guro Dida told me that in 2010, Dima went to the goldprospecting locale of Burjuji to try his luck. Reportedly, he fell into a river and was drowned; his body was not recovered.

As Borana armed men in the service of Somalia attacked and killed their own people, so did the Gujii, so much so that travel in the Gujii highlands was impossible without a military escort. Like Dima Jilo from Borana, armed Gujii men attacked people from their own communities for siding up with the "Ethiopian oppressors". For instance, Gamade Elema, the district governor of Hagere Mariam, was ambushed and killed by such Gujii men. Pastor Tesfaye Ganna, who was in charge of the local evangelical church, was also killed in similar circumstances.

It was long after the Somalia infiltrators had inflicted devastating damage in terms of killing people and plundering livestock in their thousands that the *Derg* regime sent in trained militia personnel to assist the people. The first attempt at repelling Somali-led aggression in the province was unsuccessful. In fact, Somali invaders moved *en masse* deep into Arero Province to consolidate their occupation and to invade more territories. Sometime in 1977, Jatani organised and led a local militia force to slow the advance of the aggressors. This militia force was made up of armed volunteers from around Yaballo town and the surrounding districts. The Jatani-led militia force marched 30 kilometres east from Yaballo town to confront the aggressors at a place known as Doffi, on the highway to

Moyale. In the skirmish, a prominent Borana elder and community leader named Jirmo Dida and a Burji elder named Qatto Marre were killed. The counter-attack didn't go well as it was overwhelmed by the superior firepower capacities of the invaders. Instead of keeping up the fight, the militia retreated from the battlefield. It was only after this serious military reversal that put Yaballo town in serious danger of being overrun by the enemy, that the *Derg* took the magnitude of the threat a bit more seriously. A decade or so later, Borana country and the whole of southern Ethiopia were left unarmed and defenceless as the combined rebel armies of the TPLF and EPLF took over the country at the point of the gun.

An organised assault

As mentioned, Jatani had been appealing to the *Derg* authorities either to send military reinforcement to the area to halt the Somalia invasion or send him a supply of firearms with which local peasants and pastoralists could defend themselves. His pleas started from the day of his appointment and long before the invasion was in full swing. After Borana Major Salesa Jallo defected to Somalia, some ill-informed individuals in the bureaucracy of Sidamo Administrative Region cast a suspicious eye on Jatani's request for arms, thinking that Jatani would follow Salesa's footsteps in defecting to Somalia. But Haile Eyesus Aba Hassan, then Governor of Sidamo Administrative Region, and other officials at the *Derg* Headquarters who knew Jatani personally, persisted in defending Jatani against such unfounded allegations. Jatani told me how his insistent pleas to defend the local population against Somali aggression finally reached the ears of Colonel Mengistu, Chairman of the *Derg* and Ethiopia's head of state. Colonel Mengistu ordered the suspicious elements in the *Derg* bureaucracy to give Jatani 3,000 guns; and added, "Let us see what damage he can do with the arms to the Ethiopian interests even if he defects to Somalia". After long delays, the *Derg* government finally sent a supply of 3,000 G-3 (semi-automatic) rifles and some bullets for use in antiquated guns carried by local militias.

Derg Headquarters also ordered the Southern Command of the armed forces stationed at Awassa, under the command of Major General Demissie Bulto, to launch systematic counter-attacks on Somali aggressors referred to as *sergo geb* (infiltrators). To accomplish the task, operation command posts were established in selected strategic towns in Arero, Gujii and Borana provinces. Hagere Mariam was one such post under the command of General Kebede Gashe with assistance from Major Bereta Gomara. It was tasked with clearing Gujii country from the infiltrators. Other command posts were located in lowland areas of Arero and Borana provinces; in such places as Yaballo, Arero, Mega, Moyale and Dillo. Tanks, heavy and light armaments were secured and deployed for the operations. The strategy for the assaults included attacking different units of the infiltrators and cutting off their communication facilities and surface supply lines. With this systematic approach, three groups jointly launched a counter-attack against the Somalis and their local allies. These were soldiers from the regular army, trained local militias from PAs and Borana pastoralists who received those 3,000 rifles plus some bullets to defend their communities. This joint operation was part of Ethiopia's coordinated national campaign to counter and defeat the invading Siad Barre's armies inside Ethiopia. In a few months, the operation successfully chased out the invaders from Borana and Gujii countries. Thus Siad Barre's ambition to expand into large tracts of eastern Ethiopia was cut short.

Wario Galgalo in Dirre District

Jatani transferred Wario Galgalo from Yaballo to Mega as a Governor of Dirre District, with Mega town as its capital. The Somali infiltrators controlled much of the central and eastern parts of the district with the exception of few towns. They had been using every means and opportunity to expand their control even further. Before Jatani travelled to Awassa to receive supplies of firearms for local militias, he asked Wario the number of guns needed for Dirre District. Wario's response was about 1,750 rifles. When the rifles arrived with a heavy military escort from Awassa, Wario asked community leaders to recruit capable, courageous and trustworthy men who would receive guns to defend the community against the ongoing Somali aggression. He organised the people who received the guns into a local self-defence militia force. This militia force was deployed to defend villagers from the enemy forces and sometimes for counter-attack. People like Wario had to deal with cowardly defections from battlefields; Wario told me how he, with his assistants, dealt with this matter. They would identify possible routes of retreat used by those running away from the battlefields back to their villages. They detained all those fleeing, disarmed them and gave the guns to those perceived as brave soldiers, ready to fight. Wario pointed out that this action discouraged unjustifiable or cowardly retreats from the battlefields thereafter.

The armed local militias were organised to defend the community who had to contribute in cash or in kind for their upkeep, since the government didn't have a special budget to support them. However, the contributions from the community were less than satisfactory. Wario told me how he had to dip into a fund for a community development (Birr 1.2 million), deposited at a CBE branch at Dilla, to supply the militias with basic rations.

An incident involving Wario at El Soda (literally, "salt well") in Dirre district needs recounting here. El Soda is a crater lake not far from Mega town and is where the Borana community gets salt for human and livestock consumption. It is a conical-shaped hill, the remains of an extinct volcano, and has a depression in the middle with a small salty lake at the bottom. The depression is several hundred metres deep and flanked by steep walls on all sides, except on the front side where people descend to dig salt from the bottom of the lake. The entrance to the pool is so steep in gradient that only donkeys which can carry 30 to 50 kg of salt can descend to the bottom to bring it to the surface. The dark spot in the picture below is a pool of salty water from which people extract salt by scooping out the salty water and then evaporating the water.

Salt is a vital commodity in Borana country as it is an important ingredient in both human and animal diets. El Soda was the only place where Borana from near and far could get their salt either by mining it themselves or through purchasing it at local markets. This salt mine remained under the control of the Ethiopian state despite several attempts by Somali invaders to take over the entire area. Borana villagers who found themselves in areas controlled by Somali invaders were desperate to have access to the salt as the health and productivity of their animals depended on salt intake. These Borana were not allowed to either travel to the salt mine or to markets in nearby towns such as Mega to purchase salt. The Somali invaders and occupiers banned Borana villagers under their control from having any contact with other Borana still living in areas under Ethiopian rule. These Borana were denied access to town-based markets to sell their stock in order to purchase items of clothing or other supplies. In desperation, the Somali invaders organised the people under their control to go to El Soda to dig for salt while they provided protection via an armed escort. The captive pastoralists travelled to the crater lake for salt with 77 donkeys. Wario was tipped off about this daring plan ahead of time and organised his armed men to ambush the armed escort and intercept the salt caravan. With a surprise attack Wario's men chased the armed escort away, captured the salt exploiters with their donkeys and drove them to Mega town. The people were imprisoned and the consignment of salt was confiscated with the donkeys.

The 'El Soda' salty crater lake

As mentioned before, Mega was one of the selected command posts from which the Ethiopian army would launch a counter-attack against Somali invading forces. Some soldiers dispatched from Ethiopia's Southern Army Command were stationed there. These soldiers knew little about the lives of people in the area. In part because of the language barrier, they were not equipped to read and decipher vital cultural or ethnic nuances that underpinned human interactions in the area. They had limited information as to what was going on around them. Consequently, to these soldiers the captured men at the salt mines were basically traitors or enemy agents. They proposed that all of them should be shot. Jatani and Wario who were in Mega, explained to the soldiers that the salt miners were enemy captives rather than traitors. They also argued the merit of treating the captured humanely as a strategy to win back those villagers who were still under the control of the enemy. Wario persuaded the soldiers to reconsider their views on the captured people by stressing how the captured and their communities were at the mercy of Somali invaders. He suggested a practical and symbolic way of treating the captured humanely rather than punitively, involving their conditional release, followed by an incentive that would show them the benefits of being ruled by the Ethiopian state. Wario proceeded with the plan and bought new attire and turbans for them, as they were poorly dressed thanks to their inability to access the markets. He bought the clothes and ceremonially dressed them in Borana traditional attire, complete with turbans. Then he informed them how they were free to choose between going back to their villages under Somali occupation or to stay where they were. Some chose to go and others preferred to stay. Reportedly, Somali agents mistreated those who returned by accusing them of providing vital information to the Ethiopian side.

Ethiopia's coordinated counter attack against Somali invaders was launched and gradually pushed the enemy away towards the eastern part of the province. Wario resigned from his post as the governor of Dirre District to resume his studies at university. As stated previously, Jatani appointed Kinfu Tesfaye to the position but he did not stay long in the post; he resigned soon after and Huqa Garse filled the vacancy.

Rehabilitation of victims

Somali invaders and their allies looted livestock in their thousands to sustain their war effort. This left behind hundreds of internally displaced, destitute families. The victims in Arero Province were sheltered at various localities such as at Yaballo relief camp and were provided with food items and other forms of assistance for several months. Jatani sought ways of rehabilitating them. He ordered Qamphe Debaso and another fellow to explore the possibility of settling destitute pastoralists as crop farmers. The two surveyed for farmable land west of Yaballo town. Hidi Alle and Ade Galchat were chosen as ideal sites for resettling war-affected and destitute families. The settled families received food aid as part of Ethiopia's programs for rehabilitating drought and war-affected communities. The idea was to rehabilitate them while teaching them how to cultivate land with a pair of oxen or other primitive techniques employed by Ethiopian farmers. Most of the resettled families preferred to pursue their nomadic pastoralist way of life but this would have required expensive investment in rebuilding breeding livestock over many years or even decades. Jatani raised 400 oxen from local people and distributed 200 to each site. Several farmers from the Oromo and Burji communities volunteered to teach the resetled Borana the basics of crop farming, including skills in how to use a pair of oxen for the purpose. Cultivation of land on that scale was a new and rather challenging endeavour for cattle-herding Borana. Still, it was hoped that over time, they would acquire the basic skills and become self-sufficient in food production. They were provided with farming tools and seeds to produce crops for the following harvest season. The provincial administration took care of the food supplies of these newly-settled Borana until the first harvest was ready. Many among the displaced found the skills of crop farming beneficial in giving them a more sustainable means of livelihood. A significant number of Borana pastoralists learned the art of cultivating land on a fairly wide scale as the result of this rehabilitation scheme set up by Jatani. Skills acquired there were transferred to other Borana families and later used in other localities.

The life of people in areas occupied by Somali invaders

I interviewed Murqu Liban Boru and Godana Jarso Sabo to share their experiences on the life of Borana people under Somali occupation.

Murqu Liban Boru was a middle-aged man at the time of interview but had lived in the area under the control of Somali invaders as a young man. He described his experiences with them as follows. Initially they told the people that Somalis and Oromos were people of the same ancestry in the distant past. They told the Borana that the Amhara, the ruling tribe of Ethiopia, was an alien people both culturally and religiously, who were intent on dominating these two brotherly peoples. According to the Somalis, Amhara was a common enemy which must be jointly fought and repelled by the combined efforts of the Borana and Somali peoples. They preached that the odious vestiges of the Amhara's colonial domination must be weeded out through the coordinated fight of the two communities. Accordingly, capable young or middle-aged men from both communities should go to Somalia, get arms and undergo military training to fight the common enemy. At first, the Somalis were very friendly to people they came into contact with during the earlier months of their occupation. They refrained from taking anything from the people by force. However, after they had occupied considerable areas in southern provinces of Ethiopia, their *modus operandi* suddenly changed for the worse in terms of their behaviour in treating people under their occupation. After that, no one would dare to disobey their orders. Every person was watched with suspicion and presumed to be a possible informer or agent of the enemy (the Ethiopian Government). They would send husbands on missions somewhere and raped their wives. Unmarried young girls were also victims of rape. They had no provisions of their own that would sustain them over an extended period of time and they grew predatory on the resources of the community. They slaughtered livestock from different families on a rostered basis.[28] They did not allow people under their control to have any links with their relatives in areas still governed by Ethiopian authorities or do any business transactions with those in nearby towns. As the result of the ban, the livestock of people under their control couldn't get salt, a vital mineral for human and animal health, from the markets or salt mines. To resolve this critical shortage of salt, they led people to embark on a dangerous venture of trying to access the salt mines at El Soda, as discussed above.

The people under their control became couriers and provided postal services within the territory they occupied. Sometimes, they played foul games. He reported that there were instances when the person to whom the letter was delivered instructed to kill the messenger. The person carrying a letter had no way of knowing its contents. Murqu mentioned an event in which two persons from his village were ordered to deliver a

---

[28]   I also interviewed Halakhe Dida Gobessa who was a very young boy when Somalis invaded his village. He recalled that, when Borana people under So-

letter to a certain person. While on their way to the delivery spot, they met with an acquaintance, who told them that he suspected the delivery might cost them their life. On arrival at their destination, they found that the intended recipients of the message were practising horse riding. One of the messengers requested to try the practice, and they allowed him. He made a simple attempt once or twice and galloped away with the horse. They killed his colleague who had remained behind.

The Somalis massacred prominent Borana persons who were under their occupation; Dalacha Diqa, Molu Borbor and Boru Golicha Guyo were among the victims of Somali agents. Reportedly, they took these Borana for a revenge kill to the very spot where a notable Garri named Robow Hassan Gababa was killed in a battle with Borana in 1963.

Godana Jarso Sabbo was one of the community leaders who lived under Somali occupation and had regular interaction with Somali agents. He indicated that they demanded all manner of things and services from the people under their occupation. In response to my interview about his experience, his description of Borana people's life under Somali occupation was similar to Murqu Liban's. He said many of the Somali agents and armed contingents sent to lord it over Borana areas were predominately men from ethnic Garri and Gabra tribes.[29] Godana mentioned how friendly these Somali agents were when they first arrived in the area where

---

mali occupation were liberated, out of the 60 bulls owned by his family, only one survived the practice of slaughtering bulls to feed Somali agents.

[29] To provide some context, both Garri and Gabra tribes are speakers of the Borana dialect of *Afaan Oromo* language but liked to define themselves as Somalis, with whom they shared Islam as a definer of their identity. Both Garri and Gabra sided with the Somali cause whenever war broke out between the states of Ethiopia and Somalia. Both had uneasy relations with the larger Borana Oromo tribe and laid claim to Borana grazing land. Suspicion, protracted feuds, treachery and bloody wars have defined their interaction with Borana community. Therefore, their role as agents of the Somali invaders was intertwined with their long-standing and often bloody tribal feud with the Borana people over land. The Somali invasion of Ethiopia provided these two tribes with an opportunity to settle old scores and bloody feuds.

he lived. They did not take any property by force or without making an effort to pay for it. They seemed to have their own supplies to meet their basic needs. They tended to solicit things they needed from Borana villagers in a friendly manner. He added that they would start their pleadings by saying, 'We are brothers, Please give us this or that'. However, such platitudes were short-lived as the Somalis unleashed their underlying predatory behaviour when they realised that a good part of Borana territory was still out of their control. This was despite their boast of controlling the whole region in no time, given their superior machine guns, rocket-propelled grenades or bazooka launchers. Godana said that they soon resorted to living on food items such as milk and meat, forcefully demanded from Borana families under their control. They ordered people to provide them with a daily ration of 10 to 15 live animals for slaughter for food and several litres of milk with which to make *shai*, a sweet tea boiled in milk. Community leaders who failed to enforce the payment of these "taxes" by the villagers faced severe punishment and even death. No one would dare to question their orders; whatever was demanded had to be provided immediately.

Godana said that a few months after they occupied the area, Somali agents ordered the people to identify two persons from their community who possessed unique personal qualities such as bravery in warfare and had good standing amongst the Borana. As per the order, the people presented two young men. They gave the young men a letter which they would deliver to a Somali army camp at a place called Garbi. The selected men travelled to the camp to fulfil the order but nothing has been heard of the two ever since. Borana villagers speculate that the young men were taken to the spot where Robow Hassan Gababa was killed (as mentioned above by Murqu) and executed as retribution.

To drive out the Somali invaders out of the area, the *Derg* government mobilised a force made up of soldiers from the regular army, peasant militias and armed pastoralists. Though it took a long time to mobilise, the Ethiopian fight-back force turned the tide of war against Somali invaders very quickly. When the Somalis and their supporters realised that the turn of event was against them, they apparently decided to hold the people under their control as hostages *en masse*. Hoping to get out of the reach of the Ethiopian counter-attack force, they ordered communities they held hostage to move eastwards toward the Somali border. This was to be done with all their livestock, in the middle of the day and without a water supply. Those families who were eager to be liberated by the Ethiopian forces were reluctant to fully cooperate with the Somalis, but fearing dire consequences for insubordination, they pretended to obey the orders by slowly moving eastwards. In the meantime, the Ethiopian army carried out a reconnaissance of the enemy's location and concentration from the air and started bombarding them with heavy artillery from a distance. Instead of confronting the Ethiopian forces they so often boasted at wanting to slaughter all together, they gathered together their guns and fled towards the Ethio-Somali border. Thus, Borana people in Dirre district who were under brutal Somali occupation were liberated and joined the rest of Borana at El Soda crater lake for salt or at market places.

When Somali invaders and their local backers (Garri and Gabra) realised that events were turning against them and they were unable to withstand Ethiopian counter-attack, they reasoned that those young Borana men they had forcefully recruited would surrender to the Ethiopian forces. After all, Somalis and their tribal backers often accused the Borana of being staunchly pro-Ethiopian. Instead of letting this happen, they rounded up the Borana men under their command and disarmed them. Reportedly, they executed, in cold blood, 447 of them at a place Borana call Koticha Okotu.[30] The Garri, who sponsored that bloody massacre, have since mockingly renamed the place "A Mound of Borana

---

[30] This place has since been given to Garri-Somalis who were returnees from Somalia following the defeat of the *Derg* regime by the combined rebel forces

Bones", which underscores their callousness and vindictive delight in massacring Borana men. It is necessary to mention how both the EPLF and TPLF were supported and armed by Siad Barre of Somalia as part of his agenda to weaken Ethiopia's *Derg* in order to grab a chunk of eastern Ethiopia. Both these rebel groups had offices in Mogadishu and their leaders were issued with Somali passports to travel to Arab capitals in search of arms and other supplies for their fight against the Ethiopian state. The TPLF-EPLF win over the *Derg* therefore represented an indirect win for the treacherous sympathisers of the Somali expansionist cause in southern Ethiopia.

But why did Somalis and their Garri supporters order Borana people under their occupation to move eastward *en masse*, with their livestock, as the Ethiopian forces approached? Were they planning to carry out a mass execution of all Borana hostages, just like they massacred those 447 young Borana men they once armed to fight for the Somali cause? No doubt Somali agents and their Garri collaborators would know the reason. From the antagonistic, treacherous, brutal and vindictive nature of the Garri against the Borana, the possibility of mass execution of Borana people forced to march eastwards cannot be ruled out.

Garri treachery and the continued attack on Borana and Ethiopia

The defeated invading forces of Somalia retreated to their country. Garri and Gabra, groups allied with Somalia and heavily armed by them, remained in the eastern part of Borana country where they used to live. The Ethiopian authorities seemed very forgiving of them, given their pro-Somali role against the Borana and Ethiopia. Their enthusiasm and willingness to assist Siad Barre was not the first time that the Garri exploited political turmoil to undermine the Borana's and Ethiopia's interests. Their treachery during the Ethio-Somali war mirrors a previous

---

of TPLF and EPLF in 1991 and is now part of the Somali Regional State in Ethiopia or Kilil 5.

one when the fascist forces of Mussolini invaded Ethiopia from their colonies of Italian Somalia and Eritrea. At the time when Italian forces and their *banda* (local collaborator) soldiers invaded Ethiopia, Garri used to live on the eastern edges of Borana country. During the Italian invasion and the following five-year-long occupation of Ethiopia (1936-1941), Garri allied with the Italians just like they did during the invasion of Ethiopia by Siad Barre's forces. The Garri received firearms from the Italians for their *banda* services to them. They did exactly the same thing when they rushed to embrace the invading forces of Somalia where they were given machine guns to assist the Somali cause and attack Borana to grab the latter's land. It is significant to consider how guns left in the hands of Garri and other pro-Somali tribes in Ethiopia were used once the main enemy was driven out of Ethiopia. When the Italians left, Garri and various Somali clans in the area used those firearms against the neighbouring Borana to fulfil their long-standing practice of expanding their territories at the expense of the Borana. Somali clans' and Garri collaboration with anti-Ethiopian invading forces invariably helped tilt the local balance of power against the unarmed or poorly-armed Borana (who mostly had rusty spears and sticks) to push them out their ancestral territories. Effectively, then, the invasions of Ethiopia by Italy and Siad Barre provided the Garri – and various Somali clans – with a bonanza of modern armaments with which to implement their ambition for territorial expansion. Following the defeat of their Somali benefactors, Garri kept a low profile, holding onto the firearms that came to them courtesy of Siad Barre. The Borana thus experienced a period of relative peace for a few years until another violent regime change in Addis Ababa in 1991 disrupted the lull. For the Borana, as for many other communities in Ethiopia, the defeat of the *Derg* ushered in another era of uncertainty, misrule, state-instigated persecution, and violent grabs of land. The position of the Garri and various Somali clans in the area improved dramatically with the defeat of the *Derg* regime by rebel groups from the north who had been backed, sheltered and armed by Somalia for years.

As Siad Barre's army and their local collaborators fled to Somalia, Jatani went to East Germany for the aforementioned three-month course, delegating Mesele Dhaba, his deputy, to act as Governor of Arero Province in his absence. During this period, the Borana and other groups in the area felt relief from constant attacks by the better-armed pro-Somalia groups such as the Garri and the Gabra. Some Borana men were able to purchase arms to defend their land and the peace of their communities. Still, on three occasions, Garri and their Gabra allies launched attacks on Borana at different places. Their objectives were not clear beyond their vague claim over Borana land. The first was a kind of surprise attack on Arero town (Mata Gafarsa) where they were thrashed hard by volunteer militias from that town. The second was when a column of armed men, purportedly Garri and Gabra, moved into the heartland of Borana from the east. They were attacked at Doffi Jilo Gole and were chased away. The third was a planned attack on Hidi Lola town in Dirre district. Local people detected their movement and attacked them before they reached their target. Again, the Garri and Gabra were routed and their survivors were chased away eastwards towards Somalia. After these sporadic and futile attacks, relative peace was attained in the province for a while. The lull allowed the community and leaders such as Jatani to turn their full attention to economic and social development programs.

Rural Development

Before embarking on what Jatani had accomplished in development activities in Arero Province, let us briefly look at the dismal state of road networks in that province prior to Jatani's arrival. Several half-hearted attempts at rehabilitating existing road infrastructure had hardly made much difference as the province remained as one of the least developed in Ethiopia. Invariably, all provincial governors prior to Jatani were appointees of the central government of Ethiopia and sent from Awassa or Addis Ababa. Such governors were culturally alien to the province.

The same was the case with the personnel that ran the administrative bureaucracies of the province and districts. *Fitawrari*[31] Seyoum Negash was one such appointed governors of Arero Province in the 1960s who attempted to develop the province in terms of infrastructure. On arrival, he was shocked by the state of roads in the province. In fact calling dotted lines on maps as roads hardly did justice to the dusty cattle tracks that remained impassable during the rainy season. Even considerable stretches of the international highway that linked Addis Ababa to Nairobi, through Moyale, became an impassable mud trap during the rainy season. Some stretches of this road were so steep and slippery that scores were killed every year in fatal traffic accidents. Lorries and four-wheel-drive vehicles were the only type of vehicles that could negotiate the atrociously dangerous roads to the province and within it. *Fitawrari* Seyoum planned to improve a stretch of the main highway linking Yaballo with Addis Ababa, to render it usable when it rained. His aim was to at least complete the section that ran from Yaballo town to the northern boundary of the province. He determined that the funding for this roadwork would come from imposts on people living in the province, even though the road in question didn't even touch three out of five districts in the province, namely Teltele, Arero and Burji. He set down the criteria according to which all districts in the province would contribute funds to upgrade the main highway. He ordered all district governors to raise the amount allocated to their jurisdiction by any means possible. Nomadic pastoralist communities were asked to raise the bulk of the funds although they were the least likely to benefit from such road work when compared to townsfolk. Anyway, a considerable amount of money was raised for the project despite the grumblings and resistance to pay coming from the people in the districts. Before the project got off the ground, a serious quarrel broke out between *Fitawrari* Seyoum and the district governor of

---

[31] *Fitawrari* is a traditional title in Amharic given to high-level war leader in northern Ethiopia.

Teltele, Worqu Mekuria. In those days, Teltele district was virtually inaccessible by car and it seemed that Worqu liked things to remain that way. Worqu had carved out his own mini-fiefdom in Teltele district and ran the affairs of government as though he was a minor king. He apparently didn't like Seyoum's interference in running the district nor was he willing to change his cosy life. Reportedly, the two clashed fiercely on the issue of imposing unfair monetary contribution on districts through which the main road didn't pass. Worqu was more influential than Seyoum at the regional administration offices at Yirgalem. (At the time, Yirgalem was the capital of the Sidamo Administrative Region). Apparently because of Worku's influence and lobbying at Yirgalem, Seyoum was removed from his post as Governor of Arero Province and sent to fill another post in the region. He was not given a chance to implement his road improvement project. It was difficult to determine what happened to several hundred thousand Birr raised for the road project after the initiator had left. Many people believed that the money was embezzled (as per the norm). Seyoum v. Worku-type feuds, imposed and unpopular methods of raising funds, and routine embezzlement of these funds characterised efforts at developing the province before Jatani became Governor.

Vision, programs and projects

Jatani's superiors and even casual observers admired his superb attributes as a leader. Whatever duties he had been given and wherever he had been assigned, he left behind a long-lasting legacy that changed the lives of many people. In addition to these traits, his actions and style of leadership were community-minded and aimed at improving the lives of the poor, the oppressed and the marginalised. The abovementioned conflict with Somali invaders took place from 1977 to 1980, but the social, economic and political impact of this invasion on affected communities lasted a lot longer. Securing the safety and survival of the people rather than development was the main preoccupation of political and community leaders during those years. It was only after the invaders had been successfully driven out of the country that Jatani could turn his full attention to social and economic development in Arero Province. Communities in the province were amongst the most marginalised in the country. As noted previously, in terms of development the province ranked at the bottom of the scale, even by Ethiopia's dismal human development record. Its remoteness from the centres of Ethiopia's power made the efforts of attempting to develop it even more challenging. For example, there was not a single senior high school or a modest hospital in the province when Jatani became Governor. The few primary schools in the province were created to cater for the children of government officials living in a handful of towns. Such schools were not easily accessible to children coming from farming communities dotted around such towns, let alone to children of nomadic pastoralists who lived even farther afield. Consequently, there were hardly any students from nomadic pastoralist communities attending such schools. It is safe to say that the rulers of Ethiopia only had a vague idea of the existence of Borana and other communities living in the remote southern borderlands. Focussing on the development of such isolated communities was never a pressing item on the agenda when they had wars or political squabbles to attend to. Successive regimes that ruled Ethiopia didn't have any clear or coherent policy on improving the lives of far-off communities, best known for their inter-tribal wars. At best, the approach was to leave these areas to carry on as they had done for centuries – as long as they served as a buffer zone shielding middle Ethiopia from Islamic invaders or European would-be colonialists.

The challenge for concerned persons such as Jatani was where to start in terms of developing a province that lacked the very basic institutional, infrastructural and financial foundation on which to expand. The Somali invasion and lack of development were not the only challenges faced by the people in the province. Frequent droughts had worsened the levels of poverty, forcing entire communities to seek food aid for survival. Jatani and his administration had to deal with a conundrum of trying to feed war- and drought-affected communities or build roads first, in order to get food aid donated by foreigners to the hungry. He opted for a community-centred development strategy that relied on the capacities and modest resources of the people at village or grass-roots levels. His set out to prioritise his efforts by focusing on key social and economic issues hindering community development while laying the groundwork for future development. Tackling problems related to water shortages, education of children and the lack of vital infrastructure (such as health clinics and roads both in towns and in rural areas) were given top priority. At the same time, rebuilding and strengthening organisational capacities of the community were essential so that their resources could be pooled to tackle some of these problems themselves. Organisations representing farmers and pastoralists were given prominence and offices were built to help coordinate their efforts. Public awareness campaigns were carried out to educate the community on the importance of peaceful co-existence between the various tribes as an essential prerequisite for development. Educational campaigns to reduce the effects of harmful cultural practices such as consumption of alcohol on family lives, discrimination against women and environmentally wasteful resource management practices were conducted. Human and material resources of the province were mobilised to tackle frequent outbreaks of infectious diseases that killed many people, especially young children.

*Jatani addressing the people at a fund-raising
for community development*

Such enormous undertakings could not have been accomplished without access to adequate and locally available resources or the ability to
secure funds from elsewhere. The *Derg* regime faced severe budgetary
constraints as the result of various protracted wars and could hardly
embark on any meaningful tasks to develop the country. In fact, the
regime pestered citizens to hand over what little resources they had to
finance its never-ending war efforts. As a result, the regime allowed
regional and provincial governors to have the discretion of raising funds
locally to supplement their dwindling budgetary allocations from the
national treasury. By taking advantage of this provision from the central
government, Jatani organised a fund-raising campaign to supplement the
meagre budgetary allocation of the province. His aim was to invest
locally-raised funds to build vital infrastructure projects such as road,

water wells, schools and health centres. He used his leadership and charm to persuade urban and rural communities to actively participate in fund-raising efforts. He pleaded for the people to tolerate modest and temporary imposts on goods and services as the raised funds would go towards improving the lives of all in the province.

Organising community-centred and carnival-like festivals was one means of raising funds. Individuals and groups asked for their contributions in cash and in kind during such public events. For example, on days when such events were on, hotel owners agreed to add 50 cents or 1 Birr impost on visitors who hired beds, bought meals or drinks at their establishments. Through these and other agreed-upon avenues, Jatani was able to raise over 1 million Birr.

The next step was to prudently use the money towards the key community development projects for which they were intended. Some of these development activities are discussed below.

Tackling water shortages

The supply of water from natural sources such as rain has been inadequate in most parts of the province. Frequent years of droughts exacerbated this condition even more since the 1970s drought-induced famines in the Sahelian belt of Africa. Traditionally and during most parts of the year, people relied on ground water sources both for human and animal consumption. As there was only limited capacity to store rainwater, most available rainwater was wasted through evaporation. Jatani got the idea of harvesting rainwater from a Lutheran Christian missionary working in the area. It meant constructing cisterns in strategic positions to catch rainwater from houses with corrugated tin roofs or from flooding from slopes on rocky hillsides. While this measure could not fully solve the problem of water shortages, it did help to alleviate the problem to some extent. It was too costly to build and maintain cement cisterns. Still, the idea of harvesting rainwater was taken up by some enterprising individuals in towns and has since become one additional option at solving water shortage problems in the province. Citizens continued to build their own water storage facilities with advice and guidance from local officials with expertise, without relying on funds raised for development. Those scarce funds were used in other, even more vital areas in community development.

Extending educational opportunities to nomadic pastoralists

The education of children from nomadic pastoralist communities was one of many social needs neglected by successive rulers of Ethiopia. The need to bring education to the children of pastoralist Borana was not something new that suddenly sprang to the attention of Jatani. He was fully aware of this serious gap in education and had been campaigning for it since he was at boarding school in Addis Ababa. As mentioned elsewhere, Jatani and I had been part of the group of Borana "pioneers". I was part of the first group while Jatani was part of the second and final group. It's not clear what prompted this one-off gesture from the Emperor, whose idea it was nor how the scheme was funded. At that time, however, similar policies of opening up educational opportunities to marginalised and indigenous communities were taking place in other parts of the world including Canada, USA, British Commonwealth countries, Sweden, etc. For whatever the reason, the Emperor's scheme stopped after only the second intake of students from Borana. During the following three decades, virtually no ethnic Borana children went to school except a handful who managed to go to school courtesy of foreign Christian missionaries. Of the pioneer group of Borana students, 70 per cent completed schools and a number went on to acquire university degrees ranging from bachelor degrees to a Ph.D. Many found employment in civil and military services of the Ethiopian government. See Appendices 1 and 2 for a more detailed account of the life and achievements of the group I call the "Borana Pioneers of Modern Education".

However, the reality of life for the rest of Borana children remained unchanged for decades until Jatani spearheaded the opening of primary schools in remote rural areas. Later, these became feeder schools to high schools created in major towns in the province. The first sizable number of children from the majority of predominantly rural Borana and Gujii communities went to school during Jatani's governorship, starting from the late 1970s to the early 1980s. Though small in number and mostly living outside Borana country, the "Borana Pioneers of Modern Education" were aware of the reasons that kept Borana society backward and unable to educate its children. The Borana's semi-nomadic pastoralist way of life was incompatible with the dominant education delivery system invented with sedentary societies in mind. There were very few primary schools in Arero and Borana provinces by the time the *Derg* regime came to power in 1974. Most of these schools were based in towns, catering to students living in or around such towns. It was very impractical for pastoralists, who roamed the far-flung corners of the province with their cattle, to send their children to such schools without also providing them with lodgings and essential supplies in those towns. Even then, only the towns of Yaballo and Nagelle had a school that provided education up to Grade 8. Once students completed Grade 8, they were required to travel to faraway towns such as Dilla or Yirgalem for a senior secondary school. The cost of both transport to these distant towns and student lodgings was beyond the means of most families living in towns, let alone the pastoralists. For the occasional Borana students who managed to complete primary or junior secondary-level education in towns in their province, there was no provision for them to pursue secondary education outside their province. Borana families lacked educated and successful persons from their own community to serve as role models, to justify an expensive investment in their children's education. To many Borana parents, schooling lasted an incomprehensively long period of time that often churned out many unsuccessful or troubled young men. Such perceptions only added to their mixed views on the value of education or the hefty investment in their children's education.

The small group of educated Borana, the "Borana Pioneers of Modern Education", could have served as role models to the rest of Borana but most members of this elite and reasonably successful group lived or worked in faraway cities such as Addis Ababa. Members of this group were well aware of the challenges even those few Borana students who completed Grade 8 in Borana country faced in pursuing their secondary-level education in schools in distant Dilla and Yirgalem.

Borana girls learning the basics of literacy

In 1974, 19 members of the small Borana community who resided in or around Addis Ababa sought to do their bit to help the education of Borana students. They formed an association that they called *Waal Barsimna*, a phrase that, in *Afaan Borana*, roughly means "let us teach each other". They decided to contribute Birr 10 per month to help Borana students who completed Grade 8 in schools in Borana but were unable to pursue secondary-level education in Dilla and/or Yirgalem due to a lack of resources. Jatani Ali was attending Addis Ababa University at the time and was a founding member of the *Waal Barsimna Association*. The association began its assistance with 12 Borana students, seven of whom were enrolled at Dilla and five at Yirgalem high schools. The financial needs of these students varied depending on the distance they had to travel and the cost of lodging. I was chosen as treasurer of the association and we agreed to remit a monthly stipend of Birr 10 to 25 to each student through the CBE. It was my duty to collect that Birr 10 from each member every month and remit to the students as per the arrangement. The students in Dilla were: Doyo Hallo, Golicha Wario, Dima Arero, Hamgaro Kuli, Halakhe Boru, Godana Jarso and Bagaja Duba. Those in Yirgalem were: Galma Halakhe, Dansoye Godana, Liban Dabasicha, Didole Godana and Dida Boru. There was a single girl named Jatane Jarso who went to school in Addis Ababa to whom the association also provided assistance. Several from this group of Borana students joined military and civil training courses once they completed Grades 10 and 11. The Borana residents of Addis Ababa and members of *Waal Barsimna* continued with their contributions up to 1977.

Hamgaro Kuli was one of the boys assisted by *Waal Barsimna* Association at Dilla. After having completed his Grade 11 education, he joined a military training course for army officers at Holeta. He successfully completed the course, graduated as first lieutenant and was assigned to Northern Military Command, in Tigray. He wrote a letter of gratitude to the Association, indicating how he wouldn't have been able to attain that level of success had it not been for the assistance and goodwill of those who formed the Association. He added that his turn has come for him to repay the favour by helping other Borana students who might be in need of assistance. He asked me to advise him on the amount of monthly contributions needed to achieve the *Waal Barsimna* goal. Before I responded to his letter, I was told that he had fallen in action against rebels in Tigray region of northern Ethiopia. Members of *Waal Barsimna* felt gratified with the attitude of such a considerate benefactor of the association.

Jatani would continue the ideals of *Waal Barsimna* when he was appointed the Governor of Arero province in 1976. Yaballo was the provincial capital of Arero Province and ideally located to reach other districts in Borana and Jemjem (Gujii) provinces. The contribution of funds to *Waal Barsimna* from those in Addis Ababa ceased but Jatani kept it going with a few other fellow Borana who were employed in the province. At the time, Yaballo had one junior secondary school that taught up to Grade 8. Only those with means could hope to pursue a secondary education in distant Dilla, Yirgalem or Awassa. Soon after his arrival, Jatani negotiated with the Ministry of Education and got approval to open the first senior secondary school in Yaballo.

The Auditorium of Yaballo High School, completed after Jatani left.

Jatani was well aware of the unpredictable and mobile nature of life amongst the pastoralist Borana. He knew that the single most important factor that kept the pastoralists' children away from school was the lack of equally mobile schools. The cost of building and running mobile schools was prohibitive and the next best option was to solve the lodging and food ration problems of students who had to leave their families behind and live close to available schools. He mobilised the community to address the challenges of educating the children of pastoralists. Out of this was born the community initiative to build student hostels to host pastoralist children in towns with schools. Due to Jatani's leadership in their creation, some of the hostels are informally known as "Jatani Ali Hostels". Two hostels were built in Yaballo and one each in Dillo, Teltele and Moyale. Additionally, several rural primary and junior secondary schools were also built close to student hostels so as to better reach students from pastoralist communities. The pastoralists built one of the two main hostels in Yaballo through their own initiative and contributions in cash and in kind. This hostel hosts over 300 students and residents arrive from all over the province to access the secondary school facilities in Yaballo town. Jatani Ali instructed Qamphe Dabasso to be in charge of the efforts of constructing student hotels and they called the one built in Yaballo the "Community Hostel of Yaballo". The other large hostel in Yaballo is now called the "German hostel" and it was constructed after a fund-raising campaign that secured a partial financial input from a German Lutheran Christian Mission organisation, as will be discussed below.

Residents of the community-built students' hostel in Yaballo

Qamphe was involved in the efforts of rehabilitating Borana pastoralists affected by the Somali invasion. These were settled at Hidi Alle and Ade Galchat areas, southwest of Yaballo. He recruited 120 persons from among the settled to assist with the task of building the students' hostels in Yaballo. Sixty of these recruits were chosen for their skills in lumbering and were given the duty of cutting down juniper trees on the mountains near Yaballo, splitting them into the required size and shape and piling them up. At the time, Dr Wario Godana – also a member of the "Borana Pioneers of Modern Education" group – was the manager of the Southern Range Land Development Project. He provided a truck to transport the piles of timber for the hostels to a secure storage site kindly provided by the family of Mesele Dhaba, who happened to live a short distance away from one of the sites chosen for the students' hostel. The plot was divided into blocks and students provided labour in digging the ground according to the specifications given by builders. The carpenters in the town, who hoped to secure a building contract, disagreed with the way Qamphe was handling the project and refused to cooperate. However, Qamphe claimed to have influenced two Burji carpenters willing to cooperate by paying them 1 Birr more than the prevailing daily rate. The hostel building tasks started while Jatani was away in East Germany and Mesele Dhaba was acting Governor of Arero Province. Mesele monitored the project of the building of the hostels and Borana pastoralists contributed money to purchase construction materials. On his return from Europe, Jatani visited the building site and praised all those who had worked hard to get the hostels off the ground during his absence.

Jatani described to me how he got to build the second major hostel in Yaballo, now called the German hostel. He earmarked Birr 100,000 from the funds raised for this purpose but he knew that amount was inadequate for the scale he had in mind. He went to the head of the Lutheran Christian Mission in Yaballo and explained to him the type of hostel he would like to get constructed. He explained to him the importance of the project, the amount raised locally for the purpose and how there was a shortfall to start the project. On that basis, he asked the German missionary if his organisation was willing to chip in to complete the project. The German replied in the negative by stating that he didn't have that amount of money at the time. However, he went on to express how he was touched by the request and was surprised by it all. He told Jatani, 'Since I arrived in Ethiopia years ago, you are the only person who has approached me seeking extra help after having secured a certain amount of funds towards a worthy and tangible cause', which implied that most would just turn up and beg for money without "doing their bit". He added, 'At the moment, I do not have anything on hand to give you. Please wait for a year or so while I inform my head office about your request. I hope they are willing to help you.' After a year, the money came from the German Lutheran Mission Headquarters. Jatani released the amount saved for the construction of a fully-fledged building that could accommodate 200 students arriving from remote pastoralist communities. The project of building that students' hostel started with the added financial help from the German organisation and under its supervision.

At the time, the Yaballo branch of the Ethiopian Evangelical Church Mekane Yesus – ostensibly aligned to German Lutheran Christian Mission – appeared to be the right institution to manage the new students' hostel. Jatani arranged that they would administer it with a hope that the hostel would benefit students coming from remote pastoralist communities who otherwise wouldn't continue their schooling due to lack of lodgings in towns. However, the administration of the Church unit used the services of the hostel contrary to what Jatani had envisaged. The hostel was used to fulfil sectarian and nepotistic interests that practically overlooked those students coming from remote and marginalised communities. As indicated, such students were meant to be the main beneficiaries of the hostel when the idea was floated and funding was sought. In mid-1990s I went to Yaballo on private business. Out of curiosity, I visited the German hostel to appreciate what has been achieved and to see if the boys hosted there needed any assistance. I asked a person (name withheld) who worked at the German hostel about the life at the hostel, the proportion of boys enrolled there who came from remote pastoralist villages, and related other matters. The person told me that out of 200 boys in the hostel, only 14 boys were from rural and peripheral pastoralist communities (read Borana, Gujii, Gabra etc.). I was rather stunned by the reply considering how the whole project was meant to solve lodging problems faced by students coming from distant nomadic pastoralist villages. I continued with my inquiry and asked, 'Where did the rest (the vast majority of hostel residents) come from?'

The response was that they were boys of people who lived in or around Yaballo town and had affiliation with those administering or working for the Mekane Yesus Church. Some of the boys were related to teachers who worked for the Church and most came from families in the town or from non-Borana farming villages around Yaballo town who could have easily lived with their families to attend nearby schools.

Still, through the concerted efforts of Jatani in spearheading the building of students' hostels, a few pastoralist children received lodging facilities in towns such as Yaballo. The next major concern was how to get basic food rations to such students as many of them came from impoverished and drought-ravaged communities. Jatani arranged with the local people to raise a modest amount of money on a regular basis for students living in hostels to buy them some food. A modest impost of 50 cents would be charged on every head of cattle sold by Borana persons on market day, with the proceeds used to purchase food for students living at the hostels. The effort to tackle the serious lodging problem faced by students coming from marginalised pastoralist communities, through hostel building, was a success. It encouraged quite a few children from such communities to travel to alien towns and attend school. It is safe to say that at least 90 per cent of all educated Borana young who are currently employed in a range of government institutions, provide community services or study at universities once lived in one of these hostels.

Jatani had a firm belief that the very survival of marginalised communities was tied up with their ability to educate some of their children. Wherever he went and whomever he spoke to, he tried to emphasise the need for rural and marginalised communities to educate their children. Education was Jatani's top passion. He urged people to do their bit to remove obstacles hindering the education of children coming from remote and neglected pastoralist or farming communities. He urged the population not to wait for the state to build schools and hostels for them. He showed how such things can be accomplished through community initiatives. Jatani also advised villagers and traditional leaders to take more interest in the education of their children. In Hagere Mariam (now Bule Hora) he managed to get a high school constructed with funds entirely raised by the local community.

Bariso Dukale was a government employee in the department of political affairs in Teltele. Jatani saw him as a competent person to run the new school in Bule Hora and to facilitate the education of children from remote and marginalised communities. He transferred him from Teltele to Hagere Mariam for that purpose. Later, Jatani promoted Bariso to a post in district administration in Bule Hora.

Efforts to build other service-providing institutions

Even by Ethiopia's poor standard, Arero Province lacked many basic institutions for the delivery of essential services to the people. The Province lacked resources both in terms of funds and educated manpower. Consequently, Jatani had several schemes for community development to tackle but did so one at a time.

Public health was another area of community services that was badly neglected in Arero province by successive regimes that ruled Ethiopia. There was not a single hospital in the province and the first health centre was built during Jatani's time. Before Jatani's arrival as Governor, small clinics or health dispensaries based in towns and run by foreign Christian missionaries were the only health service providers in the province. From the time he was appointed, Jatani battled with the notoriously stubborn and unresponsive Ethiopian bureaucracy to secure funds with which to build health clinics in towns and remote rural areas. His success in this effort was however a partial one at best.

In another example of Jatani's role in building community services, Yaballo, the administrative capital of the province, had no electric power. The Ethiopian Electric Light and Power Authority (EELPA) had agreed to install a generator for the town after a five-year wait. The wait could be more than that, given the notoriously slow *modus operandi* of the Ethiopian bureaucracy. Jatani had no patience to wait for that long. He explained how lack of electricity was keeping the town back, for instance, by hindering the installation of vital and efficient electric grain-milling machines. On that basis, he embarked on a public mobilisation to raise funds to bring electric power to the town. The town's residents enthusiastically raised about 1 million Birr for this scheme. Jatani earmarked Birr 90,000 for the purchase and installation of an electric power generator. He approached EELPA to waive their five-year plan and give him the skilled technicians to install the generator in the town. He was successful in convincing them to cooperate with this initiative and Yaballo got its electric power, perhaps for the first time since the Italians left the town in 1941.

In part, Yaballo was chosen as the capital of Arero Province for its location roughly in the middle of the province. The other reason was that Italians erected a handful of fine buildings in Yaballo that later came to serve as offices for government and civic administration. It is not clear why the Italians chose the town to serve as their garrison. It was possible however that their choice owed to the town being in a strategic location, flanking access routes both to Mogadishu (southern Somalia was an Italian colony) and to the British East African Dominions or Kenya Colony. Both Yaballo and Nagelle served as important Italian army garrison towns. Consequently, key public buildings in Yaballo and Nagelle were the legacy of that brief Italian occupation. After the war, many of the buildings were looted and ended up with shattered windows and broken roofs. Italian-era electric sockets and hooks for electric wires are still discernible on some of these buildings. Some of the funds raised for community development under Jatani's administration went to repair these key but crumbling Italian-era public buildings.

A shortage of essential consumer items followed the *Derg*'s regime and this condition was even worse in areas invaded by the Somalis. The regime tried to tackle the shortages by creating a parastatal trading organisation, the EDDC. This agency was tasked with the distribution of essential commodities such as sacks of grains, cooking oil and sugar to the population at a subsidised price. Ration cards were issued to people to regulate their purchases from EDDC stores as people were allowed to buy only limited quantities of scarce items on a quota basis. As usual, people living in remote and marginalised provinces of Ethiopia such as Arero Province were the last to benefit from such government policies aimed at improving their living conditions. Arero Province had to fight to get its EDDC store. Jatani explained to *Derg* officials how lack of supplies from inside Ethiopia had forced people in his province to resort to illicit cross-border trade with Kenya to meet their needs for basic consumer items such as cooking oil and clothing. He promised that he would stop the contraband trade if EDDC constructed a warehouse at Yaballo for the storage and distribution of essential commodities to the people. He managed to persuade the *Derg* officials to approve the construction of a central EDDC store at Yaballo, from where essential goods would be distributed to smaller stores located elsewhere in the province.

Displacement and loss of property due to vindictive and wanton looting by Somali invaders were not the only challenges faced by Borana pastoralists. The Arero Province (for that matter, all of Borana) is one of the localities in Ethiopia prone to chronic droughts, which habitually killed thousands of livestock, leading to famines. Jatani observed how many relatively wealthy individuals – those who owned hundreds of head of cattle – often lost most of their herd in a single year of bad drought. He noted that there was a serious disparity between the number of herds and the availability of pasture for these, especially during years of insufficient rains or droughts. A mismatch between the holding capacity of land and the number of cattle kept led to a high cattle mortality rate when droughts hit. Jatani embarked on a public education campaign where he advised Borana pastoralists to sell "excess" animals before the droughts decimated the stock. This was meant to help Borana pastoralists in at least three ways:

1. selling "excess" herd would reduce high cattle mortality rate during a drought;
2. the same would allow Borana herders to use the proceeds from cattle sales to purchase grain for human consumption; and,
3. they could save some of the proceeds in a bank or credit association to purchase cattle when the rains did arrive – cattle being both a status symbol and an economic asset.

Borana pastoralists did not seem to pay much attention to his advice. He then decided to force them to sell their "excess" animals and deposit the money in a bank. Alas! There was no bank in Yaballo or anywhere nearby at the time.

During the *Derg* and the Emperor's eras, only the CBE provided banking services in the country. According to the CBE's business expansion strategy, there was no short-term plan for establishing a branch at Yaballo or in any nearby towns. Jatani approached the bank's executive management and explained to them why he urgently needed a branch in Arero Province. After a series of lobbying he persuaded the bank management to open a CBE branch in Yaballo. In a relatively short period of time, they constructed a brand new branch at Yaballo.

His plan was to convince or even coerce wealthy Borana pastoralists to participate in a voluntary sell-off of bulls and other "excess" animals and save the proceeds in the bank. The scheme was meant to introduce a culture change in the Borana's resource management and saving practices. Unfortunately, before he could put his scheme into action, he was appointed Deputy Governor of Illubabor Administrative Region in western Ethiopia and left Arero Province.

His efforts at steering the Borana to explore alternative ways of making a living to supplement their age-old industry of cattle herding only had limited success. However, this campaign raised sufficient awareness for some in the community to try their hands at other endeavours such as retail trade and growing crops to supplement their income.

As mentioned above, some of the money raised through fund-raising campaigns for community development went towards the building of students' hostels. Some of the money also went towards restocking the newly-built high school in Yaballo with essential materials such as a library science labs and workshops. Furthermore, some of the funds contributed to the renovating and restoring of old school buildings in Yaballo and in the districts. The old school building in Yaballo was built by the Italians and urgently needed repairs. Most key government offices were located in solid-looking buildings erected by the Italians. Decades later and due to a lack of proper maintenance, many of these buildings were either decaying or crumbling. The office chambers of the Arero Provincial Government was one of the buildings repaired at that time. Part of the money raised went to buy an electric power generator for Yaballo (Birr 90,000), towards a football stadium in the middle of Yaballo town (Birr 50,000), to build the boys' hostels (Birr 100,000); towards the construction of the offices of the provincial pastoralist commission; handcraft capacity building, and farmers, women and youth associations.

As well as addressing immediate and pressing issues affecting the communities, Jatani had the foresight to invest in vital infrastructure for future development. One of these was the further expansion of the newly-built high school, with the hope that it would grow into a technical school that would provide practical and readily employable skills to students. For this, a wide area of land around the school was acquired and fenced off. He also planned to build a hospital in the middle of the town for which a rather large area was reserved while the lobbying process to get the approval for the hospital continued. Much of the land he reserved for the expansion of the high school, to build a hospital and other public institutions has since been drastically reduced in size. The municipal administration of the regime that ousted the *Derg* has doled out a good part of land previously reserved for the construction of public institutions to regime sympathisers and/or wealthy individuals who built private or rental residences on it.

These were only few examples of the initiatives and overall development achievements of Jatani in Arero Province. Among government officials who visited the province while Jatani was governor, there was hardly anyone who was not impressed by what he had accomplished in such a short period of time to improve the lives of local people in general and that of the pastoralist communities in particular. Jatani told me of the following high-ranking officials who visited the province:

- Colonel Goshu Wolde, then the Minister of Education and later the Minister for Foreign Affairs, was the first high-ranking government official with whom he met and negotiated the construction of a high school at Yaballo.

- Dr Geremew Dabale, the Minister of Agriculture, visited the community students' hostel at Yaballo and observed how students did not have beds. He promised to find beds for them but the promise failed because he didn't receive funding he was expecting to get.

- General Taye Tilahun, the Minister of the Interior, went down to the province for an ordinary visit. Jatani took him down to Dillo depression to show him the suffering of the people due to the prevailing droughts.

- Dr Feleke Gedle Giorgis, the Minister of Information, visited the province and Jatani showed him around what he had accomplished and the challenges faced by the people in the province. Jatani told me that the Minister was so impressed by his achievements that he told him that he would make sure to report what he had seen to President Mengistu Haile Mariam.

- Shimeles Adugna, the head of Relief and Rehabilitation Commission (drought relief), once visited Yaballo and told people who were around how he was in awe of Borana people's gallantry against the Somali invasion and how Ethiopia should feel blessed to have such valiant citizens. He added, "We would not have freely walked on this land as we are doing today, had it not been for the courageous struggle of Borana people against extremely difficult odds". The statement was a surprise to Jatani given the peripheral location and marginal status of the province to warrant the attention of high-ranking government officials. He did not think that many high-level government officials appreciated the magnitude of suffering endured and the sacrifice paid by Borana to defend their homeland and Ethiopia from the invading enemy.

The President of Ethiopia, Mengistu Haile Mariam, also came to know what Jatani was accomplishing in promoting the broad objectives of the revolution. Jatani told me that the President invited him to his office and held a session with him that lasted about an hour. The President asked Jatani to describe his remarkable accomplishments that he had heard so much of from other sources. Jatani told him of the struggles he overcame and the challenges he faced from the period he was appointed the Governor of Arero Province. Jatani told him about the battles he waged against the remnants of the old regime, the struggle against Somali incursions and outright invasion, his plans and visions for community development and what had been accomplished up to that point. On his part, the President told him of the challenges he had faced in promoting the objectives of the revolution all over the country. He added how, during the earlier stages of the revolution, he too struggled with people within the *Derg* circles and outside it who made attempts to reverse the forward march of the revolution. To achieve their goal, people he referred to as counter-revolutionary forces, wanted to assassinate him (Mengistu). (The President was referring to an earlier attempt on his life where Col. Atnafu Abate, his deputy, was suspected of having a hand in it.) The President advised Jatani to keep up his admirable efforts in advancing the aims of the revolution despite the challenges and temporary setbacks. Col. Mengistu also promised him all the necessary support that he might need in the future to carry out his administrative and patriotic duties. It was to be remembered that Major Salesa Jalo's decision to go to Somalia to fight against the *Derg* regime put Jatani under the suspicious gaze of the Ethiopian officials. It took Jatani years, enormous effort and patience to win back the trust of Ethiopian government officials. It is possible that their slowness in answering Jatani's requests to defend Borana against Somali aggression or to approve vital projects aimed at improving the living conditions of people in Arero and Borana Provinces was partly due to Salesa's defection.

Attempts to make peace among pastoralist communities

The major pastoralist communities in the province were Borana, Gujii, Gabra and Garri – all *Afaan Oromo* speakers. Jatani had a strong desire and worked hard to bring about peace between these communities who fought over scarce resources such as grazing land and water. He preached the virtues of peaceful co-existence and employed both traditional and modern conflict resolution techniques to bring about peace between these communities. As indicated above, Somali agents supplied automatic weapons to groups that showed willingness in advancing their expansionist agenda. Somali agents' strategy to give weapons to groups who supported them severely distorted the delicate inter-group balance of power that existed in the area prior to Somalia's full-scale invasion. However, inter-tribal feuds and wars between the Borana, Gujii, Gabra and Garri were hardly new. Borana and Gujii traditionally killed each other as a trophy of manhood. For example, a young Gujii man was required to kill a male from an enemy tribe, or a dangerous wild beast, in order to demonstrate his manhood as a condition to securing a bride. Such killings sustained a cycle of bloody feuds between the two groups where families of the victims were compelled to avenge theirs by killing a person from the opposing group. Livestock rustling was another reason that sustained attacks and counter-attacks between the Gujii and Borana. The Ethiopian government prohibited such practices when these groups were conquered and incorporated into the Ethiopian empire. However, they kept these practices going albeit in a clandestine or underground fashion. In theory, all appointed government officials were expected to totally abolish these harmful practices which were anathema to peaceful co-existence. Instead of enforcing law and order and stamping out these archaic and harmful practices, however, the officials were suspected of profiting from the very things they were meant to eradicate. During the Haile Selassie era, some officials were said to have grown very rich by turning the legal processes of investigating inter-tribal killings into a lucrative business. The officials invented a convoluted and deliberately protracted method of apprehending a person suspected of killing another person or persons from another tribe. This system was known as *awchachign* and it was an Amharic word that suggested a procedure of flushing-out the culprit through a prolonged process of collective punishment through wasteful mass enquiries. Basically, if a Borana person was suspected of killing a Gujii person, all male Borana persons in certain localities are held hostage until such a time that the suspected culprit was handed over. This process involved weeks of protracted mass gatherings in nearby towns where officials lived. This meant that all male Borana who should have been looking after the family herd or the peace of the tribe are holed up in these wasteful deliberations. The gathering was expected to narrow down the suspects to a clan, a family and a household. Often such gatherings failed to find the culprit. In this case, entire members of the suspected clan would be required to raise hundreds of head of cattle as blood money which, theoretically, was to be paid to the victim's family and to the treasury. In reality, only a fraction of the cattle were actually paid to the victims and treasury. The balance went to corrupt government officials. A similar process took place for the Gujii tribe if one of them was accused of killing a Borana. There were reports were those taking part in *awchachign* gatherings would, out of desperation or malice, hand over poor innocent persons to the authorities as culprits.

Jatani determined to change the attitudes and behaviour of the communities on such harmful cultural practices as killing other men to get a manhood trophy or cattle rustling to pay for hefty bride prices. He assembled leaders and elders from Borana and Gujii communities who discussed and agreed strategies for stopping such harmful and unlawful practices. Taking a tough measure on a person who violated the agreement was one of the resolutions. There was a practical event that demonstrated Jatani's seriousness in enforcing the covenant of peace agreed upon by both communities. Around this time, a Borana young man killed a Gujii. Jatani verified the authenticity of the case and got the culprit punished with a death penalty commuted in public. There were people who complained against the action he took, thinking it would serve as a deterrent of inter-tribal killings. Those who opposed his move argued that the suspect should have been brought to the local court of law first. He ignored them on the ground that the courts never succeeded in stopping the practice. Borana v. Gujii underground killings were stopped once and for all during his tenure as the Governor of Arero Province.

Jatani's approach to tackle conflicts that involved the Gabra and Garri communities was different from the one he used to deal with the inter Borana and Gujii feud and conflicts. The Gabra, like the Borana and Gujii, are ethnically Oromo. However, the Gabra tended to show affiliation with the Somali agenda for the region and were easily influenced by Somali propaganda. Many Gabra have been converted to Islam through Somali preachers. It appears that Somali agents and invaders exploited this co-religiosity to win over the hearts and minds of the Gabra. Most members of the Garri community, at least those within Ethiopia, spoke the Borana dialect of the Oromo language. The Garri too were converts to Islam through the Somalis and their heart has always been with Somalia, not Ethiopia. Consequently, Garri and Gabra loyalties shifted according to which side appeared to be on the winning (i.e. shifting loyalty to Somalia or Ethiopia). However, as a rule, the two groups aligned themselves to the side that provided them with a better deal in terms of securing vast grazing territories from Borana land. The Gabra and Garri have sometimes aligned themselves with the numerically larger Borana community. Borana traditional leaders have allowed them to roam Borana country in search of pasture and water for their livestock. When conditions were favourable, they often turned around and claimed part of Borana land as exclusively theirs. So, when Siad Barre's invasion of

Ethiopia was underway, as expected, the Gabra and Garri allied themselves with the Somalis. Jatani advised the Borana and Gujii to positively influence the ethnically Oromo Gabra community to come to their side. Jatani almost managed to restore peace among all these communities. These communities tried to co-exist peacefully at least up to the time when the *Derg* was violently removed from power in Addis Ababa in 1991. The ethnic Tigre-dominated regime that replaced the *Derg* favoured the traditionally pro-Somalia groups such as Garri, Gabra and various Somali clans over the Borana. That threw the tenuous inter-tribal balance of power in the region out of balance yet again.

As mentioned previously, during the Ethio-Somali war of the late 1970s, Gabra lined up with Somalia to promote Siad Barre's ambition. In the process they were totally detached from fellow Oromo pastoralists such as the Borana, among whom they lived and freely moved in search of pasture for their livestock. In the aftermath of the Somali defeat, the Gabra were driven out of Borana country along with the Somali invaders whom they had supplied, informed and backed. Many Gabra and Garri families fled to Somalia fearing a retaliatory attack from Ethiopian forces. Apparently, the almost barren territories in which the Gabra found themselves in Somalia could not accommodate their livestock with that of the Garri and other Somali clans. They found out that they had no other option but to request a pardon from the Borana and to be welcomed back into Borana country as before. This they did; however the Borana public who seriously felt the treachery and damages the Gabra had inflicted on them, jointly with Garri and the Somalis, rejected their request for pardon. Nevertheless, Jatani persuaded the Borana community to forgive them. Borana community leaders considered his pleas and arranged a site where the Gabra would settle. The Gabra were accepted back and were settled among the Borana. They resumed their life of peacefully roaming amongst the Borana as before. As far as the Borana were concerned, the Gabra were just another clan of the Borana and both resumed their practices of exchanging gifts, praying at the same shrines, drawing water from the same wells etc. as they had done for years.

After a year or so of relative peace, two Gabra boys were murdered at Dhoqqolle in Dirre District. Jatani hunted down the murderers and found two young Borana men had committed the crime. He got them executed in public at Mega town. The Gabra lived in peace among the Borana until the *Derg* regime collapsed in 1991. The Garri tried to take advantage of instability in the country before the new regime that deposed the *Derg* restored order. As usual, they influenced the Gabra to side with them in attacking the Borana. On several occasions, a good portion of the Gabra heeded Garri's insistence to attack the Borana. The new regime's ethnic-based quasi-federal system seemed to help some of the Gabra to make up their mind whether they belonged ethnically to the Oromo or the Somali. Some of them moved to the newly established Somali Regional State known as 'Kilil Somali'. The rest chose to live with the Borana as Oromo. But peaceful co-existence between the Gabra and Borana remained elusive. The Gabra v. Borana and Garri v. Borana relatively peaceful co-existence was to end in tears as an openly Somali-favouring regime (TPLF) was installed in Ethiopia after the *Derg*.

Borbur Bule Dirre is a living expert in Borana culture and oral history. He was asked how Borana and Gujii, the two main Oromo communities in the area, started killing each other for show of valour or to validate their young men's virility. In response to the question, he said that there were different versions to the story. He indicated how in the remote past, each community had its own system of government exercised through the Oromo *Gada* institution. Mostly however they lived in peace and harmony. Borbor said that one version of the story blames a minor playground incident between Borana and Gujii boys that grew into tit-for-tat inter-tribal killings. The incident was said to have taken place during the term of a Borana *Abba Gada* named Doyo Boro. The boys on both sides of the feud were playing a friendly game similar to hockey when suddenly it turned nasty and they started killing one another. That event, goes the story, was the starting point of all later inter-tribal killings not just between Borana and Gujii but also between these two and the Arsi, a neighbouring Oromo tribe.

There was another version of this story commonly heard among the Borana people. Just as in the version cited above by Borbor, peaceful co-existence said to have prevailed among the three neighbouring Oromo communities of Borana, Gujii and Arsi, until the time when Doyo Boro became a Borana *Abba Gada*. Since then, the killing of adult men was mutually tolerated as proof of valour. Over time, the practice became a self-sustaining vicious cycle of tit-for-tat inter-tribal bloodletting. This version sounds more plausible and reflects Borana's common lament of "the three enemies of Doyo Boro".

Borbor added that, according to Borana oral history, Liban Watta was the wisest *Gada* leader who came to power long after Doyo Boro's reign. He did not like the vicious cycle of killings between these three closely-related Oromo communities. As said by Borbor, Liban Watta called a general assembly of the feuding communities, to stop the animosity and the tit-for-tat killings. The assembled agreed to stop the killings and this resolution was respected during his term. However, the truce was short lived as Liban Watta himself was suddenly murdered by a Gujii sniper shortly after he handed over the *Gada* office to another person. Apparently, to avenge Liban Watta's murder, the Borana killed a Gujii. Thus, the old bloody feud between these communities was restarted and has continued on and off to the present day.

Borbor mentioned how consultative and democratic governance were aspects that Jatani recognised and tried to emulate from Borana cultural history. Borana culture and polity has been guided by two key institutions: *Gada* and *Ladu*.[32] Access to the *Gada* office is through popular elections while *Ladu* is a hereditary office. Before it was annexed to Ethiopian rule,

---

[32]   *Gada* is the Borana system of governance. *Ladu* is a term associated with Borana spiritual leader known as *Qaallu*.

Borana was governed by a *Gada* system of government where both its *Abba Gada* (supreme leader of *Gada*) and senior councillors assisting the *Abba Gada* were elected to *Gada* office through an elaborate and lengthy electoral process all over Borana country. Individuals elected to a new *Gada* term (only men stood for public office) ceremonially took power from the *Gada* in power (or *Worra Boku*). The term of office of a *Worra Boku* or *Gada* is eight years. Political office is transferred to the next *Gada* in line at the end of the eight years' term following an election. The *Ladu* (*Worra Qaallu*) is a hereditary office and is entrusted with keeping the peace and spiritual health of Borana society. While the *Gada* is the source of political power, the *Ladu*, like the church, is charged with the spiritual life of the Borana. *Gada* is an institution that made and enforced laws that governs Borana society. As such, *Gada* is the most powerful institution in Borana country and the *Abba Gada* is its supreme leader. At least, this was the case until the Ethiopian-appointed governors started to tamper with the *Gada* system by weakening it and co-opting the *Ladu* to their super-imposed and decidedly undemocratic feudal system of government. According to Borana laws and culture, these two institutions have specific and well-defined roles aimed at making Borana a peaceful, harmonious and prosperous society. Though independent from each other and seeing to different aspects of society, the two institutions often complemented one another in enforcing Borana laws and cultural norms. The two provided a counter-balance of power against each other to reduce the abuse of power by those holding office. The Borana's fairly democratic and egalitarian political culture stood in stark contrast to Ethiopia's autocratic feudal despotism, presided over by hereditary monarchs in the past and military dictators in later years. The Ethiopian leaders who occupied Borana territory, or were sent to govern it, found it hard to reconcile between the two diametrically opposed political systems, norms and values. They couldn't fathom, nor had they any experience of dealing with, a community where political power has been transferred peacefully from one group of leaders to another through popular elections. All they knew was Ethiopia's murky, violent and bloody processes that accompanied nearly all transfers of political power and the Machiavellian intrigues that defined public office. First they looked for a feudal king or chief amongst the Borana that resembled their own despots and, failing to find one, they sought traditional institutions they could co-opt, to assist their rule in Borana country. So they resorted to deliberately distorting the pre-existing balance of power between the *Gada* and *Ladu* institutions to end up with a powerless, more malleable and responsive (to their wishes) traditional institutions. Their ultimate aim was to use these watered-down institutions as a channel of communication to assist their top-down autocratic rule.

To demonstrate how this worked: the Borana society is divided into two moieties named Sabo and Gona. Marriage could only take place across the moieties, not between the clans within a moiety. Therefore, all clans that make up Borana are tied up in this across-moieties marriage arrangement or are in-laws to each other. It was a mechanism that has historically guaranteed relative peace and harmony among Borana clans. Both moieties have *Qaallu* (*Ladu*) institutions of their own headed by a *Worra Qaallu* (family of the *Qaallu*). As a norm, the Karayu clan provided the *Qaallu* for the Sabo moiety, while the Oditu clan provided the *Qaallu* for the Gona moiety. The Ethiopian rulers basically converted the *Qaallu* institution into a *Balabat* (traditional chieftain) institution that they imposed on other conquered peoples in the southern half of Ethiopia to facilitate their rule. Thus the Borana ended up with two *Balabats* (chiefs), one each for Sabo and Gona moieties. The two Borana *Balabats* were deliberately chosen from each *Worra Qaallu*. Therefore, at once the *Balabats* wielded traditional authority (for being members of the *Qaallu* institution) and acted as agents of the Ethiopian government (in their role as *Balabats*). With the interference of and support from the Ethiopian government, the *Qaallu* institution became more powerful and took away traditional authority from the *Gada* in managing certain traditional affairs. It was social engineering that distorted the foci of power in Borana society. It also confounded many as to who had what powers and who was answerable to whom.

Jatani realised the unjust interference by Ethiopian officials in Borana cultural affairs and the distortions their actions produced in the Borana's traditional power structure. He set out to correct this anomaly and entrusted the task to respected and knowledgeable Borana elders, so that the anomaly could be redressed in accordance with indigenous Borana culture. The elders reported to Jatani how in the original state of affairs, any person who wanted a nomination for service in *Gada* council used to seek it from both the incumbent *Abba Gada* and the outgoing one. The *Qaallu* office used to have anointment from the *Gada* council during certain period in the Borana calendar. Jatani made sure that this would continue as per the recommendation of the elders. He went further and restored certain distorted practices in the Borana's indigenous political culture (*Gada*). He argued that there should be a clear separation between the Borana's cultural affairs and Ethiopia's state bureaucracy. For instance, in the all-Borana gathering or assembly known as *Gumi Gayo* that takes place every eight years, it was determined that outsiders could observe the process but should not interfere in the proceedings or try to modify the agenda. He pointed out that such a meeting mainly concerned the Borana people.

As Governor, Jatani was instrumental in restoring peace and order in Arero Province. He spearheaded the development of this neglected corner of Ethiopia by conducting public awareness campaign highlighting the benefits of education and by encouraging local initiatives to build vital infrastructures such as students' hostels for children from marginalised communities.

8: As Deputy Governor of Illubabor Region

In June 1985 the Ministry of the Interior promoted Jatani to a higher position as the Deputy Governor of Illubabor region in the western part of Ethiopia. Jatani was not sure why he was promoted to a remote region that bordered on Sudan. Elders from the Gujii community learned about his promotion but expressed their unhappiness to lose him as provincial governor. Apparently, they also knew about the existence of a similar vacant position in Sidamo Administrative Region, to which Arero Province belonged. They argued, why not appoint Jatani as a deputy governor of Sidamo Administrative Region – a region where he had already been working – instead of sending him to Illubabor region? They were determined to ask the officials in the Ministry of the Interior to reconsider their decision and instead promote Jatani within Sidamo Administrative Region. However, Jatani advised them not to do so.

His tenure as Deputy Governor of Illubabor was a short lived one and lasted only six months, up to December 1985. It was not clear to many why he was sent to Illubabor when several similar vacancies existed in Sidamo region or in other regions closer to Borana country. At the time of this appointment, the governing socialist party's political head of Illubabor region was a person named Simeon Galore. Simeon was a native of Wolaita province – part of Sidamo region – and was once a governor of his home province around the same time when Jatani was also the Governor of Arero Province. As both had been governors in provinces that were part of Sidamo Administrative Region, the two knew each other quite well. They often sat in the same meetings at the Sidamo Administrative Region headquarters at Awassa. Jatani once mentioned to me how Simeon was almost the only rational person in Awassa with whom one could have a sensible conversation. Similarly, Simeon had a positive attitude towards Jatani. One could speculate: did Simeon request the Ministry of the Interior to appoint Jatani to Illubabor region, where he was also serving? Impossible to know for sure.

Notable elders in Arero Province such as the late Golissa Roba escorted Jatani up to Illubabor. On arrival at Mettu, the administrative capital of the region, he observed how the region was very underdeveloped even by Ethiopia's poor standards. He reasoned however that it was a place where one could accomplish a great deal that would have a positive impact on the lives of the population. One of his first observations was that the main street that crossed the town was so muddy that it was difficult to walk on after rain. At that time, the Ethiopian Highway Authority was constructing a bridge across the Baro River in Gambella province of Illubabor region. It so happened that some of the engineers in the construction work were his old schoolmates at General Wingate Secondary School. Among them he met with the chief engineer of the project – one of his schoolmates – who was travelling to the project site for inspection. Jatani described the pitiful state of roads in the region in general and in Mettu town in particular to the visiting engineers. The chief engineer promised him that he would lay asphalt on the main street of Mettu, once they completed the construction of the bridge on Baro River. Unfortunately, this promise did not materialise as Jatani left the area a few months after this encounter.

Still, Jatani made immediate impact in reforming the entrenched and rather archaic feudal bureaucratic culture in Illubabor regional administration offices. He didn't hesitate to take disciplinary action for improper behaviour at work. Soon after he started work, he observed that employees in the administration office were displaying strange behaviour. The official start of work used to be 8 a.m. Just before the start of morning shift, all the employees used to line up in front of the Illubabor Governor General's office to await his arrival. When he arrived, all would bow low to which he would reciprocate. It was after this ritual that they would disperse to their offices. Jatani observed this unusual behaviour in the government office for about a week and realised that it was a leftover legacy from the old feudal regime being reformed in other parts of Ethiopia. He decided to stop the ritual once and for all. He called a meeting of all the employees who were participating in the daily practice. He reminded them, "You are lining up in front of the Governor's office every morning to demonstrate your respect for him. Though there is a difference in rank and seniority, all of us are equally government employees. I admire your respect for a senior officer, but I do not approve of the way you are go about showing respect to those in a position of authority." He went on, "In my opinion, respect for a superior officer is not expressed by wasting office hours lining up waiting for his arrival but by being on duty on time and by performing one's share of work diligently." He strongly warned them, "Starting from tomorrow morning, if I find anyone idly standing in front of the Governor's office when he/she should be at his/her desk, I shall take administrative measure against him/her." The practice stopped from that day onward. Jatani told me that the Governor-General whom the matter concerned neither mentioned anything about the action he took nor showed any discernible change of attitude towards him.

Six months after he arrived in Illubabor, he received a letter signed not by the Minister of the Interior, his employer, but by Fikreselassie Wogderes, the Secretary General of the *Derg* who was the second highest ranking official in the country after Colonel Mengistu Haile Mariam. The message in the letter stated that he (Jatani) should hand over everything in his hands and urgently come to Addis Ababa. He did not like another sudden transfer from Illubabor to another place after such a short period of time. However he had no choice other than to comply with the order from the highest authority. Reportedly, the person who was appointed to Gamu Gofa region as a Governor-General ran into difficulty in solving some public service issues that arose in the region. The administrative personnel in the Ministry of the Interior who looked into the case stated that Jatani was the right person to sort out the mess in Gamu Gofa region and in regions in other parts of southern Ethiopia. It was under this pretext that his service in Illubabor was terminated after such a short time. As mentioned before, Jatani's very first public service post was to a remote corner of Gamu Gofa region as a rooky police officer.

The Ministry officials explained to him why he was called to Addis Ababa so urgently. The officials considered him an expert in handling inter-communal problems in the south of the country. They told him about the nature of the conflicts that had developed among various communities or tribes in Gamu Gofa and they sought his counsel on how to tackle them. He shared with them his approach in solving such matters. However, the Ministry did not assign him to Gamu Gofa as Deputy Governor. Instead he was laterally transferred as Deputy Governor of Sidamo region, just as Gujii elders sought before his departure for Illubabor.

Jatani thought of expressing his reluctance to be transferred from Illubabor region after such a short period of time to the Secretary General of the *Derg*. His friends who were around the office of Fikreselassie Wogderes advised him to refrain from such an action. He accepted the advice and kept quiet.

9: As Deputy Governor of Sidamo Region

Jatani's move from Illubabor to Sidamo in 1986 was a lateral transfer in terms of rank – from Deputy Governor of Illubabor region to Deputy Governor of Sidamo region. As mentioned above, the Ministry of the Interior urgently called him back from Illubabor to help them solve administrative problems in Gamu Gofa region. They didn't assign him to Gamu Gofa but instead to Sidamo region. The reason why he was assigned to Sidamo rather than Gamu Gofa was not clear to anybody that I know.

However, being the Deputy Governor of Sidamo region was the post and place Jatani enjoyed the least. Reportedly, the Governor-General of Sidamo – his senior – was only minimally concerned about the development and welfare of the community. More, the person was known for his limited leadership abilities and had unsuitable academic training to fill such a high-calibre administrative position. Instead of moving about among the mostly rural communities of the region to promote the ideals of development, he used to give priority to tedious paper work that wasted everyone's time and effort. Indeed, efficient management of administrative paperwork of the region was necessary. But red tape shouldn't have been the most important thing a governor of the Sidamo region spent his time on, given all the development, security and inter-communal challenges the region faced.

Abera Ashine was one of Jatani's best friends from school days and later in life. He recalled the behaviour of Jatani while he was the deputy governor of Sidamo region. At the time, Abera was the Dean of Wondo Genet Forestry College, about 30 kilometres from the city of Awassa where Jatani worked. In their close social relationship extending over dozens of years, Abera recalled that he never saw Jatani so frustrated and disgusted with everything around him. In his style of managing public office, Jatani couldn't have been more different from his immediate superior. He would have liked to move out of the office more and work with rural communities in tackling development, governance, inter-communal and security issues in an efficient and hands-on manner. In most parts of rural Ethiopia, peasants were victims of a series of adminis-trative abuses from the very officials sent there to ostensibly serve them. Often, the uneducated masses were left to be exploited and abused by officials sent to help them. Most of the appointees or officials came from regions outside Sidamo. They hardly understood the complexities of cultural and ethnic factors that defined inter-communal relations in the region. Most were career bureaucrats not particularly concerned with development activities that could improve the livelihood of peasant and pastoralist communities. Besides, many of these officials were often accused of resorting to illicit means of appropriating resources that should have gone to improve the lives of the people. Inappropriate use of public office for personal gains or embezzlement was rampant at the time of his appointment there. His nature and ethical values did not allow him to tolerate such practices. His admirers often described him as a man of integrity and a champion of the oppressed. However, he was not given a chance to move about among the rural communities to encourage them to be involved in development activities for their own good. Unfortunate-ly, his boss preferred Jatani to stay in his office to accomplish routine administrative chores all the time. Under such oppressive working condition, Jatani seemed to have decided to keep himself aloof from those who indulged in such mind-numbing administrative red tape, character assassination and office gossip. These practices and behaviours were against his nature.

Abera used to occasionally go to Awassa to visit him. He advised Jatani that keeping himself away from everything he did not like would, in the long run, hurt him. According to Abera, Jatani did not attempt to relieve himself from the frustration till he was appointed as Chief Governor of

Borana Administrative Region. The administrative structure of Sidamo region changed once again where a new entity called Borana Administrative Region was carved out of it. The latter was created by combining the mostly Oromo-speaking provinces of Borana, Arero and Jemjem (a Gujii locale).

Jatani was a community development-minded person. He enjoyed going out of the office and working with the community on development programs. But the Governor General of Sidamo region, a robotic individual who seemed to have little interest in community development issues, tried to tie him down to carry out mind-numbing routine paperwork duties in his office. Jatani had no difficulty in handling the routines of paper work. In fact, he was very good at this task too. But he enjoyed more the tasks that allowed him to interact with rural people through community development projects. Because of this, his stint as a deputy governor of Sidamo region in Awassa, the capital city of the region, was a frustrating one. He found it difficult to accomplish anything tangible as he had done in other places or other assignments. This was a very unfulfilling post as far as he was concerned. He had, however, made many intangible contributions even here. He learnt about and shared the many struggles and challenges indigenous peoples in Sidamo region faced during three different regimes. Some of these included: courageous resistance of many against the Italian invasion and the treacherous acts of some during this time; valiant protests of *chisegna* against landlords during the era of Emperor Haile Selassie; sacrifices paid in resisting the Somali invasion and the treacherous role of some in assisting that invasion; the struggle against the *Derg*'s often unwieldy and Machiavellian bureaucratic intrigues; and the effects of unrestrained power and inflated egos of Ethiopian leaders.

10: As Governor of Borana Administrative Region

Rulers of Ethiopia appeared to be fond of reorganising the administrative structure of the country according to the prevailing administrative jargon or their parochial tribal whims. Regime changes at Addis Ababa invariably led to reorganisation of the country's administrative structure, complete with new terms to mean a district or province. At best, these changes in administrative nomenclature were pointless and only created endless confusion to the people they purport to govern. Such changes didn't bring about any substantive change in Ethiopia's top-down rule by despots. Towards the end of their reign, the *Derg* officials reorganised Ethiopia's administrative regions citing budgetary reasons. In the new structure, the majority ethnic Oromo provinces of Borana and Arero, and the Gujii Province of Jemjem were combined to create Borana Administrative Region, with its capital in Nagelle-Borana. Up to then, all three provinces were part of Sidamo Administrative Region and governed from Awassa. It wasn't clear why the new jurisdiction wasn't called Borana-Gujii or similar, given that these two sub-groups of the Oromo were the majority in the region or to have a more inclusive-sounding name for the new administrative unit. To cut the cost of administration, the *Derg* removed a district (*woreda*) from the new administrative structure and came up with three levels of government that make up an Administrative Region. From bottom up these were: *kebele*, province and region.

Jatani was appointed the Governor of Borana Administrative Region in 1988. When he left Awassa for the new post, he felt as though he was released from a jail. Persons unaware of the policies of the *Derg* or, that of Ethiopian rulers in general, might blame him for not resigning from the oppressive post he held as a deputy governor of Sidamo Administrative

Region. According to the *Derg*'s policies, resignation from any government post was forbidden and, at times, tantamount to treason. Let alone resignation, even a transfer from one post to a similar one within the same department was not allowed without the consent of those higher up the chain of authority. However, Jatani felt that his new job and position would provide him with an opportunity to exercise his style of government in Borana region. He realised he has a chance to promote development schemes in the community in a manner he always envisaged and with a degree of autonomy from the top-down, red-tape bound, slow and often unresponsive Ethiopian byzantine bureaucracy.

A governor was not necessarily the most senior position in an Administrative Region according to *Derg*'s system of government. The regime created a parallel-operating power structure to that of the governor headed by a party apparatchik or representative answerable to the supreme leader of the party. This was meant to check or provide counterbalance to the power of governors. Colonel Mengistu Haile Mariam was simultaneously the Secretary-General of Ethiopia's Socialist Party, Ethiopia's Head of State or President, and Commander-in-Chief of Ethiopia's Armed Forces. He wielded as much power, if not more, than the series of despotic emperors who ruled Ethiopia before him. So, in Borana Administrative Region, a party representative who would keep an eye on the governor (at this time, Jatani) was appointed. The party representative was said to be the vanguard of the region's political affairs while the Governor was in charge of civil administration. Under such an arrangement, the party representative had the upper hand in determining what happened in the region. Such parallel-operating foci of power led to constant power struggles or clashes of egos between those holding the two posts. It wasn't always clear who of the two wielded more power or authority. It was often reported that people holding the two opposing posts in other regions of Ethiopia did not get along, let alone work harmoniously. Feuds between the holders of these two posts negatively impacted on regional development efforts or on public administration. In this respect, Jatani felt lucky to have a fellow Borana named Godana Tuni as the party political representative of Borana Administrative Region. Also, Godana Tuni's outlook on life and concern for community welfare and development matched Jatani's. Godana and Jatani were both "Borana Pioneers of Modern Education". Godana was also an experienced governor (of Bale Administrative Region) before he was appointed the head of the ruling party's political bureau in Borana. Godana also served as Governor of Borana region after his stint as Governor of Bale region. In both places, Godana was one of the most successful governors in the country, both in terms of his relationship with the people and with those higher up the chain of authority. Godana and Jatani were both from Borana community and from childhood they grew up together. Godana and Jatani believed the principle of peaceful co-existence between communities as a foundation for peace and development in the area. They had similar views on how to advance the economic and social development of pastoralist communities. As the result, the working relation between the two was a cordial one despite their opposing posts in the same region. They implemented their administrative, economic and social development visions in the region in a co-operative and consultative manner.

A fellow named Ilu Banata worked closely with Jatani as Deputy Governor of Borana Administrative Region from 1989 to 1991. In the previous administrative structure of Sidamo region, where Jatani was the Deputy Governor, Ilu was Governor of the predominantly Gujii-Oromo province of Jamjam (Jemjem *Awraja*). Jatani knew Ilu and had worked with him from the time when Ilu was the Jamjam Provincial Governor. In fact, Jatani recommended Ilu to be appointed as his Deputy through the Ministry of the Interior. Ilu described the character of Jatani as, 'A selfless champion for the wellbeing of the people, a fighter of corruption, a staunch believer in equality of opportunities for communities, a decisive leader with a strong vision and dogged determination for the expansion of education to marginalised pastoralist communities'.

Ilu indicated that people who did not know Jatani closely sometimes considered him to be a hot-tempered person. In reality, he added, Jatani was soft-hearted, a person who put the interests and advancement of the community ahead of anything else. According to Ilu, Jatani identified competent individuals from local communities, matched them to suitable administrative posts in the provinces and recommended them to the Ministry of the Interior for their effective appointment. When Godana, Jatani and Ilu took over the administration of Borana region, among other things, they found too many unnecessary customs checkpoints or roadblocks along the main roads used to control the movement of goods and people. Ordinary travellers regarded these roadblocks at best as a nuisance that affected the smooth flow of public transport and at worst as unnecessary hindrance to healthy business transactions. Ilu pointed out that they made sure to remove most of the roadblocks with the approval of those higher up the chain of authority.

Jatani respected those in a position of authority and expected these to discharge their public service duties honourably, according to recognised policies and accepted ethical standards. However, he wouldn't hesitate to challenge his superiors who indulged in behaviour he deemed unethical or outside established norms. His appointment to the post of Governor of Borana region started with a confrontation with those higher up the ladder of power but with questionable ethical standards. As discussed earlier, the *Derg* regime nationalised land in rural areas and houses other than the family home in towns from well-to-do persons soon after it came to power. However, some over-zealous officials went beyond the call of duty in attacking every person they deemed rich or suspected of harbouring counter-revolutionary thoughts. Injustices were committed against citizens who ran their own businesses, employed people and tried to build vital infrastructures for the development of remote provinces. There was an Ethiopian businessman who owned a heavy truck, ran a small business and used to live in Hagere Mariam town in what used to be Arero province. He was one of the victims of the *Derg*'s overzealous officials in their attempt to implement the regime's revolutionary decrees. As a protest, he defected to Kenya with his truck and resumed his business in Moyale-Kenya, just across the border from the town of Moyale-Ethiopia. Border crossing procedures between the two Moyales were often informal for residents living on either side of the border as many were related to each other. One day, the truck crossed the border into Moyale-Ethiopia and was apprehended by customs officials. They confiscated the truck and handed it over to bureaucrats working for Sidamo Administrative Region in Awassa, some 500 kilometres north of Moyale. Jatani had been living in Awassa as Deputy Governor of Sidamo region when he learnt about the truck's saga. According to him, the truck was not being used legally to assist in either government or community work. Following the new administrative structure, Moyale-Ethiopia, where the truck was apprehended, came under Jatani's administrative jurisdiction of Borana Region. Jatani got permission to use the truck to take his personal effects from Awassa to Nagelle Borana, the administrative capital of Borana region. Once in Nagelle, he asked the driver whether he would like to work with him in the new region, to which he replied, no. Jatani told him to hand over the key and leave. The driver did as he was asked – for the time being. Later, he changed his mind and returned to Nagelle, hoping to work for Jatani. Jatani however had been accused of illegally confiscating a truck that belonged to authorities in Awassa. Tefera Endalew, the previous governor of Sidamo region, and his allies loudly protested against Jatani's action and reported the issue to *Derg* authorities higher up the ladder of power. Jatani firmly stood his ground and won the charges in his favour. He kept the truck under his custody for the time being. As mentioned above, the owner of the truck was a refugee from Ethiopia whom the Kenya Government provided an asylum. He made the confiscation of his property an international issue. The Kenya Government intervened on his behalf and with the help of Jatani, the businessman regained possession of his property. As far as Jatani was concerned, justice was finally done.

Facing challenges was not something new to Jatani. By nature, he was not a type of person who retreated from an obstacle that might stop him from achieving his goals. Following the upgrade of Nagelle town from a provincial capital to the capital of the new Borana Administrative Region, key ministries in the country had to open branch offices in Nagelle too. Various ministries also sent their employees down to Nagelle but the town lacked adequate office space and rentable houses to host them. This was one the first challenges Jatani's administration had to overcome. There were no prior arrangements for accommodating these in terms of office space and residential places for the newly arrived. Jatani told me how he addressed the issue by designing short- and long-term strategies to solve the problem. In the short term, he arranged for the construction of low-cost houses for employees who were forced to stay in hotels due to the lack of rentable houses. In the long term, he managed to secure a budget of Birr 6.8 million to build complexes that could serve both as offices and residences for employees. Ilu Banata stated that a contractual agreement to build office and residential complexes in Nagelle was signed with Batu Construction Company. However, the *Derg* regime collapsed while the construction of the buildings was still underway. Jatani left his post and went into exile. The construction of both the office complex and low cost houses was completed after he left and used more or less for what they were intended. Some of the low-cost houses have since been remodelled to provide nursing education for young people from Borana and Gujii Zones or Provinces.[33]

Jatani's other accomplishments as Governor of Borana

Jatani's tenure as the governor of Borana Region was a short one, lasting only for about two years. Still, he managed to accomplish a number of

---

[33] The Amharic nomenclature for a province or administrative region has since changed to a 'Zone' by the ethnic Tigre-dominated *Woyane* regime that violently ousted the *Derg* regime.

things that had a lasting impact on the lives of people in the region. One of the first actions he took was to help rebuild businesses that provided vital services to people in the province. Many of these had been national-ised by the *Derg*'s often overzealous officials and then left idle, or were abandoned by their owners, given the regime's business-unfriendly policies. One of these was to revitalise businesses that operated petrol or gas stations. For example, the owner of Nagelle's Shell petrol station fled the country as the *Derg* came to power and the station remained idle for years. To find an alternative person to rebuild and operate the petrol station, he floated the business, seeking public bids. A businessman in the town won the bid and made it operational immediately. Another move was to improve the availability of suitable lodgings in Nagelle town to cater for increasing numbers of visitors as the town went from a provin-cial capital to a regional capital. The tourist hotel in Nagelle was fairly decent one by local standard but the owner, Gebre Hiwot Kidane, had neglected it to the point of deterioration. Jatani urged and persuaded Gebre Hiwot to repair the hotel and restore it to an acceptable standard immediately or else he would put it to public tender, seeking other individuals willing to take over and run the hotel properly. I personally knew Gebre Hiwot and once met him casually in Addis Ababa around that time when Jatani was urging him to improve the standard of his hotel. Gebre Hiywot bitterly complained about Jatani, indicating how Jatani was exerting undue pressure on him. However, Gebre Hiwot did not mention any specific grievances against Jatani's *modus operandi* in running the region.

Then Jatani looked into the conditions of Nagelle Hospital. He found that the health authorities had totally neglected it and the hospital tag was in name only. The hospital beds all had sagging bedsprings and lacked mattresses. Anyone who had to stay overnight had to bring his/her own sleeping materials from home. He reported this appalling condition to the Ministry of Health but they took no action, citing budgetary constraints. He determined to make a change on his own. He purchased 60 sponge mattresses from Kenya with money saved from the administrative budget of the region. He requested the customs office at Moyale to let the mattresses through duty free as they were for the public good. They denied the request. He tried to reason with them and said, 'What I am asking of you might be against government policy but it is not a request for personal gain but to benefit the public.' He went on, 'You tend to look the other way when certain individuals become wealthy overnight through illicit cross-border contraband trade that you let slip through this same customs checkpoint. Your refusal to show a one-off discretion in processing my request for public good highlights your lack of concern for the public welfare.' Having told them what he felt about their behaviour, he determined to take his own action. He ordered his men to smuggle the mattresses through the bush on camel back into Nagelle. This daring action gave a slight relief to the hospital service but, no doubt, raised the ire of customs officials and their bosses higher up the chain of command.

The twin towns of Moyale-Ethiopia and Moyale-Kenya are located along the Ethio-Kenya border at a distance of 775 kilometres from Addis Ababa, along the international highway that links Addis Ababa with Nairobi. A dry river bed separates the two towns. Moyale plays a significant economic role as Ethiopia's major inland port. The destruction of rail bridges on the Addis Ababa to Djibouti railway line and the disruption of access routes to Ethiopia's ports in war-torn Eritrea increased the strategic importance of Moyale as an alternative dry port. Export and import trade between the two countries passed through the adjacent customs offices in the twin towns. The central Ethiopian Government in Addis Ababa used to give export and import licenses to businesspeople who participated in such transactions. This lucrative trade and license-issuing processes attracted a great deal of corrupt practices and shady characters.

With regard to granting licenses to business people, Jatani challenged the officials in charge on two grounds. First, he argued that the priority of granting a license to trade through Moyale should be given to local people who fulfil the criteria. Secondly, all the benefits from the cross-border trade should not go to merchants who come from outside the area. Ideally, some of the gains should be invested back into the locality to improve the living conditions of the impoverished, war-torn and marginalised communities. This could be in the form of building a hotel or residential houses in the area. The dispute between Jatani and customs agents went up to higher government officials. Jatani won the case on both challenges.

Borana Administrative Region was one of the largest in the country in terms of its area. Farmers' associations were key grassroots organisations that served as conduits for good governance, delivery of services, community development, peace and security. Jatani realised that it was vital for farmers' associations in the region to have a motor vehicle to reach disparate communities. The associations had money to purchase a vehicle but the *Derg's* rather inflexible and dogmatic socialist trade policies prohibited the importation of vehicles into the country. A chronic shortage of petrol was one of the reasons for banning car importations into the country. What little petrol was imported was used by the army which was bogged down in various and seemingly never-ending wars. Jatani purchased from Kenya a second-hand pickup truck for the farmers' association and advised them to use it in the bush to avoid apprehension. This was a violation of existing government policy but, as was with the mattress importation case, he took a risk for the sake of the greater public good.

Incidents like the above were several during his period as Governor of Borana region. These are just a few examples of his determination to take daring action to advance the cause of the poor and the neglected.

I asked a few individuals to tell me their impressions of Jatani in terms of his achievements during his brief stint as Governor of Borana region. Nura Dida Halakhe was one such and he came from a Borana nomadic pastoralist family in Liban district (now in the Gujii Zone). Nura served in the Ethiopian army during the *Derg* period but was a retired army officer when he gave me his views. Nura started by saying that he was well aware of Jatani's tangible contributions towards community development both in rural and urban areas. He said, besides the business of government and trying to rebuild run-down businesses, Jatani encouraged the planting of tree seedlings in Nagelle town around government offices and in public areas such as parks. Jatani himself planted many tree seedlings and flowers and looked after these. He advised people in the offices to make sure to water and nurse the seedlings. Though some of the seedlings died, a great many did survive and grew into flowering trees. As a result, the landscape and outlook of the town has since improved a great deal. For example, Nura continued, there was an enclosure in the middle Nagelle town with young trees and flower beds. Due to neglect by the town's municipal officials, many of the plants were reduced to shrivelling twigs overtaken by weeds. Nura said that Jatani spearheaded the regeneration of trees and flowers in that enclosure and it grew into a green and pleasant public park. Town's people and visitors alike now use the park as a place for meeting and relaxation. In a way, through such activities, Jatani helped instil a strong sense of civic pride in many people.

According to Nura, when Jatani came to the region as the governor, only two persons from the large Borana pastoralist community owned houses in Nagelle town. Even Nura Dida who had been exposed to life in a town, given his job as an army officer, did not own a house of his own in that town. This was all the more puzzling given the fact that land was freely available to anyone who wanted to build a house for residence during the *Derg* era. Jatani educated pastoralists on the economic and social advantages of having houses in nearby towns. For example, many pastoralists wanted to send some of their children to schools based in nearby towns. Yet most were deterred from doing so because of a lack of lodgings for their children. He strongly advised them that they should take the plunge, apply for land grants in towns and build houses to be used as family residences, student lodges or as rental properties that generate income. Many of them, including Nura, heeded Jatani's advice and became owners of houses in Nagelle town. Jatani tirelessly educated the pastoralists in a range of areas so that they caught up with other communities in terms of their economic and social development. Among other things, Nura continued, Jatani highlighted to them the vitality of sending their children to school; the need to diversify their livelihood to reduce their precarious dependence on cattle farming; to take up small-scale commerce and handicraft trades to diversify their income stream; to establish self-help credit facilities to assist those wanting to start small businesses; to cultivate land to reduce their reliance on food relief during droughts; to look after each other in life and death matters by creating *idir* (grassroots savings guilds) and similar self-help associations, as found in other communities.

Jatani in his spare time

Inaugurating Boku Luboma's military communication post

On agreement with its Kenyan counterpart, the Ethiopian Government constructed a military communication post at Boku Luboma in the vicinity of the Kenyan border. Brigadier-General Getachew Shibeshi, Commander-in-Chief of the Southern Military Command stationed at Awassa, went down to Moyale Province for the inauguration of the centre. Both Godana Tuni and Jatani Ali were present at the inaugural ceremony attended by community leaders and other dignitaries. After the ceremony, the guest of honour praised the Borana people for their gallantry against Somali cross-border incursions and outright invasion of their homeland and Ethiopia. The general advised the gathering to keep watchful eyes on the enemy and to continue their effort in defending the country's southern borders. It was an occasion that reinforced the view that Borana people were held in high regard by successive rulers of Ethiopia. The guest of honour went to Moyale town with his entourage for a brief visit and returned to Awassa. During this time, the *Derg* regime was struggling to keep a tab on the separatist rebels fighting in Eritrea and their ethnic allies from the province of Tigray. As mentioned elsewhere, both these groups had been armed and supported by Somalia. Both groups had offices and delegations that operated from Mogadishu and other major cities in Somalia. Senior leaders of these groups travelled around the Arab world and northern Africa looking for military assistance by using Somali passports. Somalia and its local sympathisers were sensing that another opportunity to invade Ethiopia and take over Borana land was approaching.

Jatani's last meeting with government employees at Moyale

After the ceremony, Godana and Jatani remained behind to speak to all government employees in Moyale Province. The purpose was to brief them on the prevailing and increasingly fluid political conditions in the country. Godana opened the session and left.

Jatani took the floor and the session was videoed. It was the last meeting Jatani would have with people working for the government in that town or the region. Three points were the focus of the briefing and their possible implications for communities living in the province. These were: the threat posed by the combined and increasingly bold Tigrai and Eritrea Liberation Fronts on the country; the dire financial situation of the country due to the high cost of fighting rebel forces; and the possible awakening of Somalia and its sympathisers to resume their attempt to grab Borana land. Regarding the first issue, he indicated how Eritrea had broken away from Ethiopia. The Tigrai group had liberated their region and, with military assistance from their co-ethnic allies from Eritrea, had started incursions into the remaining part of the country. He told the gathering how the overall strategy of the government was not only to halt their progress but to turn them back. Jatani lamented how the regime was not succeeding in its strategy as the rebels were getting bolder by the day and continued to occupy larger areas in northern regions of Ethiopia. He said that there was no peace in regions of Wollo, Gondar, Gojjam and even Wollega. Consequently, many government employees such as teachers and other civilian employees of the state in these northern regions were fleeing to the relatively safer southern regions of the country. According to him Borana Administrative Region had relative peace compared to those being overrun by the rebels.

He elaborated on the second point and highlighted the financial constraints in running the affairs of the state in general and that of the Borana region in particular. He said that government treasury was empty. The ongoing strategy to cope with the situation was to explore different sources of fund-raising. In addition to regular taxes already levied on different sectors and economic activities in the country, the government had imposed additional taxes of Birr 70 on each business owner and Birr 40 on each farmer. Furthermore, he instructed them to solicit donations in cash from well-to-do members of the community and businessmen who had been participating in cross-border trade through Moyale. He warned the gathering to use discretion and take utmost care in not hurting those who could not afford to pay when collecting the newly-imposed additional taxes or levies. He told them that the levy was imposed on the community *en masse* and it was likely that some members might not even be alive at the time of collection and the financial situation of others might have changed for the worse since they paid taxes last time. Turning to the collection of regular taxes, he indicated that there were arrears of several thousand Birr due to sub-standard tax collection process. He urged tax agents to clear the arrears immediately.

The third issue concerned the situation in neighbouring Somalia, a country that was still nursing its humiliating defeat at the hands of the Ethiopian army a decade or so earlier. Jatani said that Somali rulers appeared calm and peaceful with Ethiopia at that point. He added that there was no guarantee that Somalia wouldn't take advantage of Ethiopia's internal instability to resume its cross-border incursions or assist the usual local sympathisers in the region to destabilise the region. He warned that the community should be alert for such a possibility. He mentioned how the central government of Ethiopia left Borana region alone twice in its nation-wide drive to recruit more militia forces to fight the rebels. The understanding was that the region was expected to organise its own militia forces and raise necessary resources for these in order to protect the local peace and defend Ethiopia's southern borders.

Jatani had great ambition to bring about fundamental changes in the lives of nomadic pastoralists and farming communities in Borana region. But his two years' tenure was too short to realise his vision. Nevertheless, he did manage to sow the seeds for community-led development. He awakened many to the realities of gross neglect, bad governance, injustices, lack of representation, lack of development and wanton regime brutality endured for decades by communities in the region. He managed to galvanise urban and rural communities to initiate and actively partake in community development schemes. These included strengthening traditional self-government institutions, building students' hostels, and building or repairing vital infrastructure such as primary schools and health facilities in remote areas. He managed to build the necessary manpower and institutional capabilities to improve public administration and delivery of vital services. He rekindled community spirit to expand educational opportunities to marginalised communities. He started the culture of community initiative to solve key social and economic problems in the region. His efforts at raising community awareness for development were simply remarkable and still bearing fruit, long after his demise.

11: In the Bush, Exile and Assassination

The Tigray People's Liberation Front (TPLF), with military assistance from their co-ethnic allies of Eritrean People's Liberation Front (EPLF), ousted the *Derg* regime from power in May 1991. As the result, all the administrative structures of the *Derg* collapsed. The incoming rulers set out to dismantle all state institutions such as the army and bureaucracy by making sure that these were dominated by ethnic Tigre officials.

In the bush and in exile

When the *Derg* regime failed, Jatani left Nagelle and went to Hoboq, an area straddling the districts of Dirre and Teltele, where he stayed for a month. He assembled the Borana people in the area and informed them about the serious political upheaval Ethiopia was going through yet again. He told the gathered how the *Derg* regime, led by Col. Mengistu Haile Mariam, has just been violently overthrown by armed rebels from northern Ethiopia. He told them that he was no longer in power to look after their interests. He warned them that they did not have power to challenge the new rulers of the country. He advised them how their only chance of survival was to live in peace with them and try to make the regime a Borana-friendly one. He told them not to trust Somalia and their surrogates in the area as they could resume their treacherous agenda of expanding at the expense of Boranaland and Ethiopia. Regarding his future, he stated that he would leave the country to seek safety elsewhere.

So Jatani, instead of surrendering to the new regime as so many officials did and were jailed, went into the bush in Borana country. He did so not to wage guerrilla warfare against the TPLF but to avoid confinement. He went to Teltele District for one month and moved to Dirre District and stayed in a secluded spot surrounded by mountains for the rest of his stay in the bush. The community provided him with sanctuary and material supplies. He kept with him the vehicle he was using while in office and its driver. The vehicle was parked at a secure place at the foot of a mountain. Villagers prepared a secure place for him to stay and supplied him with what they had in terms of the essentials for survival. The community selected seven individuals who had military training to protect him against any possible attack. They even bought some fuel for the vehicle with which he sometimes moved around. If anything went wrong with the vehicle the people would bring spare parts and his driver, who stayed with him throughout, would fix it. Close friends and prominent Borana men used to visit him where the security guards would verify the identity and *bona fides* of visitors. However, there was an opportunist individual – whose name is withheld – who came to visit him but the guards stopped him on a suspicion that he was an enemy agent with a mission. In one occasion a retired Borana *Abba Gada* (traditional supreme leader), the late Boru Guyo, visited him. Jatani told this writer how he had the pleasure of spending a night with the late *Abba Gada*, where they were entertained with a feast of goat. To conceal his exact whereabouts for security reasons, diversionary gossip was spread around, claiming that Jatani was staying in a remote locality known as Bada Huri (just across the border in Kenya).

Before going into the bush for refuge, Jatani advised a group of prominent elders in Dubuluq area about what the Borana community would likely face in the future. Jaba Kotola (name changed) was one of the elders and reported that Jatani alerted them to three major challenges the Borana community could encounter following the violent regime change. These were:

1. the possibility of a Borana-unfriendly government installed in the region;
2. resumption of Somali aggression from the east; and/or,
3. severe droughts where they (Borana) would struggle to get government assistance.

He told them that a completely new set of rulers had been installed in Addis Ababa and the implications for Borana might not be good. The ethnic and political outlook of the new rulers was completely different from the regimes the Borana had been familiar with up to that point. He warned them that all the enemies of the Borana would rush to embrace the leaders of the new regime to advance their sectarian interests, to undermine Borana authority on their own country or to grab Borana land that they failed to acquire in countless previous invasions. Jatani advised that the primary purpose of these anti-Borana elements in the area would be to serve as informers of the new rulers and identify capable Borana leaders to be killed or imprisoned on trumped-up charges. By highlighting how making the Borana a leaderless people is a strategy its enemies would use, Jatani urged the elders to be vigilant in defending Borana land, leaders and interests. He warned them that it was crucial not to give the enemies a chance to indulge in divide-and-rule tactics that would pit one section of Borana against another to render them all impotent. He advised that the community should not keep aloof from the new rulers but rather should recognise their authority and behave towards them in friendly manner in order to protect Borana interests. In relation to what could be expected from the Borana's traditional rivals from the east, he indicated that they would be quick to exploit the upheavals that follow regime change and would wage war to occupy Borana land. Jatani emphasised how the only means for the Borana's survival hinged on its ability to have a strong, well-armed, well-supplied and alert self-defence force. Regarding the effects of droughts, he said that the community had lived through recurrent droughts for centuries and had their own traditional coping mechanisms. He noted how droughts have become more frequent in recent decades and how traditional coping mechanisms have been inadequate, leaving many to rely on foreign food aid. He advised that to reduce the devastating effects of droughts, the Borana must keep the right number of stock and sell excess livestock in good times and use the proceeds to buy houses in towns to rent out or start alternative small businesses.

Jatani stayed in the bush of Borana country for ten months. During this time, agents of the new regime attempted different means to have him arrested or assassinated but failed. At the same time, the agents of the regime turned to harassing the innocent pastoralists suspected of harbouring him. To halt the pestering of the community by Ethiopia's security forces, Jatani crossed the border to Kenya in March 1992, applied for asylum and got it. He was accompanied by prominent elders until he surrendered to Kenyan authorities for asylum. Jatani temporarily settled at Thika refugee camp, about 30 kilometres east of Nairobi, where hundreds of Ethiopian refugees were hosted at the time.

Inter-communal relations between tribes living in Marsabit area of northern Kenya were often difficult. Inter-tribal feuds as the result of competition over land and scarce resources often led to bloody clashes and cattle rustling. President Daniel Arap Moi of Kenya went to the area to talk peace and reconciliation to the assembled members of the warring communities. Wario Sora, a Kenyan police man, was at the meeting. He reported that Jatani came and met with assembled Borana community members. The President advised the people to live in peace with each other within the Kenyan legal system. When the President finished his speech, Jatani asked him if he could pose three questions; he was allowed to go ahead:

Question number 1: Why was the asphalt road that started from Nairobi stopped at Isiolo instead of reaching Moyale?

Question number 2: There is no restriction on different ethnic groups in the area to carry traditional arms like spears. Why is this restriction imposed on Borana alone? and,

Question number 3: Different ethnic groups who were involved in tribal clashes in the area such as Burji, Rendille and others came from outside the area. The land on which these clashes took place belongs to Borana. You are the President of all the citizens in Kenya. Why has the Borana community been singled out for this unfavourable and discriminatory treatment on its own land?

The President told him that he would give him the answers to his questions from Nairobi, through appropriate channels. He boarded his plane and returned to Nairobi. Wario Sora (who reported this information) indicated that he did not know whether the President ever answered the questions as promised.

This author [Tadhi] had the pleasure of having a rendezvous with Jatani in Nairobi, a few months before his assassination. At the end of March 1992, I travelled to Accra, Ghana, as a representative of the Ethiopian Management Institute, to participate in a ten-day workshop organised for those working in the management area in English-speaking African countries. Before travelling to the workshop, I heard that Jatani had crossed over into Kenya and arrived in Nairobi. I realised that my travel itinerary would give me a chance to catch up with him. [34] On the return trip from the workshop, I arranged with the Airline ticket office for flexibility in my travel plans that would allow me to alter my flight itinerary in order to stay in Nairobi for three days. As per the arrangement I landed at Nairobi airport and travelled into the city. I looked around for Borana persons who might have heard about Jatani's arrival in Nairobi and could help me find him. Luckily enough, I came across a group of Borana elders who came from Moyale and Sololo areas to lodge complaints against a district governor who, according to them, mistreated them. They were Sora Ali Galgalo, Hassan Jilo Galgalo, Godana Galgalo, Guyo Halakhe Liban, Golicha Galgalo Guyo, Abdi Hassan, Mohammed Galgalo Duba, Mohammed Wario Guracha and Dida Jaledesa Dida. After we exchanged information about our respective purposes for being in Nairobi, I asked them whether anyone among them could help me find Jatani in Nairobi. They told me that he was in Thika refugee camp and Mohammed Galgalo Duba had been in touch with him since he came to Nairobi. Mohammed and I travelled to Thika camp and met with Jatani. I

---

[34] My travel route on Ethiopian Airlines was: Addis Ababa-Accra and, on the return trip, Accra-Nairobi-Addis Ababa.

asked him to come to Nairobi with me for a day or two but he told me that he could not do so without permission from the camp administration. We agreed that he would get permission and meet with me the following day in Nairobi. As arranged, we met and spent a night together, when we reminisced about the old times and talked about our personal and Borana's current predicament. Before departure, I asked him what he would like to do in the future. He told me that he would keep up the struggle from the outside till justice is restored in Ethiopia. He promised to keep me informed about what he would be doing.

On 3 July 1992 at 2 p.m. Mohammed Galgalo called me to inform me that Jatani Ali had been murdered the preceding evening at his hotel. Abdullah Guyo Jarso from Ethiopia was with him on the phone. I asked them who carried out the crime and they told me armed men from Ethiopia did that. The news about his assassination was the greatest shock in my whole life.

After Jatani had stayed in Kenya as a refugee for four months, an assassin squad was organised in Ethiopia and dispatched to Kenya to carry out the cold-blooded murder.

The assassination

During his time, Jatani was loved by most Borana. At the same time, he was admired and feared by many non-Borana. He also infuriated a few, who held grudges against him and the Borana people. Such individuals or groups plotted and waited for an opportune time to harm him. Many of his enemies were aware that the best way to approach Jatani would have to be through another Borana. It was through another Borana person named Gobba Liban that the assassins approached and murdered Jatani in a hotel in the city of Nairobi. Gobba Liban ended up living in Nairobi after a previous incident on the streets of Yaballo, where he knocked down a pedestrian with a vehicle he was driving. To avoid arrest, Gobba fled Yaballo and sought refuge in a remote rural area in Borana country. Later he went to see Jatani presumably seeking a way out or a pardon.

Jatani turned him away. Apparently, he left Ethiopia and sought refuge in Kenya. Gobba was one of the persons whom people believed to have led the assassin squad to the hotel where Jatani was staying. Another suspect escaped to the United States via Somalia and now lives in Les Vegas, Nevada, hiding himself from other Borana residents living in that city. After Jatani's assassination, Gobba returned to Ethiopia from Kenya and the government provided him with a protection for a while against a possible vendetta attack for his alleged participation in Jatani's assassination. Reportedly, the government neglected him and he got sick, was admitted to Tikur Anbessa Hospital in Addis Ababa and could not recover from the illness.

The assassination of Jatani Ali was an organised venture in which several parties with grudges joined forces to commit this heinous crime. Close observers pointed their fingers at ethnic Garri businessmen, a few Borana men, TPLF agents in Awassa and Borana region and the Ethiopian Embassy in Nairobi. One of the perpetrators of the assassination lives in Addis Ababa as a favoured investor. Well-informed people claim that this investor is a very close ally of one of the top leaders of the party that currently rules the state of Oromia. Reportedly, this man presented himself to the officials as a Borana elder.

Three gunmen assassinated Jatani on the evening of 2 July 1992 at Ngera Hotel in the western part of Nairobi where he was staying. One of the gunmen was apprehended on the spot but two of them escaped in a vehicle, reportedly provided by the Ethiopian Embassy. The late Hussein Sora, the attorney who was prosecuting this crime, accused the Ethiopian Embassy of participation in the murder in an open letter written on 21 August 1992. The full text of the letter is reproduced here:

OUR Ref: MJA/HS/2
Hussein Sora *P.O. Box 1048* *MERU* *21st August 1992*

His Excellency Getachew Zerihun
The Ethiopian Ambassador
P.O. Box 45198
NAIROBI
KENYA

Dear Your Excellency,

Allow me to revisit the issue pertaining to the assassination of MEBATSION JATANI ALI an Ethiopian refugee exiled in Kenya and murdered in cold blood on 2nd July 1992 in Nairobi, subsequent demonstration at your Embassy and your press conference thereafter.

It is alleged on the death of Mr. Ali and the allegation is maintained to date that his slaying was the work of the Ethiopian Government through its agents. It is further alleged and the allegation is still maintained that of the assassins not apprehended so far two are held up in your Embassy.

Your Excellency, the allegation aforesaid has not been denied by you for and on behalf of yourself and your government. On the contrary Your Excellency, you were reported in your press conference subsequent upon demonstration at your embassy to have stated that killing of Jatani Ali was undertaken by Ethiopian people ostensibly for a crime allegedly committed by him during the Mengistu era. While we are at pains to understand and what Your Excellency meant by the term, "Ethiopian People", we are, Your Excellency left in no doubt that you are in the know of the so called Ethiopian People who killed Jatani. We are further left in no doubt that Your Excellency did approve and maintains the approval of the place (in sovereign Kenya), the manner (by assassins, without bringing the suspect before any tribunal to establish his guilt and/or innocence), the status (a refugee seeking peace in a country other than his own) of Jatani's killing. We are further in no doubt that Your Excellency's role in the assassination of Jatani Ali was without decorum and is in violation of norms of International Law and Diplomacy.

Your Excellency, it is common knowledge that two of the assassins (the ones who actually pulled the trigger) were driven in gateway car which belongs to your Embassy from the scene of the crime and into your Embassy premises. Your Excellency, it is further common knowledge and there is ample evidence supporting the knowledge that several attempts by your Embassy to smuggle the assassins out of your Embassy premises have proven futile. Your Excellency, it is further common knowledge that you have not given up the attempts to smuggle the two assassins out of Your Excellency's premises and Kenya.

It is our contention and firmly held believe that the smuggling of the two out of the country does not augur well for your country's international image and standing. It is for *these reasons that we urge your Excellency to reconsider the other option, which is one of surrendering the two assassins to the Kenya Government and thereby atone for "The Misadventure".*

In handing over the two assassins namely:-

1.   Eweneto Tefera and

2.   Abraham (F.N.U)

to the Kenyan authorities so that they may face justice, Your Excellency would make a big contribution to making our world a better and safer place generally and more so for harmless, defenceless person who have fled their country for one reason or another and are seeking solace and respite in another country as a refugee.

I am confident that a concession by Your Excellency to our humble requests herein is not a matter of great botheration to you.

In concluding, I indulge in one indulgence which I know Your Excellency will not withhold from me. Such an indulgence being copying the letter to all who certainly appreciate your magnanimity in handing over TFERA and ABRAHM to Kenyan authorities.

Yours faithfully,

HUSSEIN SORA

CC: THE PERMANENT SECRETARY
MINISTRY OF FOREIGN AFFAIRS
P.O. BOX 30551
NAIROBI
All Diplomats accredited to Kenya,   NAIROBI

(For information and all possible action in conformity with International Law and diplomatic practice thereby restoring diplomacy and the practice thereof to the high pedestal upon which it has always rested save for few aberrations there from.)

Note the slight variation in the way the names of the three members of the assassin squad was spelt in Hussein Sora's letter as well as in a related article that appeared in the *Indian Ocean Newsletter.*

Before the conclusion of the case, Hussein Sora was reportedly poisoned and died suddenly in Nairobi.

The people in the hotel had witnessed the murder of Jatani by three persons, two of whom escaped with another being arrested at the site. The two suspects who escaped were reportedly sheltered in the Ethiopian

Embassy and smuggled out of the country without appearing in a court of justice in Kenya. The one who was apprehended defended himself in court against the charges by saying that no murder weapon was found on him at the time of his arrest. Under this pretext, the judge ignored all circumstantial evidence around the murder and acquitted the suspect on the grounds that there was no sufficient proof. It was not clear what more compelling evidence the judge required other than the testimony of eyewitnesses to the murder at the hotel, along with related circumstantial evidence. Isn't this a mockery of justice? Thus the Kenyan court set the suspect free and he triumphantly returned home (to Ethiopia) with the mission accomplished, just like his accomplices who were smuggled out of the country before facing a Kenyan court.

After the death of Hussein Sora, another attorney, Gitobu Imanyara, was appointed to deal with the recovery of Jatani's estate. This attorney wrote the following letter to a committee supposedly in charge of Jatani's belongings.

GITOBU IMANYARA and COMPANY
Tumaini House 4th Floor
Advocates
Nkrumah Avenue
P.O. Box 53234
Nairobi, KENYA
Gitobu Imanyara
LLB (Hons)
Tel: 254-2-330480
Fax: 254-2-230173
Our Ref: 95/G1/144
Date 2nd January, 1996

Mr. Dika Godana Dida
Mr. Solomon Demise
Mr. Tunga Godan
Mr Galgalo Erbe
P.O. Box 71658
NAIROBI

Comments about the alleged estate

Regarding the attorney's letter on the recovery of Jatani's estate allegedly in the custody of abovementioned individuals, there are so many dubious points. I would like to raise certain points that reflect the questionable nature of the issue from the perspective of my knowledge about Jatani's behaviour and character.

1. Where was the so-called caretaker committee organised, in Kenya or Ethiopia? Who organised it? What was its composition?

2. Where exactly was the estate amassed or stored, in Ethiopia or in Kenya?

3. What was the fundamental or real interest of the committee to urge the attorney to recover the property of the deceased 4 years after the event?

4. If the interest of the caretaker committee was inheritance, the legal heir of the deceased person should have been informed about the matter. To the best of my knowledge, such information was not available to the legal heir.

5. Jatani arrived in Kenya as a refugee in March 1992 and was assassinated 4 months later in July 1992. The Jatani Ali that I knew hardly ever kept any cash with him. I never came across a person who ever pointed his finger at Jatani for getting money through illicit means from anywhere. Where in the world had he got 60,000 Ethiopian Birr? Where did he keep that money – in Kenya or in Ethiopia?

6. I assume that any person who knew Jatani can raise similar questions in relation to the items in the list.

Why was Jatani assassinated?

There were several high ranking officials in the *Derg* administrative and political systems who took refuge in Kenya at the time of Jatani's assassination. It is possible to speculate from different perspectives why a single Ethiopian ex-official was singled out for elimination. A person who was in service of the Ethiopian government at that time was heard commenting about the attitudes of the regime toward Jatani. They knew that Jatani was a charismatic leader who was capable of easily influencing communities in the border regions of Sidamo and Gamu Goffa for causes he believed in. Kenya bordered both these strategic regions of southern Ethiopia. The EPRDF government[35] realised that they could not comfortably rule over those regions while such a person was at large "next door". Since he did not surrender to be under their control, the apparent safe measure for them was to eliminate him.

---

[35] The EPRDF is the ruling party in Ethiopia, dominated by the TPLF.

Another reason for his murder suggests a revenge killing by Garri businessmen. Garri is a community which occupied the eastern part of the Borana region before they were consolidated into the Somali region under the *Woyane* regime.[36] The Garri have been contesting ownership of Borana land for years. The Garri have allied themselves with the anti-Ethiopian agenda of the Somalis, received arms from them and participated in Somalia's expansionist wars in a bid to emerge as owners of Borana's ancestral territories. They have tried to exploit just about all political instabilities in Ethiopia to advance their cause of grabbing Borana land. The Republic of Somalia provided them with political and military backing in their effort to undermine both the Borana's and Ethiopia's interests. Whenever their attempts failed, Somalia provided the Garri with a safe haven or refuge. The collapse of the *Derg* regime in Ethiopia brought another phase of political instability to the country. As usual, the Garri and their Somali allies were quick to exploit the political unrest and the ensuing chaos to their advantage. More, the regime that replaced the *Derg* in Addis Ababa (namely, the *Woyane*) appeared to favour Somali clans over the pro-Ethiopian Borana. It is possible that this was *Woyane*'s way of repaying a debt they owed to the Somali government. As mentioned above, both the TPLF and EPLF had offices in Mogadishu where the leaders of these ethnically Tigre-dominated rebel groups also lived and freely operated against Ethiopia. Reportedly and as was previously mentioned, these leaders also travelled the Arab world and Africa with Somali passports issued to them by the government of Siad Barre. The installation of the *Woyane* regime in Addis Ababa coincided with the disintegration of Somalia's Siad Barre government in Mogadishu. The collapse of the Somali state and army enabled the Garri to have access to ample supplies of armaments needed in their wars of expansion against the Borana. These favourable sets of conditions tempted the Garri to

---

[36] *Woyane* is an informal name for ethnic Tigre-dominated regime that ousted the *Derg*.

embark on a war of aggression to displace the Borana from their ancestral territories and to occupy the land they had been coveting for years. The Borana people knew of the Garri's treacherous behaviour for years and had managed to thwart many of their attacks to grab Borana land. A regime change in Ethiopia emboldened the Garri more than ever but, as usual, Borana waited patiently for them to strike first. Garri resumed their attack on the Borana as expected but Borana hit them hard by using their limited resources and fire power at their disposal. This time, too, Borana not only hit them hard but exacted a humiliating defeat on them. Borana fighters chased the Garri out of Borana country in Ethiopia and forced them to flee to Kenya.

Under the encouragement and protection of Jatani, while he was the governor of Borana region, some Garri businessmen have acquired wealth and influence. These men alleged that the Garri's humiliating defeat at the hands of the Borana was due to the role Jatani played from his refuge. According to them, Jatani organised the Borana people against them while in the bush. To avenge the humiliation, they apparently went so far as influencing the top TPLF government officials in the area to organise a murder squad to eliminate Jatani. According to a rumour, these businessmen pledged considerable funds to partially cover the cost incurred in the mission to assassinate Jatani. The plotters recruited an assassin squad that was dispatched to Nairobi to murder Jatani Ali in cold blood. It is likely that several enemies of Jatani and of Borana people collaborated in the assassination plot, with an active encouragement and support from Ethiopia's state security agencies and its embassy in Nairobi.

Jatani had many friends and admirers. His murder was a shock to all who knew him in whatever context, in the country as well as outside the country. His murder was reported in the Kenyan media and in leading international broadcasting services such as the BBC of London. In its broadcast two days after the assassination, the BBC reported, 'A prominent Oromo leader was killed in a hotel in Nairobi Kenya.' Pertaining to his assassination, *Gaffat Ethiopia*, a newspaper published in the United States by Ethiopians in diaspora, issued two articles in Amharic in August 1992. The first one was written by Asefa Chabo, the victim's long-time close friend. The second was a piece by the reporter of that paper. Asefa's article dealt with what he knew about Jatani and the other was about a mass demonstration organised against the Ethiopian Embassy in Nairobi by Ethiopian refugees in Kenya and other Kenyan sympathisers. *Seife Nebalbal*, a private weekly local newspaper in Addis Ababa (now out of print due to a ban by the ruling regime), expressed deep sadness about Jatani's assassination in an article written in Amharic. The English version of the materials printed in *Gafat* and *Seife Nebalbal* are presented below in chapter 12.

12: Gallant When Alive, Awesome in Death

In this chapter will be discussed the various media reports of Jatani's assassination.

Asefa Chabo's article

Homage to Jatani Ali

by Asefa Chabo

I heard from the broadcast of Ethiopian Democrats' Radio station in Washington DC that a great Ethiopian citizen was murdered in Nairobi, Kenya on July 2, 1992 in a hotel where he was staying, and that the murderers and their collaborators were partially apprehended. I, then, confirmed the authenticity of the event from many of my own sources. The information that arrived soon and thereafter attested that the murderers or their associates had strong relationships with the Ethiopian Embassy in Nairobi. Till this print comes out, I have no information as to what actions the Kenya Government took against the crime. Subsequently, I have strong faith in the Kenya Government and police that they'll take appropriate action and make the matter clear to the Ethiopian public. I have no doubt about the similarity of expectations, to that of mine, of the Ethiopians I know, here, in the USA, Canada, Europe and Ethiopia. If that does not happen, the Kenya authority has a moral obligation, at the very least, to establish who killed him and why that great Ethiopian was killed.

The victim referred to above whose life was cut short in Nairobi, Kenya was Jatani Ali. He was also called Mebatsion Ali. Jatani or Mebatsion was around 50 years in age. He was one of the few Ethiopians whom I have known for the last 30 years and whom I highly respect. I think those of us who are around 50 years in age now, could recall the popularity of inter-school competitions in different events of athletics and games years back during our schooling period. In my opinion the popularity of inter-school sports was partially enhanced by the limited number of Borana boys who came from the province for education and got enrolled in different schools in Addis Ababa. Jatani was one of them. He was not, however, known for sportsmanship. He was known in the school for disciplined behaviour and seasoned thinking. He had demonstrated in practice that he could get along harmoniously with any human being.

Jatani Ali completed secondary level education in General Wingate Secondary School and joined Aba Dina police cadet from where he graduated as first lieutenant in rank. He was in the 8th batch in the cadet training course. Then, he was admitted to the School of Social Work in the former Haile Selassie I University in Addis Ababa from where he graduated with a Bachelor of Arts degree.[37] In his police career he attained the rank of Major. Starting from 1976 he joined the Ministry of the Interior as an administrator in different capacities. First he was the administrator of Arero province in Sidamo region, Deputy General Administrator in Illubabor and Sidamo regions, and at last up to a year ago he was the administrator of Borana region for a few years, where he was born.

Last year in May 1991, when the Tigray People's Liberation Front entered Addis Ababa, Mebatsion abandoned the administrative position. As is known, Borana and Kenya are immediate neighbours; besides, the Borana community inhabits a good part of northern Kenya. It can be understood that Jatani had no difficulty to freely move around up and down both in Ethiopia and Kenya in the areas inhabited by his people. He was contemplating as to how he would liberate his people from the quagmire they were in.

Soon after they entered Addis Ababa, the TPLF came to know who Jatani was and sent a messenger to persuade him to surrender on the promise that they would not lock him up as they had with other Dergue officials they rounded up in the country. When this attempt failed, they came up with a fresh promise: that was to restore him to the administrative position in Borana as he had been during the Dergue period. This did not work either. Through different means they discovered that we were intimate friends. With this information, the TPLF high officials came to me [Asefa] and asked me to persuade him to surrender. I denied any knowledge of him. They insisted that we were intimate friends. I told them our friendship could not serve the purpose they were looking to me for.

I presume, the message they asked me to deliver was the same with the one they attempted previously with others. The contents were, "You oppressed children of southern Ethiopia whom their people love were downtrodden, insulted, and subjected to all sorts of humiliation by chauvinists…" In these there were some elements of truth. The main point was, in my opinion, the TPLF which claimed to be "a new liberator" took the contents of the message from textbooks they prepared for school

---

[37] Correction: He was forced to discontinue from his third year before fulfilling requirements for a degree because of the *Derg*'s LDC.

children in southern Ethiopia. The struggle of the southern Ethiopian people, as I look at it, is not to prepare themselves for serving a new master who came with dubious promises. According to my perception, the whole idea of the struggle has been for creating conditions in Ethiopia whereby human rights are respected and the citizens live in peace with equal status and respect for each other. There can be individuals who might have been deceived by crafty policy of the regime that has been practising divide and rule in the country. I think the individuals who have become promoters of this deceptive policy by being the instrument of the regime will one day be accountable for their deeds to the Ethiopian people. If this won't happen, let common sense prick them, if they have conscience at all.[38]

Mebatsion was one of the proud southern Ethiopians who won't cooperate with such petty crafty deals. He was a gallant and respectful Borana son. I can recall what we had discussed when we met for the last time. "Asefa, you and I know this game; we cannot understand even by learning."

For instance, last year, a considerable number of Eritrean citizens opposed President Isayas Afeworki. Under the pretext of their not supporting the President or competing for the position, they were persecuted and rounded up; nobody knows where they are sheltered now nor their fate. Turning to Ethiopia, it is reported that a considerable number of members of Ethiopian Popular Liberation Party among whom are the sick and wounded, nursing mothers and physically disabled persons, were found rounded up by TPLF and imprisoned at Azezo, Gondar. Probably, it is better to say nobody knows their whereabouts. According to the report of African Watch, the human rights protection organisation, Sudan, Eritrea and TPLF made a tripartite agreement in which they jointly persecute their respective oppositions. Accordingly, the Sudan regime handed over exiled persons from the two countries that sheltered in its territory to the respective governments; in return Ethiopia and Eritrea supported the Sudan Government against the SPLA. Jatani Ali was murdered by these 'infamous' ventures.

The Ministry of the Interior of the Ethiopian Transitional Government is fully

---

[38] I had a similar experience with reference to persuading Jatani to surrender to TPLF. Lieutenant Tekle Amdebran, an Eritrean, was an intimate friend of Jatani. He introduced me to the late Kinfe Gebre Medhin who held the position of Minister of the Interior. The official told me that they had assessed Jatani's character and behaviour from different angles and came to a conclusion that TPLF had nothing against him and that he could live in peace with us if he surrendered. He went on to say, 'as he was a high govern-ment official of the past regime, if individual citizens came up with private cases against him, we cannot protect him.'

under the control of the Eritreans who conducted affairs behind the curtain. But now the Oromo Liberation Front has signed an agreement that they would openly conduct business. Of all treasons committed against Ethiopia by the joint venture so far, this will remain the most disgraceful act for years to come.

Why did the TPLF murder Jatani now? I do not have all the answers. However, I'll try to express those which appear obvious. Jatani worked with the Dergue for 17 years and gained honour and universal respect from the public wherever he went. He was courteous by nature. Added to this inherent attribute, police training and university education made him a more seasoned person. He was a born leader. He was among the few Ethiopians who disapproved from a distance the dubious behaviour of the TPLF and sought a means of redeeming the country from the regime. He was the son of Borana who had a love of people and came from a strategic geographic area. He was a proud Borana son who did not believe in nor accept narrow minded regionalism and divisions into villages. Jatani saw no contradiction between being a Borana and an Ethiopian. Since they could not suppress this inborn spirit, they set out to eliminate him. Yesterday, nobody ever thought a regime worse than the Dergue would ever come. In the 17 years of reign the Dergue did not persecute and murder a person who was in exile. Once an attempt was made in Berlin, Germany, but the outcome was futile.

Now a new disaster and adversity came. Ethiopians could not live in Ethiopia. Those who are even out of the country are being told that they cannot continue to exist in exile. People do not have a guarantee of their life. Ethiopians are experiencing a different kind of tragic treatment. Many were killed. Others ran away into exile. Families of those who remained behind dispersed. Many did not even have the time and opportunity to establish families. Jatani was one of them. There are those who believe that, by killing an individual, the causes he stands for and objectives he cherished can be killed. World history clearly shows that this is impossible. I think this assumption is confirmed by what a scholar once said. "What we learn from history is that we learn nothing from history." The objective has been to deprive Ethiopia of leaders who show concern for its welfare of the people. This is the first bullet. I can see all of us are targets.

Privately, I express deep sorrow at losing a best friend. But Ethiopia and Borana lost a gallant son. On behalf of myself and the Popular Unity Party of which I am the leader, I use this occasion to send a condolence to his family with my deepest sorrow.

From the information I have access to up to now, my brother Jatani Ali was murdered by the TPLF's bullet. The TPLF is in charge of the current Ethiopian Government. They legitimised their authority through the so-called election that even the observers they hand-picked condemned for fraudulence. This cracked open to light their real nature that they attempt to cover up. Even before, though they pretend to conceal it, their real character has been an open secret. Persecuting a person in exile and murdering is state terrorism. The countries which used to do this are now abandoning the practice. Ours is one of the newcomers to an old game. They have close relationships with those who used to perform such odious treachery.

The 'Seife Nebalbal' article

Seife Nebalbal was a private weekly newspaper published in the Amharic language in Addis Ababa. The paper is now out of print due to a government ban. It published an article on 7 July 2005 under the title, "Who Was Jatani Ali?" The paper discussed Jatani's life including his year and place of birth, his family, his schooling, his training in police academy; his services in the police force, his life as a university student in Addis Ababa, his public service work in the LDC and later as a provincial and regional governor through the Ministry of the Interior. It described Jatani's vision for improving the living conditions of marginalised and neglected communities and listed what he had accomplished in community development areas. The reporter highlighted Jatani's stature as a tireless campaigner in raising awareness around dire social, economic and political problems affecting the communities and in embarking on community-centred campaigns to improve the living conditions of the people he served. It went on to point out how, under Jatani's rule, Arero Province escaped the excesses of Derg's "red terror" campaign that resulted in bloody urban warfare that killed many young opponents of the regime in other parts of the country. In addition, the paper noted how Ethiopia's then President and dictator (Mengistu) ordered all governors in the country to either jail or eliminate any persons of Eritrean or Tigre origin, whom they suspect of being agents or supporters of rebel groups in rebellious provinces in northern Ethiopia. The paper said that in Borana region, where Jatani was the governor, no person of Eritrean or Tigre origin was targeted. It added that all persons of Eritrean or Tigre origin in Borana country lived and managed their affairs peacefully without any fear of persecution from

Jatani's administration. The paper expressed the irony how Jatani lost his life in the hands of the very people (ethnic Tigre assassins) whom he had protected against any unlawful and unjust treatment by government agents.

The writer of the article in *Seife Nebelbal* pondered why Jatani Ali was assassinated. Who carried out the crime? What would the verdict on the perpetrators be? He indicated that these and related other questions that might be raised by all concerned required satisfactory answers. He lamented how he was not in a condition to provide any answers at the time the article went to the press. The paper indicated that opinions expressed and information being spread in the country and around the world up to now, held the TPLF leaders responsible for Jatani's assassination.

Reports of the Nairobi demonstrations protesting Jatani's assassination

The Standard, a Kenyan daily newspaper, reported on Jatani's assassination in its 3 July 1992 issue. It said that Major Jatani Ali, soon after he departed with the persons who came to visit him in the evening of 2 July 1992 at Nairobi's Ngara Hotel where he was staying, four persons came to his room and shot him dead.[39] The paper said that among the four, one was immediately apprehended on the spot and the other three escaped. The people who were around at the time were temporarily detained for questioning about the crime. While Jatani's relatives, friends and other concerned individuals presented the case to a police station at the Nairobi Park, his relatives reported to *The Standard* that Major Jatani Ali was murdered because of a difference in political views with the Ethiopian Transitional Government. Pertaining to the event, thousands of Ethiopians in Nairobi, spearheaded by Kenya Borana, carried out a huge protest

---

[39]   Correction: The confirmed number of the murder squad was three, not four.

demonstration. Among the placards they carried were: "Jatani Ali's poured blood cannot be left in vain"; "We will take measures on the EPRDF (Ethiopian) Ambassador and the employees in the Embassy;" and "Measures taken on ethnic cleansing will be reciprocated in a similar manner."

According to a report for the Amharic *Gaffat Ethiopia* newspaper sent from Nairobi, as the result of Jatani's assassination, tensions and protests were escalated: attempts were made to damage motor vehicles and a policeman was seriously injured.

It was surprising to note why a number of key mass media agencies kept silent on the assassination and the heated mass protest marches that took place in front of their eyes in Nairobi, except the EPLP reporter, who explained in detail the conditions surrounding the event and the ensuing unrest a day after the assassination. Intentional or otherwise, there seemed to be blackout of information on Jatani's assassination by international mass media outlets until a reporter from *Gaffat Ethiopia* newspaper went to them and expressed his disappointment about their behaviour in failing to report on an event with enormous magnitude and significance to people in the region. Starting from 8 July 1992, many news media outlets started to report on the assassination by providing different perspectives on the event itself, as well as the unrest that followed.

The reporter added that, 'in any case Jatani Ali has passed away. The action is a case in international terrorism. Whom does an assassination and abduction benefit? In what direction would this kind of action lead the country (Ethiopia) in the future?'

The Ethiopian Ambassador in Kenya gave a press conference in which he expressed conflicting statements such as, 'How can we kill a Borana person? Another entity or agency could be responsible.' It was reported that the three escaped assassins were sheltered in the Ethiopian Embassy and later smuggled out to Ethiopia.

Other media reports

The following are examples from different sources.

The Ethiopian Review is a monthly magazine published in the United States. On 12 July 1992, it printed an article on page 9 with a heading "Murder of Former Governor". The paper went on to say that thousands of Oromo refugees from Ethiopia, who were living in Kenya, demonstrated in front of the Ethiopian Embassy in Nairobi, denouncing Jatani Ali's assassination and exposing the Ethiopian Government's responsibility for the crime. The demonstrators demanded that the two suspects sheltering in the Embassy be brought to justice. The Ethiopian Ambassador to Kenya, Ato Getachew Zerihun, came out and told the demonstrators that the Ethiopian Government had no hand in the crime.

The Indian Ocean Newsletter printed an article on 25 July 1992 with a headline, "Opponent Killed in Nairobi". In the article the paper pointed out that Ato Hailu Kindu (nicknamed 'Gemachu') was apprehended on the spot while his compatriots Ato Zinabu Kidane and Ato Tigist Mebratu[7] escaped from the site of the murder and took shelter in the Ethiopian Embassy. To get them released under a false cover-up or pretext, the Ethiopian Government declared that the two were technicians of the government-owned Ethiopian Airlines who had come to Nairobi to maintain or repair two Antonov 22 planes which had been grounded over a month at Nairobi Airport.

Radio EDAK used to transmit a program titled "Patriotic Voice of Ethiopia" on Wednesdays and Sundays. On one of its Sunday evening transmissions in December 1992, it reported that over two thousand Ethiopian refugees in Kenya made a peaceful demonstration in Nairobi condemning the assassination of Jatani Ali. It indicated how, even before Jatani left his homeland into exile in Kenya, the people in Borana region had witnessed several attempts made by TPLF secret agents to murder him. They used different means to carry out the task and this ranged from a country-wide search for him by its army and security forces to the hiring of assassins.

Even after Jatani was assassinated, the actions TPLF took in the region confirmed the fact that they had direct hand in the assassination. For example, TPLF agents harassed, severely beat and even killed several Borana persons in detention on suspicion of supporting Jatani and to force certain individuals to show them where Jatani's papers and personal belongings were hidden.

There was evidence that the TPLF used wealthy businessmen of a certain ethnic group and gangsters on the street for the assassination of Jatani Ali.

Jatani was a renowned and influential person in localities in which he had worked and among a great deal of Ethiopian people. His death was not even mentioned in support or against in any mass media in Ethiopia, whose regime at the time claimed to have restored freedom of press in the country. These conditions directly confirmed that the Ethiopian Government not only had direct hand in the assassination of Jatani but also paid special attention to it in a bid to manage its ramifications.

In conclusion, there was no doubt that Jatani Ali was assassinated by gunmen employed by the TPLF. He was a great man who loved his people and was reciprocally loved by them. He put aside his personal comforts, material benefits and interests to advance the welfare, development and progress of the community at large. He was a man of history whom generations to come will remember. Even though his life was cut short by TPLF bullets, the objectives for which he skilfully and tirelessly worked for years won't be. His efforts to improve the lives of marginalised communities will be taken up by many others to whom he was a beacon of hope and a role model. We are sure that out of this sad news would emerge a renewed and redoubled determination of his followers to speed up the implementation of his vision. We believe that the best way to avenge his death is by following his example in striving to educate ourselves in order to uplift our people from the quagmires of poverty, ignorance, injustice, hopelessness and despair. We hope that this state of affairs will arouse the determination of his followers and speed up the demise of his assassins.

13: The Funeral and Attempting a Reburial

The funeral

After the assassination of Jatani Ali the concern of close friends and admirers in Ethiopia was to find an appropriate place where his body would rest. Very close friends thought of temporarily laying down the body either at Marsabit or Moyale, with the intention of exhuming the body and reburying it in his homeland with honour, at an opportune time. One of the justifications for this option was that both localities are predominately inhabited by Borana. The perceived proposal at the Ethiopian end was communicated to those who were handling the matter from Kenya. They later agreed and implemented the option as intended.

A few days after the sad event, his funeral took place at Marsabit in the presence of thousands of Ethiopian refugees in Kenya, the Borana community in northern Kenya, friends of Borana and other admirers of Jatani from southern Ethiopia. The body was put in a temporary grave built with concrete walls with an iron-bar fence around it. The arrangement was such that it could easily be exhumed for permanent reburial in his homeland soil of Borana country in southern Ethiopia at some point in the future.

Attempting reburial

Jatani made a lasting positive impression on all those he met and worked with. As I stated earlier, he left both tangible and intangible legacies by which generations of Borana would remember him. He worked hard to fight harmful cultural practices that hindered the social development of communities. His campaigns at raising community awareness towards key social and economic problems were meant to garner community participation in development projects. As the result, a great deal of vital infrastructure had been built under his guidance with the community's active participation. These ranged from the building of students' hostels catering for students coming from marginalised pastoralist communities to the expansion of primary and secondary school facilities all over Borana country. From the date of his assassination and for the following 15 years, his name was hardly mentioned by the people who loved and honoured him in the land he so devotedly served. Are the Borana people so ungrateful? Could it be that people were so shocked by the news of his assassination and found it traumatic to mention his name in public? Maybe their decision not to utter his name was associated with a fear of giving the swarms of regime informers amid them an excuse to persecute them. The reason for silence could owe to any one of these reasons or a combination of them. The people he had served and even his enemies could not produce any evidence of Jatani's improper or illegal actions that would have justified his cold-blooded assassination. Many people in the region alleged that the government had a hand in the murder of Jatani. Under such conditions, one can see why many people opted not to mention Jatani's name in public or, in the presence of government officials, not to draw unwanted attention from the regime's many informers. Probably, many reasoned that Ethiopia remains the same old brutal place despite all the regime changes it has had, and the safest thing to do was to shut one's mouth and mourn Jatani's passing privately.

Towards the last quarter of 2007, news was spread that Jatani's body would come home for reburial. In the area where even mentioning his name was considered taboo, the news of his remains coming home for reburial became household talk. Who had initiated the idea? It was not clear. But the incumbent *Abba Gada*, Liban Jaldessa, claimed to have come up with the idea and got government approval to carry it out. In December 2007, Abdulqadir Abdi, the then governor of Borana Zone, called a meeting at which the reburial of Jatani's remains was discussed.

District governors and Borana community leaders took part in that meeting.

The gathering arrived at the following decisions. A committee would be formed to coordinate the whole issue of reburying Jatani's remains with proper dignity. The committee would be tasked with the erection of a statue that would represent Jatani's magnanimity on a permanent tomb at Yaballo. To cover the cost of reburial and to build a statue, the committee would raise Birr 1,000,000 from the people, before the end of February 2008. The cost incurred would be shared between the people living in all concerned districts, by taking into account their resources or ability to pay. The district governors were strictly instructed to facilitate the collection of the funds in their jurisdictions and to hand in their share to the committee before the agreed-upon deadline. Reportedly, more than Birr 1,000,000 was collected from the Borana community in the Zone and the committee embarked on the responsibility of repatriating the remains of Jatani and erecting the statue. A place at the entrance of Yaballo town was selected as an ideal and permanent resting place for Jatani.

Members of the elected committee:

1. Jatani Tadhi   Chairperson
2. Liban Bute   Signatory of cheques
3. Abdi Wario   Signatory of cheques
4. Guyo Halakhe   Coordinator of awareness committee
5. Galglo Jarso   Secretary of treasury
6. Dulacha Jilo   Finance committee
7. Eliyas Galgalo   Coordinator of committee
8. Galgalo Dida   Member
9. Golicha Galgalo   "
10. Jaldesa Halakhe   "
11. Qararsa Godana   "
12. Qalcha Galgalo   "

Before the arrival of the body, the committee assembled a figure that was enshrouded with a plastic material at the chosen site, ostensibly to represent the statue they were to erect. It remained there for some years without being exposed to the public. The Borana people eagerly awaited the homecoming of Jatani's remains and its formal reburial. However, nobody bothered to inform them of either the amount of money raised by the community up to that point or what had been accomplished with it. Furthermore, the committee did not report to the people any obstacle that might have prevented it from carrying out the responsibility put on its shoulders. There was no audit carried out by any agency in order to ensure a transparent and proper use of the assets collected.

Utukan Malo was one of the Gujii elders and community leaders whom I interviewed towards this biography. After the formal interview was over, the interviewee expressed his concern about the fund-raising scheme meant to repatriate Jatani's remains for reburial. He stated that he was not comfortable with the manner in which the then Borana Zone Governor, Abdulqadir Abdi, went about it in 2007. Utukan recalled how the governor called a meeting of Borana people at Yaballo, where the main item on the agenda was to raise money for bringing home Jatani's body. Utukan lamented how members of the brotherly Gujii and Gabra communities were not invited to the meeting nor were they asked if they wished to take part in this scheme. He said that Jatani governed all communities in the Borana Administrative Region (since renamed the Borana Zone) in a fair manner. He said that Jatani's assassination in a foreign land was a sad event for all of these communities, not just the Borana. He added that many in the Gujii and Gabra communities would also like to see his body brought home and reburied with dignity and in the land he so devotedly served. Utukan said that he could not figure out why the governor summarily excluded the two communities from such a symbolically and historically significant scheme. He finished his remarks by expressing his deep disappointment with the conduct of the whole affair.

An attempt at auditing

Gujii elders were not the only ones expressing their frustration with the way the delicate issue of repatriating Jatani Ali's remains had been mishandled. Elders and concerned individuals have tried to get a tab on the raised funds as well as get some answers as to why the project failed to achieve any of its intended aims. The matter was viewed as part of a moral decadence affecting the Borana community at large and the issue has been raised as part of a series of gatherings to tackle many of these social and economic problems affecting the Borana.

In recent times, increased consumption of addictive substances such as alcohol and the chewing of *chat* leaves have had serious detrimental effects on family and community life of the Borana. Community leaders are determined to address this crippling moral decadence through indigenous norms and institutions of governance. As an expression of this, the incumbent Borana's supreme indigenous leader, *Abba Gada* Guyo Goba, convened a community meeting at Alonna in Arero District from 7-10 June 2013. The gathering was made up of three main sub-groups comprising: traditional leaders of clans; representative of elders from all lowland districts including Liban; and educated groups represent-ed by employees in government and civil agencies such as NGOs. The composition of the gathering was deliberate; each sub-group had distinc-tive social and moral issues to tackle according to the social norms each was more comfortable with. Members of each group were allowed to speak their mind to identify the root causes of the moral corruption that affected them and the community at large. On that basis, it was hoped that group-appropriate and -targeted solutions would emerge out of the sessions. Another important issue was to determine why many Borana have abandoned known traditional social norms and embraced damaging alien vices and conducts. The participants agreed not to waste a great deal of time on what has gone wrong with any group or individuals in the past and instead chart corrective measures to move forward as a community. Accordingly, they agreed that chewing *chat* and excessive consumption of alcohol was un-Borana and such practices were doing enormous damage to family and community health. On that basis, they unanimously agreed to ban the selling of *chat* and alcoholic beverages in Borana villages. The meeting participants also agreed to work hard to eradicate the damaging vices of chewing *chat* and imbibing alcoholic drinks by any self-respecting Borana. They went even further and imposed monetary penalties and public-shaming measures on Borana persons that sell or consume addictive substances. To enforce the fulfilment of the covenant, they formed committees that would keep a watchful eye on those who violated the agreed-upon norms of behaviour at zone, district and *kebele* levels. They agreed on a penalty of Birr 500 for those caught consuming or selling addictive substances. The fines (penalty money) would be used by the committee in educational public campaigns against damaging vices or in enforcing the new rules. As a follow-up to the fruitful gathering at Alonna and to assess progress made, the gathering agreed to meet up again at El Waye in Yaballo district in two months' time.

The conveners of the meeting felt that there has been a serious break-down in the lines of communication between various sub-groups in society and between these and the government. They agreed to speak up against any ill-feeling that lurked in the hearts of people and pitted one section of the community against another. It was felt that the lack of transparency in managing public finances was a dark spot in the moral compass of those leading the community. One such blemish was the saga surrounding the committee tasked with the repatriation and reburial of Jatani Ali's body.

The entity neither reported on the failure of the scheme nor on any progress made in erecting a statue for Jatani with money raised from Borana people. This was all the more worrisome as there have been rumours doing the rounds accusing the committee of embezzling the funds intended for the repatriation of Jatani's body. Though there has been ongoing grumblings by the general public against the committee for some time, the committee made no serious attempt to audit the funds or explain why the project has stalled. This delicate and prickly issue in the hearts of the people was also raised at the gathering at Alonna. Some members of the committee tasked with the repatriation of Jatani's body were in the meeting. They indicated that a proper audit would be carried out to clear them from any blame of embezzlement.

Five years after a committee was formed to coordinate the repatriation of the body and build a statue, it has nothing tangible to show for its efforts. In fact, a dark cloud of doubts hangs over the whereabouts of the funds contributed by Borana pastoralists and friends of the Borana towards the project. Those gathered at Alonna elected an audit committee of six members. The mandate of the committee was to carry out the audit and report its findings to a forthcoming meeting scheduled to take place at El Waye, near Yaballo. The audit committee members were:

1. Halakhe Dida   Coordinator of the Committee
2. Boru Tunne
3. Galgalo Arero
4. Dabano Guyo
5. Jatani Godana
6. Galma Boru

The El Waye meeting was held from 17-19 August 2013. Halakhe Dida, the coordinator of the committee, reported the following audit findings to the assembled.

According to that report, there were two critical issues in the working procedure of the committee and its propriety. In the first place, the committee was made up of 12 members but only four of these actively participated in its workings. These were Jatani Tadhi, Liban Bute, Guyo Halakhe and Eliyas Galgalo. Secondly, they did not show any formal business plan on how the money would be spent nor kept proper or clear records of expenditure. The way they carried out the tasks was outside known or acceptable norms of handling public money. Accordingly, the audit committee found it very difficult to make sense of the state of the finances. It made no progress in its effort to follow the trail of spent monies. In frustration, the audit committee laid down its own working procedures. These were to:

- Check the accounting records of the coordinating committee and other related documents in the conditions they were presented to it;
- Interview the chairperson and other members of the committee who actively participated in the project; and,
- Visit the site for erecting the statue and examine the progress.

As mentioned earlier, at the first meeting in December 2007, the community agreed to contribute Birr 1,000,000 towards the project of repatriating Jatani Ali's body and to build a statue that reflected his stature. All districts were given a quota of funds to be collected from Borana people. However, according to rumours, the amount obtained was in fact a lot more than the agreed total. But the audit committee could not find any record or receipts to indicate the exact amount each of the districts contributed. The understanding was that whatever was collected would be deposited into an account specifically opened for the project at Yaballo branch of the CBE. However, the amount the audit committee found deposited in the Bank was Birr 813,545. The audit committee learnt that that additional Birr 70,000 was planned to be raised on top of the total but only Birr 65,000 was reportedly collected. This raised the total amount deposited in the Bank to Birr 878,545.

The next step was to find out what the money was spent on and locate the records of these expenditures. The committee found no proper records of expenditure or receipts. All they found were haphazardly and casually made lists of expenditures on loose pieces of paper. In the records presented to it, the committee learnt about items purchased with no receipts to show for them and building works carried out with no recording of the name of builders or signatures of those to whom money was paid. The major cost items listed were matters related to: the carving and erection of the statue; *per diem* and transport costs for travelling back and forth to Addis Ababa; the travel costs within the districts of Borana; the travel costs to Kenya; the costs involved in organising meetings; the fees paid to individuals hired for work in Ethiopia and Kenya; and the cost of a prepaid plane ticket for the anticipated transport of Jatani's remains back home. Some of the listed expenditure included:

- The statue: carving, infrastructure (fencing, lights and plumbing) and the guard's wage: Birr 357,641; for workers who erected it: Birr 3,500;
- The processing costs of the remains coming back home: Birr 286,689;
- Transport and *per diem* to various places: Birr 143,531;
- Meetings at Yaballo and Moyale: Birr 72,774.50;
- Fees for individuals who facilitated films, songs and other matters: Birr 3,700;
- The committee in charge of the project signed a contractual agreement with an individual who carved the statue, to pay him Birr 346,862 for his services. The task was said to have been completed according to the stated agreement. The audit committee however found no evidence of the agreed-upon payment to the carver of the statue, nor a signature or receipt from him of having received the payment;
- Birr 120,000 was directly paid to a certain individual named Jarso Wario without passing through any proper channel of payment, nor was the reason for such hefty payment given; and,
- Birr 70,000 was deposited in a Kenyan bank for the anticipated cost of transporting or repatriating Jatani's remains back home.

As per the working procedures they laid down for themselves, the members of the audit committee reported that they have interviewed the persons who were actively involved in the implementation of the scheme and examined the documents and financial records presented to them.

But rather intriguingly, they declared that they did not visit the site of the statue, located in the same town where members of the committee resided.

The problems the audited committee tasked with the repatriation of the body and statue building reported to have faced in executing the task were:

- Going back and forth to Addis Ababa and Nagelle, looking for recorded speeches of Jatani in videos;
- The lack of support from the Governor of Borana Zone who had started the whole scheme made their efforts become arduous;
- The Kenya Government did not allow the body to return home; and,
- They faced unspecified political problems in completing the task.

In conclusion, the audit committee reported that:

- They found no authentic financial records and evidence of income and expenditures; and,
- They recommended an immediate suspension of all activities in relation to the project for the good of the public who contributed money.

The chairperson of the committee in charge of the project tasked for the repatriation of Jatani's body protested against the damning charges. He claimed that the auditors did not make a fair assessment of their efforts and failed to properly report what has actually been accomplished. The auditors rebuffed that counter-claim and reported that their assessment was objective and based on documents they were shown and on what they had been verbally informed. The chairperson of the committee insisted that key documents that would clear the committee from these charges were in the possession of the secretary of the committee, who was away at the time. Amid such confusion, those at a community gathering to hear the findings of the audit committee agreed to postpone the date for making any decisions. They felt that they needed to wait for the return of the secretary who was allegedly in possession of vital evidence. According to the auditors, the posture adopted by the coordinating committee for the repatriation of Jatani Ali's body was nothing more than a time-wasting exercise. They indicated that nothing that the secretary might produce would substantially change their damning findings on the improper use of funds meant for such a worthy project.

The unfinished statue of Jatani Ali at the entrance of Yaballo Town.
The statue is nothing more than a pitiful-looking plastic dummy meant to be a replica
of a bronze statute promised to the public. The figure is covered with plastic materials
covered in dust and gradually being worn down under the elements.
[Photos by Tadhi Liban]

14: Tributes to Jatani Ali

Borana at home, those in diaspora and friends of the Borana people touched by the assassination of Jatani have used the occasion to ponder on his legacies. Borana living in diaspora have been observing the anniversary of Jatani's assassination every year on 2 July. Below are some tributes presented at the 5th, 7th and 10th anniversary of Jatani's assassination by Borana living abroad.

The 5TH anniversary of Jatani's assassination

To commemorate the 5th anniversary of Jatani's assassination, Borana living in diaspora made a roll call of famous Borana and Oromo heroes noted for their gallantry in the past. This was done to add Jatani to the roll as an heroic figure of these communities in modern times. The sacrifices and gallantry of heroic figures of the past from Borana, Gujii, Arsi and North Kenyan Oromo communities were used as a fitting backdrop to honour Jatani's lifetime achievements in advancing the cause of these communities. The following is the full text of their tribute.[40]

The Oromo Nation has produced several great men and women, who gave their lives on the front lines of the struggle for freedom. These heroes are not only honoured and remembered, but will continue to live in the minds and hearts of the people forever. The historic mark and symbol of freedom they left behind is always there. The great jobs done by these heroes can't be found in any books, but in our live memories.

Many of the martyrs we mourn and remember fought in defence of our human dignity, land, water and its attributes. These great men and women kept the life of Borana Oromo possible by their gallant death. The respect we enjoy among the

---

[40] In the tributes, the spelling used to write Jatani Ali's name or the name of other persons was not consistent. They are included here as they appeared in the brochures prepared for the commemoration(s).

*family of other tribes is therefore, the direct result of their big deeds. The Borana people had great political leaders like Halake Guyo Tuye, Anna Guyo, Galgalo Gedo, Dima Kula Korolle, etc. and leaders of modern politics such as Mr. Dabasso Wabera, Haji Galma Dido, Godana Tuny Kano, **Major Jatanni Alli**, Waqo Guttu Usu, and others, the exemplary deeds of whom will never will fade away both from our history and life memories.*

These national heroes did not get the recognition they deserved indeed, only due to the prevailing colonial legacies as history will assure it. It is, therefore, up to us to honour our heroes and remember our dead, and in so doing continue in the way of struggle they paved until freedom.

As a part of this effort, we, the Borana Oromo in exile have decided to com- memorate our heroes on the third [sic] of July from now on, and urge all our compatriots and country men to do the same! July was selected, because it is the day we lost our great leader and father of our beloved land and people, Major Jatani Alli, who was assassinated by the EPRDF thugs in Nairobi as we all know. Additionally, this day shall be honoured as a national mourning day to remember all those, who were sacrificed on the battle field. Needless to say, this day is not a day to drink and dance, but a day of silence and mourning as Abba Gada Madha did when his comrade Dido Gawalle was killed, until our independence when we are able to celebrate and honour them with military parades. The true Dido Gawalle of today's Borana was and is evidently Major Jatani Alli Tandhu'u. He was a hero, he was a man of great wisdom, he was kind and a humanist. In short, he was the best of the best.

On the other hand, to resort the short message we would like to convey on this horrific 5th memorial occasion of Jatani's assassination to all Oromo in general, and to the Borana, Gujii and Arsi whom he served, in particular is:

- *Promote and work for unity, to the best of your ability, which is the only source of strength to overcome the enemy!*

- *Mourning Jatani's assassination means pulling all he started to the designed goal in all walks of life, as Akko Haamanoye said, "…sob hayeet, sobaat hayeet…" We say, "waan Jattannin, Yayabe fulaan gaha hayeet!!!"*

- *Mourning Jatani's death by assassination should also mean not to forget and forgive his killers, above all if we don't abandon the cause for which Jatani was shot, it is an inseparable part of the essential and historic national task of lib- erating Oromiya and of ensuring that his killers are brought to justice. Until then, no deal, no peace, with the merciless enemy, who invaded Oromiya, killed Jatani and fed the body of the murdered Abba Gada Boru Guyo, to wild scav- engers on a land he once led.*

- *Mourning Jatani's assassination should finally mean, honouring all the heroes like Abba Gada Boru Guyo, Daabasso Wabara, Haji Galma Dido, Major Salessa Jallo Boqo, Boru Liban Dinne, Saar Jarso Molu, Tary Jarso Molu, Hussein Sora, Liban Dabasicha Dhado, Arero Galgalo Kosy, Abgudo Tary, Badhane Gashu Gadessa, Gamede Elema his father Mr. Elema, Bekele Elema, Galchu Chule, Major Anna Guyo, Nuura Guyo Ramata, Golicha Huqa. Boru Dido, Dido Boru, Abraham Duba, Djirom Dida, Dub Dawiti Sore, Dub Dhane Korolle, Woqo Lugo, Jarsso Waqo, etc.*
  The cause of these heroes will live in the souls of all Oromos. Their death is a driving force of the ongoing struggle for the liberation of Oromiya.
  LONG LIVE THE OROMO STRUGGLE
  KAAYO QAMNA!!

The 7th anniversary of Jatani's assassination

For the commemoration of 7th anniversary of Jatani Ali's assassination, Hussein Huqa Jillo contributed the following article for the occasion.

JATANI ALI'S VISION FOR HIS PEOPLE

Jatani's Vision was to see a United Boran. He denied himself all the luxuries of the world in order to concentrate and dedicate his efforts towards the liberation of his people socially, politically economically.

During the time he was the governor of Borana Province in Ethiopia under the government of Mengistu, he did all he could to ensure that his people are at par with the rest of the world. He was a bitter man all through his life time not because of his personal problems, but because of his desperate society whose rights were violated by all the successive regimes in Ethiopia. His people were denied the right to self-determination, rights to health facilities, Education, the right to their social activities, the right to their religious beliefs and to economic liberation.

As a major step to Economic Liberation for Oromos he urged them to fight hunger by advising them to engage in farming activities besides raising cattle. He created good market facilities for livestock in Ethiopia and advised the Oromos to sell their animals and engage in business activities.

In order to strengthen his people, he encouraged them to enrol their kids in learning institutions. All along, Oromos were denied the rights to education. Addressing Boranas at Yaballo, he said, "enemies of Education are enemies of freedom, a society founded on knowledge is more viable and better equipped to survive than those built on fear, intimidation and ignorance. Oppressors use ignorance and bullets to intimidate and rule and we must overcome this."

At the time he took power as a provincial governor of Boran Province, literacy rate of the Oromo/Boran was only 2% for men and virtually nil for women. Jatani moved very fast to improve this situation. He did this by organising fund raisings which he used for constructing schools and hostels for nomadic children. He further introduced a fee of one Ethiopian birr on every head of cattle sold in that region. He built two hostels in Yaballo alone to accommodate over five hundred children. A German NGO helped to cover 50% of the expenses for the hostels. Majority of those children who were enrolled in those schools and who were accommodated in the said hostels are now in the Universities undertaking different fields of studies.

He particularly emphasised the education of the girl child. He managed to achieve this noble objective despite difficulties which arose at the time due to the cultural bias. Oromo cultural belief took the education of girl child as abomination. He changed this belief and set up boarding schools for girls under very strict discipline. His argument was that girl child education is/was the education for the whole family unlike that of the boys which benefited that particular individual as a person.

While at the middle of this project, Mengistu regime was overthrown by a coalition of liberation forces. Meles Zenawi took power. Jatani was then turned into an opposition activist of Meles government. He was in Nagele Borana when the Mengistu government fell. At that time (June 1991) some garrisons resisted the takeover by Zenawi. Nagele garrison planned to resist, but led by Jatani Ali, they eventually defected to the bush taking some vehicles and the remaining "die hard" soldiers. He moved down near Lake Stephanie, near Kenya border.

The Oromo Liberation Front (OLF) pulled out of regional election in 1992, because the dominant TPLF were using violence and harassment in the pre-election run-up. OLF defected into the bush and started serious armed resistance against Meles Zenawi's government. (Zenawi said the government was at war with OLF, roads had been mined and that armed men had walked out of Government sanctioned OLF encampments).

For a while, "Oromo" was seen as synonymous with rebellion. As part of their strategy, the Oromo Liberation Front contacted Jatani Ali in the bush. His usefulness was increased by the fact that he was familiar with Kenya as a former governor, had contact with the higher echelons of the Kenya government. Though he did not become a signed-up member of OLF, Jatani literally accepted to join forces with OLF to fight the Zenawi Government. He was therefore advised to come to Kenya because he would be more useful here to co-ordinate and communicate with others for the above stated reasons. He then crossed the border and came to Nairobi in April 1992.

This development threatened the Zenawi government and plans were immediately put in place to assassinate him. Reliable sources confirm that Kenyan and Ethiopian officials held a meeting on the Ethiopian side of Moyale town on 23rd June 1992 to plan the murder. Gunmen were then hired by the Ethiopian government to move to Nairobi and liquidate him.

SEVEN YEARS AGO TODAY that was on 2nd July 1992, three hired killers assassinated Mebastion Jatani Ali in his room at the Tea Zone of Hotel Ngara (Nairobi). It was proved beyond any reasonable doubt that two of the assassins were hosted in Ethiopian Embassy in Nairobi and that an Embassy car was used as the get-away vehicle. Two Ethiopians, Haile Kidu and Goba Liban, were later arrested. The two were finally brought to stand trial for murder on 6th November 1995. The delay in taking them to Court indicated that there were more than usual "behind the scenes" obstacles.

After a three week trial, both men were acquitted. In his judgement the judge acknowledged that "murder was well organised and carefully executed". He said that "Jatani Ali, while living Kenya was always fearful of his safety, fearing the possibility that the agents of the existing government of Ethiopia may want to follow him and eliminate him". However, despite all these observations, Justice Oguk erroneously found that there was insufficient evidence to convict the two suspects.

JATANI DIED A HEROES [sic] DEATH that is why we are here today to commemorate his death and those of all the persons who died while trying to accomplish the task that he left incomplete. As I had said earlier in my opening remarks, "HE WHOSE HEART IS FIRM AND HIS CONSCIENCE RIGHTFULLY APPROVES HIS CONDUCT WILL PURSUE HIS PRINCIPLES UNTO DEATH". That was exactly what Jatani did. The onus is now on us to pick up from where he left.

COMPILED BY YUSSUF HUQA JILLO
CHAIRMAN DARARA
2nd July 1999

Note: there is a factual oversight in the above tribute by Huqa Jillo. Goba Liban was one of the suspects who led the assassin squad to the hotel where Jatani Ali was murdered. He was not arrested and stood trial in a Kenyan court. He returned to Ethiopia and died in a hospital due to illness.

The 10TH anniversary of Jatani's assassination

The 10th anniversary of martyr Jatani Ali's death was commemorated. TPLF mercenaries assassinated Jatani Ali in Nairobi, Kenya on 2nd July 1992. Jatani was born in 1941 to Borana-Oromo parentage at a place called Melbana in southern Oromia. He was an extraordinary public servant even through the most difficult times. He served our people with distinction. That is why he is one of the most beloved sons of Oromia and history will remember him in that light. TPLF decided to assassinate Jatani because of his involvement with and support of the Oromo cause. We all miss him deeply.

15: Jatani Ali: The Person

The people of the world can be classified into three categories:

- The few who make things happen;
- The scores who watch them happening; and,
- The multitudes who have no idea what is happening.

A similar assertion to the above classification was stated by another person, one Nathaniel Hawthorne, thus: 'The world owes all its onward impulse to men ill at ease.'

Anybody who knows what Jatani Ali accomplished in life, in his different positions, would characterise him as amongst "the few who make things happen" and those who are 'ill at ease' with the *status quo* in which they found themselves.

Jatani Ali was a person with special and unique personal attributes. He exuded positivity and love for his people. In my opinion, his love and positive attitude towards the people was often expressed non-verbally, via his warm demeanour and gregarious personality. Consequently, he managed to have many close and devoted friends, as well as many casual admirers

In the preceding chapters, I have provided a brief portrayal of Jatani's life from early childhood through to schooling; from professional life to the termination of his life by an assassin's bullet. He was a visionary leader who strove hard to improve the general welfare of those he deemed marginalised. He upheld the principle of justice, no matter how difficult it was to do so in a country such as Ethiopia, always ruled through the barrel of the gun, where despotic rulers have been the law unto themselves. Jatani has been portrayed in this book as a unique and model human being. Indeed, he was a legendary figure who was loved by many people.

However, such a glowing portrayal of Jatani's character could lend itself to the illusion that he got along very well with all people he came in contact with, in life and work. This could hardly be the case as he was far from being a perfect individual. Jatani had frailties like any other human being. He worked under pressure and in a challenging neighbourhood where constant balancing acts of conflicting sectarian interests were needed. He was an outstanding personality who had managed to channel a positive interpersonal energy to render the lives of many people better. Snippets of his social life described below are intended to give the reader a glimpse into his *joie de vivre* [love of life] and should not cast a shadow over his otherwise legendary achievements or his positive relationship with people. As mentioned elsewhere, Jatani's off-duty socialisation with close friends was sometimes colourful and exposed his said love for life and human frailties. A few incidents that provide a glimpse into Jatani's socialising and love for life are given below.

I was so close to Jatani starting from our school days that he used to share with me even minute incidents in his life. Out of many, I would like to share four incidents that give a glimpse into Jatani's social life. These are: "a comment by a would-be mother-in-law"; "his generosity and limitations in handling his own money"; "the loss of a wristwatch"; and "a flying car that landed on the roof top of houses in Addis Ababa".

A comment by a would-be mother-in-law

When he was working at Addis Ababa Traffic Police Unit, Jatani rented a house with two cadet course-mates named Workneh Belihu and Eshete Damote. He had a lady neighbour named Manhaile Lemma, a vocalist singer in the Ethiopian Patriotic Association, who lived with a beautiful daughter called Elizabeth Tiku. Because of her beauty, Jatani used to call Elizabeth "Mona Lisa". The admiration was mutual as the girl was as interested in him as he was in her. Her mother apparently knew about their relationship and showed a respectful and favourable attitude toward him. Her father was a high-ranking government official in Haile Selassie's regime and lived in another part of Addis Ababa with a new family. Jatani's interest in the girl went as far as a desire to ultimately marry her. One evening, he went out with housemates and friends and returned home drunk. The neighbourhood knew Jatani and his house-mates as highly disciplined police officers. That night, under the influence of alcohol, Jatani displayed unusual and out-of-character behaviour. Jatani was loud and used very colourful language with his friends, within an earshot of his potential mother-in-law. The mother of his "Mona Lisa" came out of her house and witnessed his behaviour. She commented, 'Is this not a dangerous drunkard?' Jatani overheard the comment. The following day he met with me and told me, 'Last night I got drunk with friends and embarrassed myself in front of my potential mother-in-law'. His sense of shame was compounded even more, given a reverence and respect with which mothers-in-law are held in Borana culture. It was from this perspective that he commented about the embarrassment.

The gossip about Jatani's interest to marry "Mona Lisa" reached the ears of her father. He was heard commenting, 'She is not ready for marriage; I have a plan to send her abroad for education.' When Jatani's friends in the police service heard about the father's reluctance to endorse the marriage, they advised him to abduct her for marriage. Marriage through abduction was an archaic tradition that was still practised in many parts of rural Ethiopia. Jatani turned down the idea. The father sent her to France where she stayed for about two years and returned without achieving much in the way of education. She had met a man from the republic of Congo while in France. The Congolese followed her to Ethiopia, apparently in pursuit of her. She introduced him to her father with gratitude that he had been her benefactor when she was in financial difficulties. The father suspected the real intentions of the young man and was heard commenting, 'If this is the case, why doesn't she get married to an Ethiopian?' Learning about "his" Mona Lisa's love interest in other man, Jatani commented that he had no interest in marrying her anymore.

How Jatani handled his own money

Jatani hardly took his salary home. Some might say that this behaviour was a demonstration of extravagance. Others may argue to the contrary, indicating that Jatani's rather relaxed and casual attitude towards money was an expression of his extreme generosity. Jatani was exceptionally generous with his money and saw no real need to accumulate wealth. He spent his money not only to socialise with friends but also to help anyone, even those he hardly knew. Persons who knew him closely often remarked that his unreserved generosity towards the poor was indicative of his love for people. There was an occasion when his expenditure of money was closely managed by me. Salaried persons who took part in the *Derg*'s LDC in faraway rural corners of Ethiopia often delegated someone to collect part of their monthly salary on their behalf to pay house rent or bills. Jatani delegated me to manage part of his salary from Addis Ababa while he was in Arero Province, partaking in this campaign. I opened a bank account to deposit the amount of money he entrusted to me and arranged with the bank that I would manage the account on his behalf. One can appreciate how Jatani used his money in the context of what is discussed below in Chapter 16, "Others' Impressions of Jatani". That was probably the first time his salary was ever deposited in a bank!

Losing a prized wristwatch

Occasionally and when socialising with friends, Jatani indulged himself a bit more than usual. Because of that, his friends saw him as "the life of a party". Such nights out were sometimes followed by harmless youthful pranks that got out of hand. This was what happened one evening when Jatani was attending Addis Ababa University. Friends took him out in the evening where they enjoyed themselves in nightclubs and bars. Finally, their "bar crawling" session ended up in a bar in a district with a colourful nightlife called Merkato. Soon, Jatani's group was involved in a brawl with another group of drinkers. It was not clear which group initiated the brawl or the reason behind it. Members of the two groups engaged in a heated squabble to the point of fistfights. Which group won the contest? An outsider could not tell. Later that night, Jatani realised his prized wristwatch awarded to him in Harar for successfully conducting the "youth leadership development program", was lost in the melee. He told me that he did not know how he lost it except that he found his hand stripped of the watch when the commotion ended.

A car on the rooftop of houses in Addis Ababa

Another event, among several, that embarrassed Jatani involved a Volkswagen car. A visiting friend from outside the city picked up Jatani and two other friends in his Volkswagen Beetle car to have a good night-out in Addis Ababa. They visited a few bars and got drunk. While driving around in the city, they came to the bridge on the road that leads from the Palace to Tewodro's Square. A blind curve down a hilly road served as an approach to the bridge on a river. Several rows of houses with corrugated tin roofs clung to the sides of the hilly gorge leading to the river. Their little car overshot the curve in the road, flew over the edge of the road, down the hill and landed on top of the roofs of the houses with an almighty bang. As Jatani told me, the landing of the vehicle sounded as though a heavy object dropped from the sky or a thunder. The residents rushed out in shock and still half asleep, to find four persons in a car perched on a rooftop looking dazed and terrified. Among the people who came out to look, there was a police officer who knew Jatani. The officer couldn't believe his eyes and uttered words to the effect of, "Mebatsion, what a shame?!" He knew Jatani as a seasoned and disciplined police officer. The officer suspected the incident was the result of a night out by a group of youthful friends, fuelled by alcohol. Jatani spoke about the deep embarrassment that incident caused him. Still, he saw the humorous side of the story and often told it with sound effects that made people roll with laughter.

Such anecdotes serve to depict Jatani as a human being, not merely as someone on a pedestal – a flawed human being but one whose strengths and positive character traits far outweigh his weaknesses.

16: Others' Impressions of Jatani

I interviewed several individuals who knew Jatani, to get their impressions of Jatani as a governor, a community leader, a work colleague and a person. I felt that the interviewees might desire to share with me certain views of Jatani as a person that were not raised during the interview process. Most expressed similar feelings and observations about his nature as a human being, as a governor and a leader. The following are a few of such impressions. Effort has been made to provide the social and/or work-related context in which these individuals came to know Jatani.

Galgalo Liban

Galgalo is a Borana elder who now resides in Addis Ababa. He indicated that he knew Jatani from the time when both travelled from Borana country together to Addis Ababa and were admitted to Medhane Alem School in September 1952. They attended the same grades both in Medhane Alem Elementary and General Wingate Secondary schools. The author asked Galgalo what type of person Jatani was. He said, "Jatani never discriminated against any person: young or old, big or small, rich or poor. He looked at all persons whom he came across with the same eye." He never saw or heard about any involvement in physical fights with boys in the schools.

General Yadate Gurmu

General Yadate Gurmu is a retired Ethiopian police officer who now resides in Addis Ababa. The General knew Jatani from the time when he was transferred from the third police station in Addis Ababa to Addis Ababa Traffic Police Unit. With the rank of captain at the time, he was

Jatani's immediate superior officer. When he was asked what he knew about Jatani, he described his impression of him in terms of Jatani's performance of assigned tasks, his relationship with colleagues of all ranks and his attributes as a human being.

The General praised Jatani's performance highly in completing assigned tasks. He indicated that Jatani never failed to accomplish an assignment he was given and often was commended by his superiors for his professionalism and thoroughness in completing assigned tasks. He remembered how Jatani was very popular and worked in a collaborative manner with his superior officers, colleagues and rank-and-file constables. He added how Jatani had unique human characteristics: he loved people around him, was loved by all who came to work with him as well as those outside his work area. He said Jatani was respectful of colleagues and, in turn, was highly respected by them.

Colonel Teferedegn Yigezu

Colonel Teferedegn is a retired police officer who now works in the International Red Cross office in Addis Ababa. Jatani and Teferedegn worked together in Addis Ababa Police Traffic Department for one year in 1971. Thereafter, their social relationship continued. Teferedegn described Jatani as a person who was honest, a man of integrity, open-minded, as one who expressed what he believed in without fear or retreat, as one who believed in the value of constructive dialogue to solve issues, as a person who easily worked cooperatively with his superior and junior officers, as a person who valued and respected people in all walks of life. Teferedegn highlighted how Jatani was fair in settling traffic offenses. Once Jatani investigated a traffic accident in which a grandson of Emperor Haile Selassie was involved. According to Jatani's finding, the prince was the offender of traffic regulations. Jatani told him the facts and the consequences by citing traffic rules that applied to all citizens in the land. In a country where the Emperor and his family were revered as living gods, Jatani's approach was regarded as a daring move that won him respect from his superiors, work colleagues and the public. Jatani's interpersonal skills and ability to get along with high- and low-ranked officers had won him admiration. For example, when Jatani was part of the Ethiopian police delegation touring Japan and Western Europe, his mediation abilities were vital to reduce tensions between senior members of the delegation. Colonel Negussie Wolde Michael and his deputy, Major Abera Ayana, were senior officers in that delegation but the two some-times bickered. On their return, Colonel Negussie charged Major Abera for misbehaviour in foreign lands and presented the case to the then Police Chief Commander, General Dereje Dubale. The Commander organised an *ad hoc* committee which would investigate the charges. The committee called Jatani as a witness, as he was with them throughout the entire trip to Japan and Western Europe. Jatani described what he had witnessed as he saw it and for what it was. The committee accepted Jatani's views of the events as valid and an impartial observation, and compiled a recommendation for the Police Commander. On that basis, the Commander dropped the charges as insignificant. Jatani reported the committee members told him to his face, 'You are an honest Ethiopian'.

Mesele Dhaba

Mesele closely worked with Jatani in both Arero provincial and Borana Regional Administrations. The two knew each other from the time when they took part in the LDC in the region. In Arero Province, Mesele worked both as a district governor of Teltele and deputy governor, to Jatani, of Arero Province. In Borana Administrative Region, Mesele held a high political post. Mesele noted how several ethnic groups lived side-by-side in the province. He indicated that Jatani looked at members of all ethnic groups with the same eye and treated them as equal citizens of Ethiopia. He said that Jatani wouldn't tolerate any form of corruption, discrimination and maladministration within the community or in the administrative system. He indicated that Jatani stood for the welfare of the oppressed and worked hard to improve the lot of the most marginalised in the region. Mesele added that Jatani believed in upholding the rule of justice for all. Most of all, Mesele remembered Jatani as a decent human being, as a development-minded governor who worked hard to improve the living conditions of the people in the region. Mesele now lives in Addis Ababa.

Ilu Banata

Ilu is member of the Gujii community and now resides in Addis Ababa. He is a manager of an NGO called Girja that operates in Gujii Zone. He worked with him in two capacities. When Jatani was deputy governor of Sidamo Administrative Region, Ilu was governor of Jamjam Province – one of the provinces under Sidamo Administrative Region. When Jatani was appointed as a Governor of Borana Administrative Region that combined Gujii and Borana districts, Ilu became his deputy. He described Jatani thus, as 'a selfless person, who had no time for himself, he who devoted all his time and energy for the betterment and welfare of the community.' Ilu Banata said that Jatani was fair in settling issues that arose between the personnel in the bureaucracy or between communities in the region.

Teshome Dahesa

Currently Teshome is a coordinator of the Save the Children Program in Borana Zone. He worked as a district governor when Jatani was the governor of Arero Province. During this period Teshome worked as a governor of Teltele, Moyale and Arero Districts. He described Jatani as visionary and resourceful leader in times of war and peace. According to him, had Jatani not been a governor of Arero Province when Somalia invaded Ethiopia, Somalis would have overrun the whole of Borana country. Teshome indicated that Jatani was a leader with strong stamina and superb "people skills", able to tolerate any kind of challenges. He added that Jatani encouraged open expressions of views and welcomed fair discussion on issues with his subordinates. Teshome agrees with others' views regarding Jatani's insistence to have a non-discriminatory approach in outlook and action in dealing with all communities under his administration.

Teshome said that Jatani wouldn't hesitate to intervene on behalf of a person whom he deemed was mistreated. An incident in Teshome's life is a case in point. Teshome was a governor of Awassa District in Sidama Province before he joined Jatani in Arero Province. He did not get along well with the then-governor of Sidamo Administrative Region, Tefera Endalew. He resigned from his post of district governor of Awassa and applied for a job in the Southern Range Land Development Unit located at Yaballo. Tefera used his position and blocked Teshome from getting that job. Jatani went to the Minister of Agriculture, Dr Geremew Dabale, and explained to the Minister about the unfair political interference of Tefera Endalew in blocking Teshome's application for a job in Yaballo. Jatani was able to convince the Minister to remove the blockade and ordered the officials in charge of Southern Range Land Development Project to employ Teshome.

Huqa Garse

Huqa is currently head of SOS-Sahel development program in Borana Zone. He worked under Jatani in various capacities, ranging from a governor of Dirre District to the head of office for provincial security services. Huqa agrees with Teshome about Jatani's visionary leadership and resourcefulness during both war and peace. He helped Jatani design and implement a fund-raising strategy for economic development in Arero Province. Huqa said that Jatani was a man born to open the eyes of the Borana people to modern ways of life by creating educational opportunities. Jatani urged and encouraged communities to take up crop cultivation and other trades to reduce the unpredictability of nomadic pastoralism. Huqa pointed out how Jatani was a lot more than a governor who served a regime that appointed him. To Huqa, Jatani was a great mobiliser, a tireless campaigner for community-led development, a model and teacher of proper ethical behaviour at work and in social relations. Huqa added that Jatani also had a weak point that certain unscrupulous individuals often exploited to their advantage. In this regard when a certain issue arose and was reported to him, he had a tendency to listen and accept at face value what he had just been told, without exploring the other side of the coin. This tendency was borne out of his belief in the decency of most humans. Huqa indicated how at times Jatani was inflexible in changing his mind on issues. However, this inflexible approach improved as he spent many evenings with elders, learning about their patient approach to issues and their listening, reasoning and oratory skills that were vital in persuading people.

Abebe Zeleqe

Abebe is now a hotel owner in Yaballo. When I asked him what type of person Jatani was, at first he could hardly control his emotion to speak. With tears in his eyes, he said, 'No one like him was ever born in this community before him, nor will one ever in the future.' He went on to describe what he had observed about him. Abebe said that Jatani went around and encouraged everyone in any occupation to strive to improve their lives and, through that, the lives of the community. In this, he took time to chat with carpenters, blacksmith, farmers, cattle-herders, students or people going about their business or just walking along the streets. Following some fatal traffic accidents along the main highway linking the region with the rest of the country, Jatani undertook memorable and, at times, colourful public education campaigns to reduce such accidents. Abebe said that Jatani often stopped people and gave impromptu lessons on proper, safer and legal ways of walking along the highways. Sometimes he would get out of his car and instruct locals to change their habit of walking on or in the middle of the asphalted highway. Abebe remembered one particular traffic incident that was the talking point of the town for a while. While driving towards Yaballo town from the outlying areas, Jatani came across a group of prominent residents of the town walking abreast in the middle of the highway. He offered them a lift to the town, which they accepted. Then, he drove them to Yaballo police station where they were charged for intentionally and deliberately violating a traffic regulation for pedestrians. Jatani's justification was that, instead of being exemplary to the uneducated peasants, the charged carelessly walked in the middle of the highway, thereby endangering lives. They were imprisoned for 15 days and the incident became an important piece in the province's accident reduction educational campaigns.

Abebe recalled an incident that once brought him before Jatani. At the time, Abebe and his partner were engaged in a contraband trade using a camel. On one occasion, two customs policemen stopped them on suspicion that they had an illicit load on the camel. The policemen put down their guns to search for possible illicit items in the camel's load. Daringly, Abebe and his friend picked up their guns and chased them away. The policemen reported the incident to their superiors, saying that contraband gangsters robbed them of their guns while on duty. The head of the local customs police station came to Jatani and reported what had happened to his men while on duty. Jatani sent a message to local people to search for persons that fit the description of the alleged contraband gangsters or had arrived in town around that time. They brought to him six suspects including Abebe and his partner. Other innocent suspects were released as Abebe and his partner admitted to the charges. Jatani collected the guns from them and returned them to the customs office. On his part, Jatani awarded them a gun each for their honesty in admitting to the charges and in acknowledgement to their previous notable services in the defence of the community. [41]

---

[41]   A gun is a favoured gift to a Borana man and in Ethiopia.

Saar Arero

Saar is at head office of Gayo Pastoral Development Initiative in Addis Ababa, working as Coordinator of Administration and Human Resource Development. He told me that he had seen Jatani Ali several times in Borana. But he recalled two incidents which he would never forget about him. The first was when Saar left his rural village and travelled to Yaballo in September 1981 to attend school. One Saturday morning, a market day in Yaballo, Saar with a group of other boys who recently joined school was at goats' market watching the transactions. Jatani drove up, parked the vehicle nearby and walked towards them. Saar was the smallest among the group, only about seven years old. Jatani tapped him on the head and addressed the boys. He went on to say, 'now you have joined school, among you there will be some who might reach high positions and others who might drop out without achieving anything. Study hard to reach high positions.' Saar could recall all the names of the boys who started school with him. Some dropped out of school and others became successful in life and career.

The second incident remembered by Saar involved several Borana boys of different ages who joined the school, occupying the same dormitory. They had no regular food suply at all. The older boys could go out into the town, buy something to eat or simply loiter around for food and return. But younger boys like Saar did not know where to go to buy food nor had the skills or courage to approach other people for pocket money or food. Saar said that they often reached a point of starvation while trying to study and sleep in dormitories without adequate lighting. One day the bigger boys took the smaller ones to Jatani's office and explained to him the situation they were in. When he came out to see them some of them collapsed in front of his eyes. He was shocked by the sight and ordered his driver, Halakhe Tuni, to take them to a restaurant in the town for immediate feeding. Saar added that in the provincial government headquarters where Jatani had an office, there was a room used to store emergency food supplies for war and drought-affected villagers. Jatani broke the door and told the boys to take as much kilograms of grains as they could.

Halakhe Dida Gobesa

Halakhe Dida Gobesa, who was working for CARE Ethiopia Borana Project when interviewed by this author, also reported a similar experience of extreme hardship when he first started school at Dida Hara. Halakhe had a vivid memory of his first day in the classroom with several other boys who already had basic learning elsewhere. One day, Jatani parked his car in the school compound and went straight into the classroom where Halakhe was. He wrote an Amharic word on the chalk board and asked whether any one among them could read it. Many of them shot up their hands to read. He was happy to see so many hands up. He thanked them and proceeded to give them a piece of advice stressing the need to study hard to be successful. Halakhe specially remembered how Jatani cited the ups and downs of life in general where some of the students could drop out and reach nowhere while others would be successful leaders of their people. In this case, Halakhe was one of the successful few out of the many who were in that classroom in Dida Hara. He had since obtained a master's degree in anthropology.

Godana Arero

Godana is now a middle-aged person employed by the SOS-Sahel office in Nagelle-Borana. Godana said that he did not directly work with Jatani but was a political appointee in Moyale when Jatani was a governor of Arero Province. Godana was invited to a meeting held in Yaballo by pastoralist community leaders to share ideas on the need to construct hostels for students coming from marginalised pastoralist communities. Godana remembered how his own brief statement helped persuade the participants on the virtues of constructing hostels for such students. Godana started his speech by mentioning how several years earlier, by the order of Emperor Haile Selassie; boys from Borana went to Addis Ababa for education. He added how one of those boys was Jatani Ali himself. He lamented how that was a one-off process after which no more students were sent away to boarding schools in Addis Ababa or elsewhere for decades afterwards. Godana noted how for decades the community could not send their children to school due to their nomadic way of life and lack of role models in the form of successful educated Borana persons. He noted how a mere lack of student dormitories in or near towns where the schools were found was a major barrier for pastoralists to send some of their children to schools. As a result, whole generations of Borana were brought up without seeing any educated Borana person until people like Jatani Ali appeared on the scene. A massive educational gap was created between the few Borana who got an opportunity to attend school earlier on and the rest of the people. Godana stressed how this gap could only be bridged if the community constructed students' hostels to accommodate children who must leave their rural communities and travel to towns to attend schools. Godana remembered how the participants were touched by what he expressed and applauded the idea of building students' dormitories as a community development initiative. The gathering agreed to contribute in cash and in kind to bring the initiative to fruition. Godana left the province as he was transferred to another organisation in Addis Ababa, but he kept in touch with Jatani whenever he came to Addis Ababa on business.

Godana shared what others had to say in terms of Jatani's effort to encourage students and communities to strive hard in whatever line of work they were engaged in. He advised people not to give up easily and to try hard to improve their lot. Godana noted how in Borana country the dry season was a particularly stressful time for both humans and their livestock. He added that when expected rains finally arrived, Jatani used to go to the localities that received the rain showers first and would advise locals to take advantage of them to build ponds to store rain water or to sow the seeds in their farms early.

Guro Dida

Guro is a Borana elder who resides in Dida Hara. His descriptions of Jatani's character and work behaviour were no different from the others. He attested that Jatani looked at all members of communities within his jurisdiction in the same way. Without his skilful leadership in mobilising people to withstand the invasion, Somalia would have overrun the whole of Arero and Borana Provinces. Jatani had special advice for Borana pastoralists:

- educate your children, both boys and girls alike;
- take care of your health through hygiene and sanitation;
- wash your hands, body and clothes;
- harvest rain water by constructing earthen dams and cisterns;
- drink clean water (boil it if necessary);
- protect what little is left of wild animals as they too are your property;
- do not cut down big trees as they provide shade and other benefits;
- improve the techniques in building houses and the location of settlements to benefit from service delivery points; and,
- do not walk in the middle of the highway to avoid motor vehicle accidents.

Guro praised Jatani's effort in encouraging the building of primary schools in rural areas as well as students' hostels that went with them. With contributions from the community, many primary schools and students' hostels were built in rural areas during the years when Jatani was a governor.

Borbor Bule

Borbor now resides in the locality of Dubuluq and is an expert in Borana culture and oral history. He described how Jatani recognised the erosion of the Borana traditional system of government and culture by the encroachment of the institutions of the Ethiopian government. Borbor indicated that Jatani took measures to halt this encroachment by making sure that the boundaries between government institutions and the Borana traditional system of government, way of life and culture were clearly demarcated. The Ethiopian government annexed Borana to the central administration in the late 1890s. Borbor explained how Borana society and culture are guided by two distinctive institutions that largely operated autonomously except when they were allowed to complement each other's functions through elaborate rituals. These two institutions are: the *Qaallu* for spiritual life; and *Gada* for secular, political and social life of the Borana. Following conquest, Ethiopian rulers often co-opted pre-existing indigenous power structures of the vanquished tribes to exert their rule. In the case of Borana, Ethiopian rulers recognised *Qaallu* institution as the one that could easily be co-opted as an effective channel of communication with the Borana community. Perhaps this choice owed to *Qaallu*'s elaborate rituals that reminded them of their own royal pomp and ceremonies. In their attempt to co-opt the *Qaallu* institution, Ethiopian officials blurred the boundaries between the *Qaallu* and *Gada* institutions. They took away certain traditional powers of the *Gada* and gave it to *Qaallu*. Jatani enlisted the help of knowledgeable Borana elders and traditional historians to correct the distortion in Borana polity. Based on the recommendation by the elders, Jatani restored the boundaries between the *Gada* and *Qaallu* institutions as they were before government interference. Particularly, Jatani has been instrumental in restoring the powers of the *Gada* institution according to pre-conquest Borana tradition. Borbor said that Jatani recognised the defined roles of each institution and insisted that there should be no mixing up of indigenous institutions with those established by Ethiopia's central government. According to Jatani, indigenous and government institutions can operate side-by-side in the life of the community without any conflict.

Jirmo Dida Gandhile

Jirmo is an elder and community leader in Dillo district. He too is an admirer of Jatani in terms of his character and his efforts in improving the welfare of marginalised pastoralist communities. He said that when Jatani first came to Dillo, a salt-bearing crater lake like El Soda, he met with him and others. Jirmo vividly remembered how Jatani climbed down to the bottom of the lake which is several hundred metres deep. During the visit, Jatani advised the people to tax the salt mineral exploited from the lake to supplement their income, to sell cattle before these are severely affected by droughts and to educate their children. At the time, Dillo was a neglected locality defined as a peasant association under Dirre district (it has since become a district on its own right). The locality was often hit by severe droughts, causing a great deal of suffering among the people. Jatani showed this suffering to the Minister of the Interior, General Taye Tilahun, and his entourage by taking them down to the bottom of the Crater Lake.

Jatani observed how Jirmo was an influential person who could mobilise the community for positive change. Jatani decided to show Jirmo what other parts of Ethiopia looked like and to appreciate a progress made in these other regions of the country. He took him all the way to Addis Ababa on one 12 September, the anniversary date marking the fall of Emperor Haile Selassie's feudal regime. On the occasion, the country put on different kinds of shows including military parades with convoys of armaments and carnival-like colourful marches staged by various civilian organisations. Jatani told Jirmo how what he had witnessed were examples of progress made as the result of education. Jirmo indicated how impressed he was by what he saw during the trip and what could be achieved through education. Jatani took the opportunity to advise Jirmo on the needs of educating the pastoralist Borana children as an avenue to catch up with the rest of the country. Shortly after that, Jatani travelled to East Germany for a three-month study tour. Jirmo returned home and used what he saw on the way to and in Addis Ababa to mobilise people in his locality to contribute money for the building of schools. On return from his study tour, Jatani was impressed by the progress made in raising funds and in building primary schools in outlying rural areas. He awarded

Jirmo a gun in acknowledgement of his achievement in fund raising for development. Jirmo observed how on Sundays, Jatani used to travel to different rural areas where he observed the challenges of life and progress made to overcome these. During such visits, he interacted with all members of the community, ranging from the young to the old, from nomadic cattle herders to farmers, on the need to work cooperatively to improve living conditions. Jatani urged all to diversify the community's income source to reduce dependency on farming or cattle-herding as the only source of income.

Jirmo reported that seven days after he had heard the assassination of Jatani, he fled to Kenya. The Ethiopian Government forces followed him and attacked his village killing or wounding 16 members of his family. Later, government agents persuaded him to return and live in peace with a promise that he would be compensated for the damages he had sustained. He said that he was still awaiting the fulfilment of that promise.

Utukan Malo

Utukan is a Gujii elder who now resides in Bule Hora District (formerly, Hagere Mariam). He said that he was a teenager when he first saw Jatani during the LDC in Hagere Mariam. When Jatani became the governor of Arero province, Utukan was around 20 years of age. One day, Ethiopian army recruitment officers came to Hagere Mariam town looking for new young recruits. Utukan said that he went to the recruitment centre to join the military but the recruiting officer turned him away, declaring that he did not look strong enough to carry a gun. The disappointed young man went to Jatani and explained the matter to him. Jatani asked him whether he had enough strength to carry a gun; he answered positively. Jatani took Utukan back to the recruiting officers, persuaded them and got him recruited. He stayed in the military for a few years and then ran away. His views on Jatani's contributions to the administration of the province, his interpersonal characteristics, his efforts to improve the living conditions of marginalised communities, his impartial treatment of all in the community, mirrored those of the others.

According to Utukan, Jatani grew up during Haile Selassie's oppressive feudal regime. He had a very good understanding of the norms and the damage the feudal regime had inflicted on people in southern parts of Ethiopia. He said that Jatani was an experienced and well-qualified person and wanted to help communities to remove the vestiges of the oppressive regime. He worked tirelessly to effect peace between warring communities in the province. Utukan said that Jatani established a platform for sustainable peaceful co-existence especially between the Borana, Gabra and Gujii communities. He urged all members of these communities to observe how what they had in common far outweighed what separated them. On that basis, he asked them to work hard collaboratively and to enjoy the fruits of their labour as brotherly people.

Mesele Bassaye

Mesele is a middle-aged person who works in agricultural office of Hagere Mariam District. He came to know Jatani when he was attending Yirgalem High School. Masele indicated that whenever he passed through Yirgalem, he stopped and visited students of Gujii and Borana origin to encourage them to study hard. He advised them that education is the most important tool to fight oppressive practices in society and government. After graduating from the school, both Mesele and Jatani were elected to the Parliament of the *Derg* era; the former representing Hagere Mariam district and the latter Arero province. Mesele said that this job brought them closer and allowed them to exchange ideas on how to better use the ongoing revolutionary change in favour of the oppressed masses.

Jatani would not tolerate the mistreatment of any individual. In this regard, Mesele cited a case about Paulos Muuda. Paulos was a physically impaired person who moved around in a wheelchair. He ran a health clinic for which he needed to apply for annual renewals of the work permit with relevant authorities. This one time, they denied him a permit on the grounds he was crippled. Paulos appealed to Jatani; his physical disability was never a hindrance for him to provide a competent service to the community. Jatani intervened on his behalf and told the permit-givers how their action was a clear violation of human rights. Mesele added that Jatani went further and told them that physical disability should not bar a person from working and earning a living in a profession for which s/he is qualified. He pointed out that what they did was totally unjust and illegal. On that basis, he instructed them to renew Paulos' work permit immediately.

Abera Ashine

Jatani was a very likeable person who earned himself many friends. Some of these were very close to him socially and knew intimate details of his life and work. One such close friend of Jatani's was Abera Ashine who knew Jatani from the time when both attended Medhane Alem School in Addis Ababa. Abera is a softly spoken, gentle and humane person who loves people and is loved by almost everyone he came in contact with. When I interviewed him about what he knew about Jatani, Abera shared so many positive attributes and stories of Jatani, similar to those that many other people had expressed. On his part, he recalled a piece of advice that Jatani had given him soon after his marriage to Beletech Eshete. In Ethiopia marriage tends to be an elaborate, expensive and extravagantly lavish undertaking. Face-saving is a key consideration in organising a wedding. Families often exhaust their life savings or borrow heavily to put on a wedding ceremony they deem worthy of their social standing. Often members of the extended family, neighbours and even friends chip in by contributing money, gifts or labour towards such weddings. At Abera's marriage ceremony, Jatani was entrusted with the responsibility of collecting contributions from close friends. Only persons who are very close to the groom could be given such a delicate responsibility. Jatani managed to collect Birr 850 in donations towards the wedding, a respectable sum at the time. Such money was used to purchase a wedding gift such as a refrigerator or kitchen appliances, per the social conventions of the time. Jatani broke the convention and decided to instead donate the money directly to the bride and groom. He knew that the two would be broke the day after the hustle and bustle of the feast. Abera often told this story to underscore Jatani's concern for the welfare of people, his foresight and his ability to make rational decisions.

Abera now resides in the United States with his family but occasionally comes to Ethiopia with his wife to visit friends and relatives. Whenever the two come back to Ethiopia, Abera invites his old schoolmates, including this author, to rekindle their friendship and to reminisce about the old times. One such encounter between Abera and over 15 former schoolmates of Medhane Alem took place in March 2013. In that get-together, Abera fondly spoke about Jatani's generosity, loyalty to friends and foresightedness that saved him from economic strain following his marriage.

Abera mentioned how Jatani's words of advice carried enormous weight in his household. Abera told his guests how Jatani's mediation in his domestic affairs helped save his marriage during the early years of his marriage. He cited one particular day when Jatani came to visit his family to catch up. He arrived when Abera and his wife were amid a serious domestic squabble. Jatani told Abera, 'Beletech is our beloved sister. If I ever see you mistreat her, I shall never come to your home again.' Abera told his guests that he took Jatani's threat very seriously as he couldn't even entertain the idea of losing Jatani's friendship. Since that intervention, Abera and his wife have never had any fights as it helped them grow and appreciate the value of friendship. He added, 'from that day onward I found that my wife has been my soul mate, my right arm and I felt uncomfortable wherever I went out or did something without her.' He finished by saying how she was the social glue that kept all friendships going and gave the credit to her for preparing the feast that enabled old acquaintances and friends to catch up once again on that day.

Liban Wako Adi

Liban is a native of Yaballo town and was a student when Jatani was the Governor of Arero Province. His father, Wako Adi, was a teacher in Yaballo and had shared a dormitory with Jatani Ali at Medhane Alem School in Addis Ababa. Liban now lives in Sydney, Australia, where he works as an educator.

Liban's earliest recollection of Jatani was when he visited his father and family at their house in Yaballo. At the time, Jatani was an officer working for Addis Ababa Traffic Police Department. He said that Yaballo was then more of a village than a town, with his family being one of two or three ethnic Borana families living there. Liban remembered being kept busy fetching supplies from the local market for a feast to welcome Jatani. He said that the two old friends spent the whole evening reminiscing and chuckling about their time as school boys in Addis Ababa. Liban recalled how Jatani gave his father a picture of himself dressed in the ceremonial regalia of a traffic police officer. He added that this photo adorned the walls of his family home for years afterwards.

After his services in *idget be hibret zemecha* (LDC), Jatani became the Governor of Arero Province where he soon became the pride of the Borana people. However, Liban noted how many non-Borana in Yaballo and the province were forced to begrudgingly accept the fact that an ethnic Borana could be a competent, bright and assertive leader.

Though there are many things by which to remember Jatani, Liban said that he personally recalls Jatani through his distinctly booming voice; his brightly-lit rolling eyes; his sharp and briskly-paced stride; his use of an Amharic phrase *"yigermal ekko"* in between his statements, to dramatically emphasise a story, and his ability to attract a small crowd of captivated onlookers whenever he was in town.

As a student and youth leader, Liban attended some public meetings convened by Governor Jatani and partook in the efforts to mobilise local resources to defend the province against Somali *"shifta"* aggression. He was sent to Ade Galchat resettlement site west of Yaballo to assist with the rehabilitation of Borana refugees affected by both the Somali invasion and drought. Liban remembered how Jatani was able to effectively use an incident to underscore what needed to be done. He recalled a day when Jatani made a brief stopover at Ade Galchat with an entourage of high-ranking officials from Awassa. The visit was to show what was being done to rehabilitate war-displaced and impoverished communities. Jatani and his entourage crowded into the small thatched hut used as living quarters for those assisting with the rehabilitation efforts. Liban and his student colleague didn't have food or drinks to offer the visitors. Liban excused himself and set out to look, without much success, for a cup of potable water among the settlers. The nearest waterhole was a day's walk away and it was a puzzle to him how the spot was chosen as a settlement site. All he could find was a cup of muddy water that smelt like cow's urine with the consistency and colour of a *tella*, an Ethiopian home-made beer. Considering that some members of Jatani's entourage were high-ranking officials, Liban was not sure whether to offer the visitors such foul-smelling water and thought that Jatani would be embarrassed by it as well. In *Afaan Borana*, the local language, Liban informed Jatani how bad the water was, expecting him to say not to offer the water. To the contrary, Jatani emphatically told Liban to give the water to them so that they had a taste of life in neglected communities. Jatani used the episode to highlight the desperate need for clean and safe sources of water in the province. The visitors endured the harrowing experience of sampling the foul water and promised to do all they could to look at the water supply issues once they returned to Awassa.

Liban said that Jatani occasionally visited his school to address students and teachers. A few times he also attended ceremonies marking the end of school year (known as *sene-selasa*). During one such occasion, Jatani arrived with a visiting dignitary, the Governor of Sidamo Administrative Region. The two were asked to hand over prizes to students who excelled academically in their classes. As the roll call of students who came top of their classes was made by the school director, it was clear that ethnic

Borana names such as Boru and Galagalo eclipsed other ethnic names. Liban indicated that he could see a warm glow of pride palpable on Jatani's face as the names were called. At one stage during the ceremony, the Governor of Sidamo leaned over and uttered some words in Jatani's ear; they both roared with laughter. Days later, Jatani was asked if he would share the joke that made them laugh. He said, 'the governor was joking how there must be something unique in the diet of the Borus and Galagalos as distinct from that of the Getachews and Tesemas [typical Amharic names].'

Later, when Jatani was the Deputy Governor of Sidamo Administrative Region and lived in Awassa, Liban used to drop by Jatani's house to greet him on his travels between Addis Ababa (where he worked) and Borana country to visit family. Occasionally he stayed at Jatani's house overnight or for few days. He recalls Jatani being an exceedingly generous man and a father figure to him while he tried to establish himself as a young employee in the Ethiopia's notoriously murky bureaucracy in Addis Ababa.

In his spare time, Jatani used to dote over a small grove of orange and mandarin trees in the compound of the house he rented. Liban remembered how visitors, neighbours and total strangers were invited to help themselves to Jatani's rather bumper harvest of fruits. He particularly remembered Jatani's demonstration on how to properly eat oranges without wasting the inner flesh of the fruit, as most Ethiopians do. This was done with an air of military seriousness, leaving a bemused and confused look on those invited to eat his oranges.

A visit from a fellow Borana was an occasion that Jatani cherished while in Awassa and his house often resembled a small Borana guesthouse. He would invite visitors to one of his favourite mind-teaser games that resembled television quiz shows. One of these involved a knowledge test on subjects ranging from geography to history; from world current affairs to Borana stories. Another one involved an English language dictionary, where random pages of a dictionary would be opened and contestants were asked to define the meaning of words. Jatani excelled in these quizzes and would give a light-hearted commentary on the origins and hidden meanings of certain words from the dictionary. Liban recalled how Jatani's knowledge of world history and affairs was outstanding and he was by far the brightest man in a room. Jatani also enjoyed watching international tennis matches on television with visitors to his home in Awassa. He would tell amusing stories on the antics, outbursts and tantrums of the then famous American tennis player, John McEnroe. He often mimicked the sound and mannerisms of McEnroe to the delight of those present.

Liban remembers how Borana people who travelled to Awassa to seek medical assistance used to stay in Jatani's house, sometimes for weeks at a time, free of charge. At times his lounge room resembled a Borana *gaadissa-koraa* (traditional gathering).

Liban said that Jatani was direct at speaking his mind and often this rubbed some people up the wrong way. He was a person who doggedly insisted on strict observance of law and order. Liban thought that Jatani's insistence in upholding the rule of law and fairness was reinforced by the egalitarian ethos flowing from nomadic pastoralist societies such as Borana in which he grew up as well as by his training as a police officer. Liban noted that Jatani's directness and honesty stood in stark contrast to Ethiopia's feudal, underhanded egocentric and vindictive ethos that informed social relations, bureaucratic norms and governance in that country.

Despite all this, Liban indicated that Jatani saw no contradiction in being a proud Borana, Oromo and Ethiopian simultaneously. After all, he was the product of all three cultures. He said that he had been able to observe and appreciate this view of Jatani during his visits to his house in Awassa. For example, one day Jatani was hosting a few Borana visitors at his home when a discussion around the status of 'Ethiopian Borana' v. 'Kenyan Borana' was raised. Jatani told the gathering how the Borana were part of a much larger group called Oromo and how the vast majority of Oromo clans were part of Ethiopia (this concept was new to many at the time). He explained how the Borana and Oromo people suffered just like all other tribes in Ethiopia at the hands of the country's invariably cruel and unimaginative rulers. He said that the Borana are respected in Ethiopia as part of the larger Oromo group and their interests are better defended as citizens of Ethiopia. In Kenya, he added, the Borana are seen as an offshoot of an Ethiopian tribe, implying that they may not be considered 'proper Kenyans' by upland Kenyans. He concluded his remarks by stating that the peace and fate of Borana people was intricately linked to that of Ethiopia's.

Liban said that Jatani often lamented the uncompromising, top-down, dictatorial and unimaginative style of leadership adopted by successive rulers of Ethiopia. He reasoned how such a brutal style of leadership has made the country a harsh and sad place for most of its citizens. He grew uneasy about how Colonel Mengistu Haile Mariam, the then dictator of Ethiopia, was elevated by party cadres to the status of a demigod, akin to that reserved for past emperors. He would say: '*namicha [Mengistu] waaqan dhahani, lafa [Ethiopia] qilee kahani*'.

Liban indicated that he saw Jatani for the last time in his house in Awassa when he, Liban, was preparing to travel abroad. He went to Yaballo to bid farewell to his family and stopped at Jatani's to say his good byes. He remembered having a special farewell dinner based on one of Jatani's favourite dishes, a roasted fish from Lake Awassa. Liban said that after he ended up in Australia, he sent Jatani a letter about his progress. He added that shortly after that letter, he learnt about the collapse of the *Derg* regime and the sad news of Jatani's assassination.

Liban said that Jatani Ali remains a beacon of hope for current and future generations of Borana, Oromo and Ethiopians. He believes that one way of honouring Jatani would have to be by trying our best to improve ourselves in whatever endeavour we choose or through education so that we can all do our bit to advance his legacy. Liban wanted to express his heartfelt gratitude to me as the author of this 'immensely valuable biography'. He concluded by saying that Jatani Ali was a decent and honourable Borana, Oromo and Ethiopian. Consequently, it is the duty of all concerned members of these communities to build on his legacies and make sure those who committed the cowardly murder of Jatani are brought to justice.

'Seife Nebalbal'

Shortly after the assassination of Jatani, an article in *Seife Nebelbal* newspaper reflected many people's view of Jatani as a person and his achievements as a leader. In his tribute peace, the author expressed a deep sorrow felt by many as the news of Jatani's assassination filtered through. He discussed at length many of Jatani's achievements. He echoed the views held by many on the character and stature of Jatani both as a person and as a competent, admired and influential leader. Translated extracts from *Seife Nebelbal* newspaper is presented below:

Since the Derg's revolution broke out in Ethiopia in 1974, Jatani unreservedly devoted his energy, knowledge and time to improve the welfare of the general public. He related to people, mingled in public and worked with them for the common good. In the process, he taught them what he knew and learned from them what he didn't. He was a governor of Arero province, then made up of 7 districts, from March 1976 to June 1985. Without substantial help from the central government at the initial stages of his governorship, he organised the human and material resources of the local people to resolutely contain the expansionist dreams of Somalia's invaders from 1978 to 1980. The invaders were finally pushed out of the territory they so ravaged with a belated but vital assistance from the central government.

When he was appointed as the governor of Arero province, there was hardly any development activity going on in any one of the 7 districts of the province. Virtually, no progress has been made in preceding decades under a succession of appointed governors. With the technical help from the Southern Range Land Development Unit, he interconnected the districts with a network of vital rural roads. By encouraging collaboration between government agencies, NGOs and the local people, he accomplished numerous tangible development projects in the province. He organised several very successful fund-raising campaigns to fend off Somali invasion as well as build key infrastructure. These included: the erection of new office buildings for mass organisations; paving new rural roads and the maintenance of the

existing ones; repairing dilapidated old buildings that served as schools and offices;
building a large students' hostel with the help of an NGO; installing electric power
in major towns and the construction of a sizeable football stadium also used to stage
other community events. He helped construct the first high school in Arero Province
after securing an approval from Ethiopia's Ministry of Education.

He led public awareness campaigns exalting the benefits of education. Many
primary schools were built in remote rural areas with the help of the community. He
campaigned tirelessly and facilitated the construction of students' hostels near such
schools. As the result, scores of children from marginalised and isolated rural
communities went to school for the first time. He was an ardent campaigner in
weeding out harmful cultural practices in the community. He opened the eyes of
nomadic cattle-herding communities in appreciating the advantages of modern ways
of life such as educating their children, cultivating land to reduce the ravages of
droughts and the need to acquire new skills in trade or commerce. During the
Derg's infamous "red terror" campaigns in which hundreds of young people were
killed all over the country, no single life was lost in Arero Province under Jatani's
watch. He did not even take any action against those who publicly plotted to kill
him at the beginning of his tenure as a governor. A few years before it was thrown
out of power by rebels from the northern provinces of Tigre and Eritrea, the Derg
regime ordered governors in the country to hunt down and eliminate persons of Tigre
and Eritrean origin suspected of secretly collaborating with the rebels. He ignored
the order at his own risk and, consequently, no one was apprehended or killed in
Borana region where he was a governor at that stage. The targeted people remained
blissfully unaware of the drastic measure by the Derg authorities, continued to live
and go about their business peacefully as they had had done for years. Open-minded
people or even those who hated Jatani begrudgingly admired his hard work and
dedication to improve the lives of communities.

Individuals or groups whose class interests were affected as a result of Jatani's
stand against exploitation, racism, corruption, nepotism and other forms of social
malaise despised him. These were people imbued with toxic ethnic chauvinism who
or whose parents used to make a fortune out of the ignorance of peasants, pastoral-
ists and ordinary people, who either did not know the extent of their rights as
citizens or were not able to protect such rights. They branded him as a narrow-
minded ethnicist. Indeed, most of the victims of the mentioned feudal exploitation,
racism and gross human rights abuses happen to be members of Jatani's own ethnic
group. Other victims were related other communities who also endured decades of
abuse at the hands of appointed chauvinist feudal officials sent down from the centre
of Ethiopia, to lord over, milk-dry and brutalise uneducated farming communities.

My Personal View

I have known Jatani Ali for most of his life. I knew him from September 1952 when he arrived in Addis Ababa to start school, to April 1992, few months before his assassination. All in all, I knew him for about forty years. For this biography, I interviewed several persons who knew Jatani in the context of work or socially. Almost all expressed his character, behaviour or inter-personal qualities in the same tone. These include integrity, diligence, concern for the welfare of the downtrodden, non-discriminatory outlook on people, dedication of his life for the service of the community, hard-working, farsighted in outlook, loyal to friends and work colleagues, and love of country. I also share the views of Jatani described by those whom I interviewed.

I would like to include some other points such as Jatani's attitude towards owning property. Although he could afford to do so, he never cared to deposit money in the bank or accumulate wealth. He did not show any overt concern to own a piece of property or a real estate. Because of our close friendship, I often advised him to revise his casual attitude towards having a property by highlighting the uncertainties of life and career prospects in a poor and misruled country such as Ethiopia. I tried to cajole him to own a piece of land near Addis Ababa on which to build a house. For example, there were people who owned large tracts of land in Addis Ababa and in the surrounding areas before the fall of Haile Selassie's regime in 1974. Some of these landowners started to sell parcels of their land to organised groups at the rate of Birr 1 to 2 per square metre on a one-year credit repayment arrangement. Purchased plots would be used to build residential houses. I joined a group of people wanting to purchase a piece of land from a landowner in Aqaqi, on the outskirts of Addis Ababa, at the rate of Birr 1.50 per square metre. I managed to persuade Jatani to join my group to partake in the land-purchasing scheme. He decided to buy 1,000 square metres of land, the payment for which was Birr 125 per month. I knew Jatani could afford a repayment regime of Birr 62.50 per month for 500 square metres of land.

Since there was no extra piece of land left to be sold to new members of the group such as Jatani, I decided to share my land allocation with him where he would get 500 square metres of land and pressured him to pay Birr 62.50 per month for it. All other members of the group completed the repayment in one year as had been agreed with the landowner and started changing the title deed to their names at the municipality of Aqaqi. While the process of changing the title deed was underway, the Ethiopian revolution broke out and, subsequently, the *Derg* nationalised all private landholdings in the country. However, the regime allowed individual citizens to own a maximum of 500 square metres of urban land free of charge on which to construct a residential home. Jatani never settled down nor showed any interest to take advantage of this offer as many others did, including me. When he was the governor of Arero Province with its capital on Yaballo town and later the governor of Borana Admin-istrative Region centred on Nagelle-Borana, he encouraged members of the pastoralist communities to register in order to acquire a piece of urban land on which to build houses in Yaballo and Nagelle towns. Yet, he did not pay any attention to his own lack of interest in applying for a freely-available piece of land in these or other towns on which to build a family residence for himself. It appears that lurching from one set of crises to another and his nomad-like existence where he had to hop between various posts of governorship in different parts of Ethiopia, didn't allow him to think about the idea of settling down and taking root in one place.

Incidentally, my perseverance with the idea of owning a piece of land and systematically pay for it rather amused a fellow Borana named Jatani Muda who also lived in Addis Ababa. My mortgage repayment schedule for the abovementioned piece of land was on the first Sunday of every month. Once in a while I used to meet up with Jatani Muda on my way to the office where the monthly mortgage repayment was made. Whenever I told him how I was on my way for mortgage repayment for land, Jatani Muda jokingly laughed and said, 'You spend your money on a land which we will soon be available free of charge.' What great foresight that was!

Jatani Ali had seen bank buildings from the outside and even campaigned for the erection of a branch in Yaballo township but never entered one to deposit his own money. As mentioned previously, during the LDC he delegated me to collect part of his monthly salary from the Police Headquarters. The first amount I collected was Birr 344 in May 1976. I deposited the money in a new account at the Selassie Branch of the Commercial Bank of Ethiopia. Since I knew the behaviour of Jatani with regard to handling his own money (he gave much of his money to whomever he perceived as poor, hungry or badly-dressed). With his approval, I retained control of the account for a while. After the revolution, Jatani did not settle down in Addis Ababa though he occasionally used to come to the city on business for few days at a time. It was during such visits when I withdrew money from the account I had opened on his behalf and gave him the amount he needed. On 2 April 1989; I made my final withdrawal from that account and gave him Birr 96.80. The balance left in the bank account was Birr 5.75, the minimum amount required for the account to stay open. When I asked the bank about the status of the money in March 2014, they told me that they have changed the operating system and made all the savings below Birr 5 totally inactive.

To reiterate what many who intimately knew Jatani as a person said before, Jatani Ali was a sincere man of integrity who dedicated his life for the fulfilment of what he believed was a just cause. He seldom failed to fulfil what he set out to achieve due to his hard work, ability to persuade and influence people and his dogged persistence. This was true for all jobs he was given and wherever he was posted as a public servant. As a person he was an articulate speaker, a logical thinker, a highly persuasive person due to his warm and engaging demeanour and a methodical organiser. He never sacrificed or twisted the truth to appease his superiors or the regime. He did his best to present his side of an argument logically by highlighting the pros and cons of any course of action. His presentations were often peppered with anecdotes from real life incidents to add humour and a human dimension to his argument. He had a gift to win over the hardest of people due to his warm and gregarious nature. He could easily twist the arms of officials with his persuasive ability, charm and the authenticity of his demand to get what he required for the good of the community. In his nature, personal gain or interests had no place. He was a loyal public servant who understood well the intricate power play in the often murky and byzantine politics of feudal Ethiopia. Whatever task he was assigned to, he persevered and worked hard to have a successful outcome. The task in hand had priority over anything else in his way. For instance, in his role as a provincial coordinator of LDC, Jatani's leadership ability contributed to the relative success of the undertaking in his sector despite many shortcomings due to the haphazard and ineffective management style of those running the campaign from Addis Ababa.

17: Measure of Jatani's Effectiveness as Leader

Once in a while, Jatani would come in conflict with individuals who had characteristics contrary to his expectations and his fundamental principles in life. As a person he had an uncompromising character that can be generalised under having honesty, integrity, sincerity, selflessness and a willingness to champion the causes of the voiceless and the underdog. If he had problems with persons with whom he worked, they were invariably with those who demonstrated behaviours contrary to his principles and expectations. His priority in work and life was in upholding the interests of the public above any other thing.

Regarding who said what about him, two inherent attributes stand out, wherever he had been: he was a born leader and an effective manager or executor of work.

From time immemorial, people have used four parameters with which to gauge the effectiveness of people at work. Such measures go under different designations. But they tend to measure essentially the same inherent qualities of people. Here below I employ the parameters that Ichak Adizes, a renowned US management consultant, used to gauge the effectiveness of managers[42]. They go under an acronym PAEI, each representing the following roles managers are expected to play to demonstrate effectiveness in assigned tasks.

P stands for *Producer*

A " " *Administrator*

E " " *Entrepreneur*

I " " *Integrator*

---

[42] Ichak Adizes, *How to Solve the Management Crisis*, Adizes Institute Inc., Santa Monica, USA, 1979.

According to Adizes, managers who can play these four roles with equal effectiveness are rare to find. Ordinarily, managers are strong in one or two roles but weak in others. In such situations subordinates or colleagues who are strong in the role in which a given manager shows limitations, cover up for his/her shortfalls. Adizes went on to designate a leader or manager who is equally strong in all the roles as a statesman.

We can apply the four parameters against Jatani's standing in terms of his effectiveness as a person and a leader in different situations and circumstances, ranging from his schooling to his career trajectory.

Producer represents an individual whose priority in the assignment is in producing tangible results. Let us apply this role to Jatani by giving a few outstanding concrete examples in his assignments and career. As the governor of Arero Province, he mobilised the community to build students' residential hostels for the pastoralist children in a few towns in the province; he arranged the installation of an electric power generator for Yaballo town; he influenced officials of the CBE to open a branch in Yaballo; he arranged the construction of a football stadium in the town; and he rehabilitated internally displaced people rendered vulnerable by wars and droughts. As the governor of Borana Administrative Region, he organised the building of low-cost houses for employees living in hotels; he began the construction of office and residential complexes in Nagelle; and purchased 60 mattresses for Nagelle Hospital to alleviate critical material shortages.

Administrator is a person who gives priority to the observation of rules and regulations, by which an organisation is governed. Several examples can be cited to show his efforts in following legal, transparent, non-discriminatory and modern administrative procedures. His unilateral action to challenge the existing practices in Illubabor Administrative Region can suffice here. As mentioned above, he observed that the behaviour of employees in the head office of the Region was outside of accepted norms. He did not consult his superior whom the matter directly concerned when he set out to change the employees' subservient feudal behaviour towards their bosses. Jatani alone took measures to stop the practice that was against the accepted norms in government offices. In other places where he was posted, he didn't hesitate to take corrective measures whenever he observed behaviour in his subordinates that was against the established rules and regulations or was simply unjust.

Entrepreneur stands for initiating new ideas or undertaking new ventures to bring about change. An entrepreneur is not satisfied with the *status quo*; s/he wants to effect change. Wherever possible, Jatani didn't hesitate to embark on measures that led to changes in how things were done, even if doing so was often a risky move. For example, the purchase of mattresses for the hospital in Nagelle and importing these into the country, bypassing customs, was a move that lead to policy change for the benefit of the public. His determination to purchase a truck from Kenya for the Farmers Association in Arero Province, by bypassing existing bureaucratic red-tape, reflected his flair for enterprise and his ability to improvise in order to solve urgent problems affecting the community. This truck played a vital role in the defence of the province against Somali invaders when, for example, it was used to transport local militias and get provisions to them. In addition, examples of Jatani's efforts mentioned above under a manager's role as 'Producer' were changes that clearly demonstrate his behaviour as an effective entrepreneur. These included the mobilisation of local human and material resources to defend the region against Somali invasion; the constructions of hostels, a bank branch, a stadium, residential low-cost houses and office complexes; and the installation of an electric power generator in the town.

Integrator is a person who unites and influences the behaviour of people for a cause or activity for the greater public good. In this role Jatani was outstanding. Wherever he had been, he was loved and admired by people with whom he had any interaction. In this regard, examples were plenty from his childhood up to the end of his life. To mention just a few: in General Wingate Secondary School he was elected captain of the Red House from among many room-mates; after completing his training as a police officer at Aba Dina Police Academy, he received 92 per cent of his course-mates' votes as the most popular cadet; and senior police officers with whom he went to Japan, Britain, Germany and France accepted his arbitration whenever there were conflicts among them, although he was their junior. He also excelled in mobilising people for a cause. His ability to lead a cohesive team of teachers and students on the LDC in Arero Province led to many productive outcomes for the people. His LDC station was lauded as being one of the most successful and relatively trouble-free in the country. His success in mobilising the people in Arero Province to resist the Somali invasion and to raise money for development activities are all examples of his ability as an integrator of the people he worked with or came across.

What can we conclude about Jatani's character in terms of the roles he had played in life by using the four parameters? From the examples cited above, Jatani Ali adequately met the requirements of all four roles, which according to Adizes, qualify him to be one of the rare leaders able to operate effectively in different and often challenging circumstances. Accordingly, he was one of the few who, using Adizes' criteria of the roles managers play, qualify for **statesmanship**. This confirms what Asefa Chabo stated, that Jatani Ali was a great leader and a statesman whose life was cut short by an outrageous international crime.

18: Jatani's Awards and Certificates

*A Certificate with a Medal awarded by the Derg
for his contributions to the country and to its revolutionary movement*

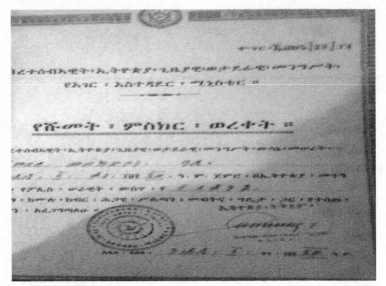

The certificate of appointment from the rank of Captain to Major in the Ethiopian Police Force

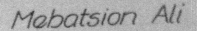

Mebatsion Ali

has successfully taken part in a

ACADEMIC COURSE

for qualifying
leading co-operators of State organs
at the
Academy of State and Law
of the German Democratic Republic
at Potsdam-Babelsberg.

The course took place in the period from
September 23rd until December 15th, 1979.

In the following topics basic knowledge was imparted

- Role of the Working Class and Its Marxist Leninist Party
- Socialist Theory of State and Law
- Structure, Rights, Duties and Working Methods of the Central and Local State Authorities
- State Management and Planning of National Economy

Potsdam-Babelsberg, December 15th, 1979

The Rector

Prof. Dr. Schüßler

A certificate awarded for participation in leadership training course in East Germany

A certificate of leadership training awarded by the Ethiopian Management Institute

Appendix 1: *Ijoolle Bulguu Kennani*: The "Borana Pioneers of Modern Education"

The brief five years' occupation of Ethiopia by the Italians ended in 1941. Emperor Haile Selassie returned from exile in the city of Bath, England, and was reinstated to his throne as the supreme leader of the country. Immediately, he embarked on various measures aimed at modernising the country. This included the creation of a modern bureaucratic system of government that required educated local manpower. Facilitating the education of the youth of the country was one way of overcoming the deficit in educated manpower necessary to operate Ethiopia's post-war government.

The end of Emperor Menelik's reign ushered in a period of political uncertainty and confusion in the Ethiopian Empire. As usual, the country went through a chaotic and bloody power struggle between families or individuals vying to emerge as the inheritors of the imperial throne. After the Emperor passed away, over a period of less than 15 years, three members of the royal family succeeded him as rulers of Ethiopia. These were: his grandson, Lij Iyasu, whose reign was regarded as short-lived and chaotic, even by Ethiopia's awful standards; his daughter, Empress Zewditu; and Emperor Haile Selassie, his distant relative. The Italian invasion of Ethiopia interrupted Haile Selassie's reign for five years, between the years of 1936 to 1941.

Menelik II laid down the foundation of modern education in Ethiopia, then known as Abyssinia. A school in Addis Ababa that still bears his name is an enduring legacy of Emperor Menelik's effort to modernise Ethiopia through education. However, very little of this modernisation trickled down to the vast majority of Ethiopians who lived in rural areas in abject poverty, under a regime of oppressive feudal despotism presided over by the Emperor and his various regional vassal kings. The two immediate successors to Emperor Menelik II who preceded Emperor Haile Selassie did not add anything to the educational foundation of the country. Mussolini's Italians who occupied the country for five years were too busy with their own agenda of consolidating their grip on the country or fighting those resisting their fascist rule. They did little to promote the education of the indigenous people. In any case, their colonial venture was too brief and was marred by armed opposition from within and outside the country to make any difference in the education of Ethiopians.

One could argue that in post-war Ethiopia, Emperor Haile Selassie started modern education from scratch or from a very basic foundation. Before the Italian occupation, only a handful of government schools existed in Addis Ababa and even fewer in the provinces. The Emperor added government-sponsored boarding facilities to some of these schools in Addis Ababa in order to admit limited number of children recruited from outlying provinces, up to then untouched by modern education.

What prompted this unusual, out-of-character policy by an Ethiopian monarch was not clear. Nor was the criteria used by government officials to recruit students to be enrolled into these boarding schools from disparate parts of the country. Nevertheless, the children of recognised patriots who had led the war of resistance against the Italian occupation were among those who got priority admission. The Emperor gave further consideration to include boys from neglected and remote pastoralist communities such as Afar, Borana and Somali.

How exactly did the group I call the "Borana Pioneers of Modern Education" get the opportunity to be admitted to boarding schools in Addis Ababa? In the mid-1940s two Borana *balabats* (chiefs) made the long and arduous trek to Addis Ababa for an audience with Emperor Haile Selassie. The primary objective for their travel was to present a complaint against the unjustified encroachment of Somali clans on Borana grazing lands. The delegation comprised Galgalo Gedo; the *balabat* for the Sabbo moiety; Anna Guyo; the *balabat* for the Gona moiety; and Tefera Nura helping as interpreter. The *balabats* explained to the Emperor how land encroachment by Somalis started mildly with the arrival of Somali traders with camel caravans. The Borana people allowed the traders a piece of land on which they could temporarily graze their camels. They told the Emperor how the people whom they treated as guests extended their stay and invited more of their people and their livestock to encroach on more Borana grazing territories. They warned the Emperor how the same people who were disturbing and trying to uproot them from their ancestral lands would later do the same thing to threaten the boundaries and territorial integrity of the Ethiopian Empire.

The Emperor listened to their grievances and told them that the best way to defend one's rights was to have an education. Accordingly, he instructed them to send 100 Borana boys to Addis Ababa to be educated. After returning home, the leaders passed the order of the Emperor to the Borana community at large. Culturally, the Borana community is divided into two moieties known as *Sabbo* and *Gona (Goona)*. Each moiety breaks down into clans and sub-clans headed by clan leaders or senior families within these. The order to recruit young boys to be sent to boarding schools in faraway Addis Ababa was passed onto clan or sub-clan leaders. Instead of the hoped-for 100 boys, only 36 reported to the recruiting site and started the momentous trip to Addis Ababa. Two boys absconded on their way to Addis Ababa and returned home. Some 34 arrived in Addis Ababa and were admitted to Medhane Alem Boarding School in September 1947. Five years later in 1952, the Ministry of Education arranged a transport service to take this first cohort back to Borana to visit their relatives. Before their departure for home, the Borana students made a courtesy call on the Emperor. He expressed satisfaction with their academic performance. He often awarded prizes to several of them who excelled academically by coming first or second in the overall ranking from their classes or schools. He instructed them to bring their younger brothers to Addis Ababa for a similar education or to follow their footsteps. In 1952, 31 additional boys arrived in Addis Ababa from Borana and were admitted to the same school as their predecessors. In Table 2 below, the two groups of Borana boys are listed as "1947 cohort" and "1952 cohort" respectively. Tables 3 to 6 show the status of their achievement in education and career since that time. This group of boys was colloquially referred to as *"ijoollee bulguu kennan?"* by the Borana people.

When we turn to achievements in education and career, the first graduates with university degrees and the first to be formally employed were shown below in the photos. When the draft of this document was compiled in 2014, most members of this group of Borana were approaching or were above 70 years of age. By this time, 16 from the first cohort and six from the second were still alive. All in all, there were 20 drop outs from the school: six from the first cohort and 14 from the second.

Table 2: List of the Pioneers

1947 Cohort	1952 Cohort
1. Abakano Karayu	1. Abdub Jaldessa
2. Adi Huqa	2. Adi Bulbule
3. Dabassa Arero	3. Bagaja Jirma
4. Dambala Guyo	4. Baraqo Chummo
5. Dhera Jatani	5. Bilal Dida
6. Dida Liban	6. Bonaya Jarso
7. Dub Galma	7. Boru Guyo
8. Dub Jarso	8. Boru Halakhe
9. Dub Liban	9. Bukure Dawa
10. Dima Jatani	10. Bule Dida
11. Galgalo Doyo	11. Dida Golicha
12. Galgalo Harisama	12. Galgalo Arero
13. Galma Jatani	13. Galgalo Liban
14. Gebre-Ab Goddo	14. Gayo Halakhe
15. Godana Adi	15. Godana Dhadacha
16. Godana Liban	16. Godana Qotto
17. Godana Tuni	17. Golicha Godana
18. Guyo Godana	18. Golicha Halakhe
19. Halakhe Guyo	19. Huqa Jirmo
20. Jarso Halakhe	20. Jatani Ali
21. Jarso Karra	21. Jatani Liban
22. Jatani Dambala	22. Sora Jarso
23. Jatani Mudda	23. Tache Adi
24. Jatani Sora	24. Taro Liban
25. Kasa Guro	25. Wako Adi
26. Liban Katelo	26. Waqo Molu
27. Qanchora Adi	27. Wario Arero
28. Salesa Jalo	28. Wario Dida

1947 Cohort	1952 Cohort
29. Sora Adi	29. Wario Godana
30. Tadhi Liban	30. Wario Guyo
31. Tadhicha Jirma	31. Wario Jirmo
32. Tadhicha Jirmo	
33. Tari Dida	
34. Wario Huqa	

Some 70 per cent of these groups attained different levels of education and were employed. The remaining 30 per cent dropped out of school and returned home. Details are:

Table 3: University Graduates and Careers

University Degrees earned		Remark/Achievement
Abakano Karayu	3rd degree	Head of regional veterinary service
Dabassa Arero	1st "	Parliamentarian & governor of province
Dida Liban	2nd "	Expert in animal science
Dub Galma	2nd "	Agricultural economist
Dub Liban	1st "	Economist in national accounting
Galgalo Arero	1st "	Building architect
Galgalo Liban	2nd "	Educator
Godana Qotto	3rd "	Physiotherapist
Godana Tuni	1st "	Governor of region
Jatani Mudda	2nd "	Ethiopian Airlines Deputy Manager & university lecturer
Jarso Karra	1st "	Expert in foreign banking
Sora Adi	2nd "	Expert in animal science
Sora Jarso	1st "	Expert in physical education
Tadhi Liban	2nd "	Educator & management expert
Wario Huqa	2nd "	Regional education administrator
Wario Godana	3rd "	Head of Veterinary Department, Ministry of Agriculture

Table 4: Employment in High-Level Jobs	
Pioneers in high-level jobs	*Remarks*
Abdub Jaldessa	Teacher in physical education
Adi Huqa	Teacher of high school
Bilal Dida	Aircraft technician (Ethiopian Air Force)
Baraqo Chummo	Artist in Ethiopian Air Force
Boru Guyo	Road construction supervisor
Dambala Guyo	Expert in pest control
Dima Jatani	Banker & branch manager
Galgalo Doyo	Army captain, governor of province
Galma Jatani	Technician in printing technology
Gayo Halakhe	Teacher of junior secondary school
Jarso Halakhe	Governor of province
Jatani Ali	Major in police service, governor of region
Jatani Dambala	Agricultural extension supervisor
Salesa Jalo	Army major, instructor in military academy
Tadhicha Jirmo	Agricultural extension supervisor
Wario Jirmo	Police major in police service

Table 5: Employment on Lower-Level Jobs

Pioneers in lower-level jobs	Remarks
Dhera Jatani	Teacher, provincial education administrator
Gebre-Ab Goddo	Parliamentarian, elementary level teacher
Godana Dhadacha	Police service
Golicha Godana	Lower-level service in administration
Guyo Godana	Elementary school teacher
Halakhe Guyo	Elementary school handicraft teacher
Jatani Liban	Lower-level service in administration
Jatani Sora	Elementary school teacher
Kasa Guro	Elementary school teacher
Qanchora Adi	Elementary school teacher
Tache Adi	Police service
Taro Liban	Lower-level service in administration
Wako Adi	Elementary school teacher, school director

Table 6: Drop-Outs and the Discontinued	
Drop-Outs/Discontinued	*Remarks*
Adi Bulbule	
Bagaja Jirma	
Bukure Dawa	
Boru Halakhe	
Bonaya Jarso	
Dub Jarso	
Bule Dida	
Dida Golicha	
Galgalo Harisama	Died while attending school
Golicha Halakhe	
Godana Adi	Dropped out because of mental illness
Godana Liban	
Huqa Jirmo	
Liban Katelo	
Tadhicha Jirma	
Tari Dida	
Waqo Molu	
Wario Arero	
Wario Dida	
Wario Guyo	

Appendix 2: Pictures of the Pioneers

It would have been wonderful if the pictures of all Borana boys that went to a boarding school in Addis Ababa had been located and included in this document. Unfortunately, I only found 36 pictures (or 55.4 per cent) of the group I call the 'Borana Pioneers of Modern Education' out of the total of 65. As can be seen, the pictures are not uniform or clear. I included them into the list in the condition in which I found them. Some of the pictures date back to when the boys were students and others are photos of adults in employment. Nevertheless, they represent the individuals concerned.

Abakano Karayu (Dr)   Abdub Jaledessa   Adi Bulbule

Adi Huqa   Boru Guyo   Dabassa Arero (Lt)

Dambala Guyo

Dhera Jatani

Dida Liban

Dima Jatani

Dub Galma

Dub Liban

Galgalo Arero

Galgalo Doyo (Capt)

Galgalo Liban

Galma Jatani

Gayo Halakhe

Gebre-Ab Godo

Godana Qotto (Dr)   Godana Tuni   Jatani Dambala

Jatani Ali (Maj.)   Jatani Liban   Jatani Muda

Jarso Halahke   Jarso Kara   Kasa Guro

Salesa Jallo (Maj.)   Sora Jarso   Sora Adi

Tadhi Liban   Taro Liban   Wako Adi

Wario Godana (D)   Waio Huqa   Wario Jiro (Maj.)

Below are the first degree graduates from the then Haile Selassie I University and its campuses in 1963 (since re-named Addis Ababa University).

Left to right: Tadhi Liban (University of Addis Ababa), Dub Galma (University of Alemaya) Dub Liban (University of Alemaya), Sora Adi (University of Alemaya)

These three (below) were the first to be employed from the group in 1957 as teachers in government schools in the towns mentioned.

Dhera Jatani   *Gebre-Ab Godo*   *Tadhi Liban*
Yaballo   *Yaballo*   *Nagelle*

Appendix 3: Poem Dedicated to Jatani Ali

The following is a poem dedicated to Jatani Ali (*Shaalaqa*) by a graduating university student who had been a resident of "Jatani Ali Students' Hostel" in Yaballo.

Tokkocch gumii kheessaa

Laf ibseen hinjirretti,
beekh deemmaan jijimmiftuu
Waan akk alkan roobaa,
kha guyyaan dimimmiftuu
Alaqaan naxxi malee,
itittuun kham khurooftu
Yo moohaan kheess hinjirre,
gosittiin himmiyooftu
Guyyaan guyyaa ororetti,
alkan alkan tuulanii
Dhaanicchaa-dhaaneelleen,
oolanii inum bulanii
Sittuu obsaan nu dhangiyee,
tanaaf afaan qabannaa
Akk aadaan tahuu maltellee,
duub ifii nuu inumbeennaa!

Kha gargarii hingorree,
akkii dhalchaa dhalootaa
Tokkotti khum kheessaa baa,
moohaa khiyyaa ma doota?
Garaa Waaqaa jalii ballaa,
kheessaa aduu nnuu ibsaa!
Jaatanii Alii Tandhuu,
abboo Booranaa qorsaa

Bakkalch barii Booranaa,
tokkocch gumii kheessaa

Meelbanaa bbulguu si khennani,
sittuu ilmee iyyeessaa
Shaggari gamaan fullaatee,
Abbaa Diinaallee ggaltee
Aadhaa-abbaa Booranaa taatee,
nuu cuf dhiibattee dhalte
Jaarrolee te dhageettetti,
khahim khankee gorfattee
Jaalal gos tanaa qabdu,
cuf luuxaan buqqifatte
Waan egeriillee erreddee,
diqqaa khe guddifattee

Beettee namaan hinsobduu,
afaan murtoo murullee
Khe dansoomii khophum jira,
duruu garree abbaallee
Warr waliin barattani,
cufumaa waayelfattaa
Daallee ifiyyuu hinbeennee,
gar jiruu middee meelfattaa
Warrii akk khankeetii,
edduun adoo jiranuu
Gam cufaan mimmidhaaddetti,
te hinbaaftu biraanuu
Jannoom khe jennaan Diidumaa,
gurbaa aabb Gaawwalee
Qaroomii kham Liiban Waataa,

waan akk abbee sihum dhalee
Barannootallee inqabdaa,
akkum warr olii khaanii
Warr dudd Boorana ggale,
si ennaan kheessaa dhabanii
Uwwaa dhiirtii laf tanaa
maqaa kheen dhaadattii
Jaarroleen geerrii teetii,
qom ifii siin dhaanattii
Tam tolchaa tam hintolchuu,
cufum siin mariyattii
Sidii Booran jidduu lamaan,
siin beettee siin wallaalti
agum guyyaa ardhaallee
Biyyitii akkan jettii
"Atoo Jaatoon jiraatee,
eent cuuqqisaa anatti?"

Ati asi jiraattee hindubbattu,
ilmummaan teenn nu fixxee
Gosaan gargar walqoonnaa,
Boorantittiin ya daaxxee
Ati il ilaan hillaaltuu,
namii cuftii sihii walqixxee
Ilmum namaa guddiftaaf,
ifii akk dhadhaa baxxee
Cuftii ilmee tiyy jettetti
daaraa dabarfacchuu diddee
Nuu aloo warroomsitetti
fulum awwaalaallee dhabdee

Ta Jaatoo nutt hinkaasinaa!,
maant imamee obbaha!
Wom ujii guyyaa tokkoollee,
Eennuutti imee kheessaa baha?
Taraarrii kharaa tolchetti,
saankullee gamaa dhugeessee
Ilmaan iyyeessaa iyyeettii,
guuree angaasuu ggeessee
Moromaa mamaa baasetti,

raaq kheessaa nu guuree
Tissituullee hintuffatuu
dheed waliin abuuree
Marroo irr jirtii teennaa
nabsee ifii gurguree
Kharaa jireennaa jiruu,
cufum booranaa ure

Liibanii-Dirree dhaqetti,
akkan jedhee nu gorsaa
Dureessii malkaa ilmaan aayyaa,
orii qabdan jabeessaa!
Qaroomii malkaa raatole,
dhiiraa dubr wa barsiisaa!
Hosteelii isanii jaaree,
maant amm isan rakkisa?
Jannilleen gurmuu gosaatii,
dhiir garaa jajjabeessaa!
Beekhaa wallaalalleen,
yo cuf walii wa obsaa!
Akkam dheedaa qar tahee,
namii dheetaa qar taha?
Kha boorannii laf hinargin,
anin abbaa warra tahaa?

Ifii ya wa baraddhee,
qaataa biyyaan qixxaaddhee
Lafaa fi lafee tiyy dhiisee,
eessaa bbaha baqaddhee?
Tan cuf jettettiin abboo,
kha abbaa gosaa nuu taate
Siyaasaan baraa amtuu,
dhuftee warraa si aate
Qaroo akk billaacchaa,
fulaa edduu nuu ejjatte
Jabaa akk dhagaacchaa,
fuutee biyya nnu darte
Balchaa akk galaanaa,
kha iltii teenn siin banamte
Adoo akk goolaa ifi dura si laalluu,

ag qaanqee nnurraa dhaamte
Ekheraa jabaa badee,
aatii gaaddisaan ooltee
Gaaddis jal boqott dhabdee,
te aatii guddoo bootte

Aabb Godaanaa Tunii,
Galgaloo Dooyyoo kheenna
Jaarrolee edduu dhibiillee,
waliin isan qaabanna
Bokkuu Alakhee Guyyoo Xuuyyee,
Ulee Tafarraa Nuuraa
Atin warr irraa fuutee,
maandhaa dhabuun waan ceeraa
Dhaltee dhibii hinqabduu,
akk biyyaa ijoollee dhuuga
Nulleen faan tantee jirraa,
ishoo ibboo abbaa dhugaa!
Fulaa tantee ciisii,
biyyeen sii sabladdhinnaa!
Waan atin nuu tolchite,
Egerillee inqaabannaa!
Maqaa khankeetillee
guddum waayelfannaa
Shalaqaa Jaatanii Alii
ilm gudeedaa ssi ddhaamanna!

Glossary of Terms

Abba Gada	Borana traditional supreme leader
AESM	All Ethiopian Socialist Movement
Afaan Borana	indigenous language of the Borana; dialect of the Oromo language
Afaan Oromo	indigenous language of the Oromo
agents provocateurs	(French) literally, "provoking agents"; people employed to associate with others by sympathising with their aims, with the intention of inciting them to commit acts that will land them in trouble
Ato	Mr
awchachign	protracted public gatherings conducted by judicial authorities to force the identification of a criminal
Awraja	Province
balabat	tribal chief
banda	local collaborator
CBE	Commercial Bank of Ethiopia
chisegna	landless tenant farmer
Derg/Dergue	revolutionary regime under Col. Mengistu Haile Mariam (1975-1991)
ECA	Economic Commission for Africa
EDDC	Ethiopian Domestic Distribution Corporation
EELPA	Ethiopian Electric Light and Power Authority
en masse	(French) all together as a group

ensete	species of flowering plant, similar to a banana; a traditional staple food in south and southwestern Ethiopia; also known as *worqee*
EPRDF	Ethiopian People's Revolutionary Democratic Front, the ruling party in Ethiopia, dominated by the TPLF.
EPLF	Eritrean People's Liberation Front, also known as *Shabia*
EPRP	Ethiopian People's Revolutionary Party
ELF	Eritrean Liberation Front, also known as *Jebha*
Fitawrari	traditional Amharic title given to a high-level war leader in Ethiopia
gaadissa-koraa	traditional Borana gathering held under a shade-giving tree
gult	piece of land or a farm allocated to the employee of an Ethiopian feudal emperor; a primitive form of salary
gultegna	employee of an Ethiopian feudal emperor who earns a living from land or farm allocated to him
Gumi Gayo	all-Borana assembly or gathering, taking place every 8 years
idget be hibret zemecha	(Amharic) literally, "development through collective effort"; Literacy and Development Campaign (LDC)
idir	self-help community association; grassroots savings guild
Kebele	sub-district; basic unit of government that comprises a locality within a district
Kebele Associations	association of farmers, producers and/or consumers based on a *kebele*

Kifle Hager	(Amharic) Administrative Region (formerly known as *Teklay Gizat*)
Kilil	new name coined to replace an Administrative Region under the *Woyane* or TPLF rule (post-1992)
Ladu	term associated with Borana spiritual leader known as *Qaallu*
LDC	Literacy and Development Campaign
malmalo	decorative ribbon of Gabra women of the Golbo area
neftegna	(Amharic) gun-carrying colonist-settler; a "conquistador"
OAU	Organisation for African Unity
OLF	Oromo Liberation Front
PA	Peasant Association
Qaallu/Qallu	Borana spiritual leader
rist	tract of privately-owned land
ristegna	private owner of *rist* land
sene-selasa	ceremonies marking the end of the school year
sergo geb	infiltrator
Shabia	informal name for the Eritrean People's Liberation Front (EPLF)
shai	sweet tea boiled in milk; similar to Indian *chai*
tej	honey-based wine; honey mead
tella	Ethiopian home-made beer
TPLF	Tigray People's Liberation Front
Worra	family in *Afaan Borana*
Worra Boku	family of *Boku*; those wielding power within the Borana *Gada* system of government

(Worra) buyo	resident family of a grass hut
(Worra)-dase	resident family of a mat-thatched house
Worra Qaallu/Qallu	family of the *Qaallu/Qallu*
Woreda	District
Woyane	informal name for the ethnic Tigre-dominated regime that ousted the *Derg*, the TPLF (1991-present)

Sources of Information

The major sources of information for this book were people who knew Jatani Ali intimately, as a result of having contact with him through work and/or social life. These include people from his schooling days, people who knew him from police training academy and in the national police service, people who knew him when he was an employee of the Ethiopian Ministry of the Interior, as a governor posted in different parts of the country, and respected elders from the communities he had served.

School

- Galgalo Liban: schoolmate; and,
- Abera Ashine: schoolmate and friend

Police Training and Services

- Major Eshete Damote: course-mate and housemate;
- Colonel Solomon Abiy: work colleague and companion on an international tour;
- Colonel Teferdegn Yigezu: colleague in Addis Ababa traffic police;
- General Yadate Gurmu; and,
- Colonel Workneh Belihu: course-mate and housemate.

Regional and Provincial Administration

- Alemayehu Legesse: district governor;
- Huqa Garse: in charge of government political affairs, district governor, head of provincial security bureau;
- Ilu Banata: provincial governor, deputy in regional govern-

ment;

- Mesele Dhaba: district governor, deputy provincial governor, head of regional political affairs bureau;
- Teshome Dahesa: district governor; and,
- Wario Galgalo: employee of government political affairs bureau, district governor.

Community Elders and other Individuals

- Abebe Zeleqe
- Borbor Bule
- Endale Fayisa
- Godana Arero
- Godana Jarso
- Guro Dida
- Halake Dida Gobesa
- Haro Duba
- Jaledesa Tache
- Jarso Boru
- Jarso Halahke
- Jirmo Dida Gandhile
- Kassa Chiriqisa
- Liban Wako Adi
- Mesele Bassaye
- Murqu Liban
- Nura Dida Halake
- Qamphe Dabaso
- Saar Jirmo
- Utukan Malo
- Wario Sora

Printed Materials

Books

- Adizes, Ichak. *How to Solve the Management Crisis*. Adizes Institute Inc., Santa Monica, California, 1979;
- Brigadier General Moges Beyene, *Policena Gize* (Police and Time) 1941 to 1971, Addis Ababa, 1972;
- Zenebe Feleke, *Neber*, Addis Ababa. 2004;
- Tabor Wami, Yewugana Dirsetoch Ena Yetarik Ewinetawoch, *Biased Essays and Historical Facts*, Addis Ababa, 2013; and,
- Teferra Haile-Selassie, *The Ethiopian Revolution, 1974-1991*, New York, 1997.

Other Materials

- *Gaffat Ethiopia*, August 1992 (monthly newspaper by Ethiopians in diaspora);
- *Indian Ocean Newsletter*, 25 July 1992;
- An Open Letter to Ato Getachew Zerihun, Ethiopian Ambassador to Kenya, 21 August 1992, by the late Hussein Sora, Attorney at the time in Nairobi, Kenya;
- Tributes commemorating various anniversaries of Jatani Ali's assassination;
- *The Ethiopian Review*, 12 July 12 1992; and,
- *Seife Nebalbal*, a local weekly newspaper in Addis Ababa, 7 July 1995 (now out of print).

About the Author

Tadhi Liban – the author – is a native Borana. He is among the pioneers of Borana boys who gained access to modern education through the order of Emperor Haile Selassie in 1947. He pursued his education, firstly, through a university degree in Ethiopia and, secondly, in the United States of America. He was an educator who served nine years as high school director. Later he moved into consultancy services in management and the training of employees in government and private organisations. He was one of the founders and board members of both the Oromo Self-Reliance Association that runs in West and East Shoa Zones and Wasasa Micro Finance Institution that operates in four Oromia Zones. He initiated the establishment of the Gayo Pastoral Development Initiative that functions in all lowland pastoralist districts in Borana region of Southern Ethiopia.

Tadhi knew Jatani from when he was admitted to Medhane Alem Boarding School in Addis Ababa in 1952, the same school he himself had joined five years earlier in 1947. Although Jatani was his junior in age and schooling, they became close friends in later days, when they grew conscious of and became concerned about the dire living conditions of people in their home region of Borana. Because of their close relationship, Tadhi knows almost all of where Jatani had been and what he accomplished. He knew many of his friends and colleagues. To enhance the authenticity of the material presented in this biographical piece, Tadhi interviewed many people who had known Jatani Ali socially or had worked with him at different times, contexts and often in challenging circumstances. Many of these were still alive when the draft of this document was compiled in 2014.

CPSIA information can be obtained
at www.ICGtesting.com
Printed in the USA
BVOW08s1149191017
498137BV00001B/54/P